IT
GIRLS

IT
GIRLS

PIONEER WOMEN IN COMPUTING

John S. Croucher AM
BA (Hons) (Macq) MSc PhD (Minn) PhD (Macq)
PhD (Hon) (DWU) PhD (UTS) FRSA FAustMS

AMBERLEY

Dedicated to all those inspirational pioneering women whose incredible achievements have helped shape the modern computer age

First published 2023

Amberley Publishing
The Hill, Stroud
Gloucestershire, GL5 4EP

www.amberley-books.com

British Library Cataloguing in Publication Data.
A catalogue record for this book is available from the British Library.

ISBN 978 1 3981 1229 2 (hardback)
ISBN 978 1 3981 1230 8 (ebook)

Typeset in 10pt on 12pt Sabon.
Typesetting by SJmagic DESIGN SERVICES, India.
Printed in the UK.

Contents

Preface	9
Introduction	11
Sarah Allen	15
Ruth Leach Amonette	18
Kathleen Rita 'Kay' Antonelli	20
Růžena Bajcsy	23
Joan Ball	26
Jean Bartik	29
Carol Bartz	32
Mavis Batey	34
Gwen Bell	36
Mary Adela Blagg	38
Gertrude Blanch	41
Sharla Boehm	44
Kathleen Hylda Valerie Booth	46
Anita Borg	49
Ellen Broad	52
Joy Buolamwini	54
Alice Burks	57
Margaret Burnett	59
Karen Catlin	61
Beatrice Mabel Cave-Browne-Cave	63
Edith Clarke	65
Mary Clem	68
Lynn Ann Conway	70
Joëlle Coutaz	73

Kate Crawford	76
Klára Dán von Neumann	78
Eleanor Dodson	80
Elizabeth Feinler	82
Christiane Floyd	84
Sally Jean Floyd	86
Alexandra 'Sandra' Winifred Illmer Forsythe	88
Margaret R. Fox	90
Timnit Gebru	92
Adele Goldberg	95
Adele Goldstine	97
Shafi Goldwasser	99
Evelyn Boyd Granville	101
Irene Greif	104
Margaret Elaine Heafield Hamilton	106
Mary K. Hawes	108
Grete Hermann	110
Susan M. Hockey	112
Dorothy Crowfoot Hodgkin	114
Frances Elizabeth 'Betty' Snyder Holberton	120
Erna Schneider Hoover	122
Grace Brewster Murray Hopper	125
Mary Jane Irwin	128
Mary Lou Jepsen	131
Katherine Johnson	134
Karen Spärck Jones	138
Susan Kare	140
Mary Kenneth Keller	143
Maria Margaret Klawe	145
Sandra Kurtzig	148
Hedwig Eva Maria Kiesler – 'Hedy Lamarr'	151
Ailsa Land	154
Henrietta Swan Leavitt	156
Nicole-Reine Lepaute	159
Barbara Jane Huberman Liskov	162
Joyce Currie Little	165
(Augusta) Ada Byron Lovelace	167
Marissa Mayer	170
Marlyn Meltzer	173
Ann Katharine Mitchell	175

Contents

Maria Mitchell	178
Vera Molnár	181
Sudha Murthy	183
Susan Hubbell Nycum	185
Ellen Lauri Ochoa	187
Cathy Helen O'Neil	190
Christine Paulin-Mohring	192
Radia Perlman	194
Rózsa Péter	197
Maria Petrou	200
Rosalind Wright Picard	202
Johanna Camilla ('Hansi') Piesch	205
Hu Qiheng	207
Virginia Marie 'Ginni' Rometty	209
Jean E. Sammet	212
Lucy Sanders	215
Patricia Selinger	217
Priti Shankar	219
Stephanie 'Steve' Shirley	221
Megan Smith	224
Cynthia Jane Solomon	226
Frances Spence	228
Janese Swanson	230
Janet Taylor	233
Ruth Teitelbaum	236
Janie Tsao	238
Dana Lynn Ulery	240
Manuela Maria Veloso	242
Mary Allen Wilkes	244
Sophie Wilson	246
Anna Winlock	248
Beatrice Worsley	250
Irma Wyman	253
Kateryna Yushchenko	255
Lixia Zhang	257
Bibliography	259
Photographic Credits	284

Preface

This book was inspired by the reception accorded two previous works, *Mistress of Science: The Story of the Remarkable Janet Taylor*, which I co-authored with Rosalind Croucher, and *Women of Science: 100 Inspirational Lives*. Janet Taylor was an outstandingly gifted mathematician, navigator, author, teacher and compass adjuster in nineteenth-century England. This volume concentrates on those women who made significant contributions to the evolution of computing, some perhaps unknowingly, going back several hundred years. In all cases they serve as an encouragement to other women who have a yearning to follow in their footsteps. One of the hardest tasks was to limit the number of women included to just one hundred. There are many more who could have been included but space did not allow it. And so I had to make a selection from different times and countries and disciplines. It is not as comprehensive as an encyclopaedia but should provide a valuable reference tool and starting point for those who wish to further expand their knowledge of those women included. A number of early female astronomers have also been included as computing and astronomy have been intertwined, with objects now being able to be observed with extreme accuracy in high resolution with the aid of computers.

The research involved spanned several years and numerous sources were called upon to create the final product. In some cases there were discrepancies in the backgrounds of the women, but all efforts were made to include the true version. There are around 400 references provided and special thanks must go to the very talented Macquarie University researcher Stephnie Hon whose exceptional efforts were instrumental in creating and formatting a comprehensive list that the reader can easily access. This was no easy assignment and she performed it with great distinction.

Much appreciation goes to the historian Dr Annette Salt who took on the challenge of not only finding appropriate photos of the women included but to obtain copyright permission where it was required. This was a daunting assignment that involved liaising with many people worldwide, sometimes frustratingly so as in some cases nobody knew who owned the copyright. In the end, Annette was able to secure photos of the vast majority of the women, an incredible achievement that warrants much well-deserved praise. For the reader, being able to see an image of the woman brings her story to life and arouses the imagination.

Thanks also go to Alex Bennett at Amberley Publishing for believing in the importance of these stories and enabling us to bring them to life. Together we have breathed life into the historical reecord to create this book, in tribute to the life of these remarkable women.

To my wonderful wife Rosalind goes a special mark of appreciation for her patience and good nature in understanding the long hours of work that necessitated my being locked away in my study for endless hours, night after night and on weekends, working on the manuscript.

John S. Croucher AM

Introduction

IT Girls: Pioneer Women in Computing celebrates an eclectic mix of women who have contributed significantly to the world of computing over three centuries – from Nicole-Reine Lepaute, born in 1723, to the youngest of the women chosen, Joy Buolamwini, born in 1989. The book provides a selection of talent and achievement, in concise biographical cameos, presented alphabetically.

Diversity is recognised through inclusion of women from a spread of nations. The subjects chosen are predominantly from the United States, or moved there (like Kay Antonelli, from Ireland; Shafi Goldwasser, from Israel; Janie Tsao, from Taiwan; Lixia Zhang, from China; Timnit Gebru, from Ethiopia; Vera Molnár and Klára Dán, from Hungary; and Irma Wyman, from Germany). There are also women from Canada, or who moved there (like Joy Buolamwini, from Ghana); from a range of European countries – France, Austria, Slovakia, Russia, Hungary, Greece, Portugal and Germany; from the United Kingdom, or who moved there (like Stephanie Shirley, from Germany); from India, China and Australia. Diversity is also recognised through celebrating the achievements of pioneering black women (Evelyn Granville, Katherine Johnson, Timnit Gebru); two transgender women (Lynn Conway and Sophie Wilson); and Megan Smith, one of the most influential LGBT people in the US (*Out* magazine, 2012, 2013).

The world of computing celebrated in the cameos of the women included is written broadly. It spans contributions in mathematics, data analysis and calculation; computer design and programming; software and computer language design (like Mary Hawes, COBOL; Beatrice Worsley, Transcode; and Radia Perlman, who developed a child-friendly version (TORTIS) of the educational robotics language LOGO); human-computer interactions; robotics and artificial intelligence; applications of computing in a wide range of fields (including, like Joan Ball) in computer dating and social networking; teaching and textbooks across the range of information technology, computer science and related fields (like Lynn Conway, Joëlle Coutaz, Sandra Forsyth,

Rózsa Péter, Janet Taylor and Kateryna Yushchenko); cryptography (Shafi Goldwasser), crystallography (Eleanor Dodson and Dorothy Hodgkin) and astronomy (like Mary Blagg, Henrietta Leavitt, Nicole-Reine Lepaute, Maria Mitchell, Janet Taylor and Anna Winlock); design of icons (Suan Kare); the legal protection of intellectual property in the computing world (Susan Nycum); and contributions in the ever-expanding corporate side of the computing and information technology sectors (like Ruth Amonette, Carol Bartz, Adele Goldberg, Margaret Hamilton, Sandra Kurtzig, Marissa Mayer, Ginni Rometty and Megan Smith).

The earliest women included were brilliant mathematicians who applied their talents to the complex calculations in the application of Charles Babbage's device (Ada Lovelace) and astronomy. The Second World War opened up the opportunity for a number of the women included, as 'human computers', doing manual calculations of things like firing tables for guns and ballistic missile trajectories. Six of the women included were the group of such 'computers' in the mid-1940s, associated with ENIAC (Electronic Numerical Integrator and Computer), bult by the US Army. ENIAC was the first all-electronic digital computer, an enormous machine comprising 48 eight-foot panels, eight feet high and eighty feet long, weighing around 30 tons, occupying 167 square metres of space and consuming 150 kW of electricity. It was rumoured that its power requirement led to the lights across Philadelphia dimming every time it was switched on. Without the programming tools available today, the complex computations were carried out be a team of six female programmers, who had to physically manipulate the 3000 switches and dozens of digital trays to route the data and program pulses through the machine. When ENIAC was unveiled to the public on 15 February 1946, the U.S. Army failed to mention any of their names. All of them are included here: Kay Antonelli (McNulty), Jean Bartik, Bety Holberton, Frances Spence, Ruth Teitelbaum and Marlyn Meltzer (Wescoff). In 1997 all were inducted into the Women in Technology Hall of Fame. The ENIAC group of women also inspired the award-winning 2013 documentary, *The Computers*.

Two of the women were part of the Bletchley Park code-breakers, a British government cryptological establishment in operation during the Second World War – Mavis Batey and Ann Mitchell. Their contribution is recognised in Tessa Dunlop's, *The Bletchley Girls: War, Secrecy, Love and Loss: The Women of Bletchley Park Tell Their Story* (2015).

Two launched self-help groups to advance networking. After attending Symposium on Operating Systems Principles in 1987, and finding only a few women present, Anita Borg and a group of other women attendees developed the 'Systers mailing list', a private, safe online forum for women involved in technical aspects of computing. Timnit Gebru founded 'Black in AI', a community of black researchers working in artificial intelligence, after seeing that she was the only black woman out of 8,500 delegates at an AI conference in 2016.

Many have been recognised and celebrated in documentaries (like Joy Buolamwini, whose research into AI inaccuracies in face recognition is the subject of the 2020 documentary film, *Coded Bias*), biographies and special editions of journals (like Lynn Conway, Maria Petrou and Dana Ulery). Ellen Ochoa was featured in the episode 'Astronaut Ellen Ochoa', in a children's TV program. Some wrote autobiographies – like Jean Bartik, Sandra Kurtzik and Hedy Lamarr.

Dorothy Hodgkin won the Nobel Prize in Chemistry in 1964; and Barbara Liskov (2008) and Shafi Goldwasser (2012) won the equivalent of a Nobel in the computing world, the AM Turing Award from the Association for Computing Machinery.

There are many inductees into Halls of Fame, including the Women in Technology International Hall of Fame (the ENIAC group of six women, 1997; Adele Goldberg, 2010;) the National Inventors Hall of Fame (Erna Hoover, 2008; Hedy Lamarr, 2014; Edith Clarke, 2015; Radia Perlamn, 2016); the Electronic Design Hall of Fame (Lynn Conway, 2002); the Internet Hall of Fame (Elizabeth Feinler, 2012; Hu Qiheng, 2013; Radia Perlman, 2014) the National Women's Hall of Fame (Katherine Johnson, 2021); and the International Air and Space Hall of Fame (Ellen Ochoa, 2018). There are also many winners of awards for pioneers: the IEEE Computer Pioneer Award (Betty Holberton, 1997; Jean Bartik, 2008; Lynn Conway, 2009; Jean Sammet, 2009); the Electronic Frontier Foundation Pioneer Award (Anita Borg; Hedy Lamarr); and the Pioneer in Tech award of the National Center for Women in Technology (Katherine Johnson, 2015; Lynn Conway, 2019; and Cynthia Solomon, 2016).

There are also many 'firsts' among the selected subjects. For example, in 1847, Maria Mitchell was the first woman elected to the American Academy of Arts and Sciences. In 1926, Edith Clarke was the first woman to present a paper before the American Institute of Electrical Engineers and the first woman elected as a Fellow of the precursor to the Institute for Electrical and Electronic Engineers. In 1950, Kateryna Yushchenko became the first woman in the USSR to become a Doctor of Physical and Mathematical Sciences in programming. In 1965, Mary Keller was the first woman in the US to be a awarded a PhD in computer science. In 1973, Grace Hopper became the first American and the first woman of any nationality to be made a Distinguished Fellow of the British Computer Society. The same year, Rózsa Péter became the first woman elected to the Hungarian Academy of Sciences. In 1978, Christiane Floyd became the first woman in Germany to be a professor in the field of computer science. In 2019, Janie Irwin was the first woman to receive the Kaufmann Award of Electronic Design Automation.

A number of the women are featured in the Notable Women in Computing cards, selected after receiving multiple, high-level awards from more than one institution, such as being named a Fellow of the Association for Computing Machinery, a Fellow of the Institute of Electrical and Electronics Engineers, and receiving the Turing Award. Those on the cards include: Augusta Ada Lovelace King (King of clubs); Ellen Ochoa (ten of clubs); Jean Bartik (two of clubs); Sophie Wilson (three of clubs); Mary Lou Jepsen (five of clubs); Barbara Liskov (King of hearts); Shafi Goldwasser (Jack of hearts); Mary Jane Irwin (ten of hearts); Irene Greif (nine of hearts); Grete

Hermann (seven of hearts); Manuela Veloso (six of hearts); Maria Klawe (Joker); Grace Hopper (Queen of spades); Jean Sammet (seven of spades); Ruth Teitelbaum (three of spades); Radia Perlman (Ace of spades); Anita Borg (Queen of diamonds); Rozena Bajcsy (six of diamonds); Kay McNulty (two of diamonds); and Lixia Zhang (four of diamonds).

Several women have asteroids and moon craters named after them (Mary Blagg, Henrietta Leavitt, Nicole-Reine Lepaute and Maria Mitchell). Some have ships or spacecraft named in their honour (Maria Mitchell is recognised in the cargo ship *SS Maria Mitchell*, a Second World War cargo ship; Katherine Johnson – the supply vessel to the International Space Station is named the SS *Katherine Johnson*; Grace Hopper – the USS Hopper (DDG-70), nicknamed 'Amazing Grace', is named in her honour). Ada Lovelace and Anita Borg have medals named after them.

The most unusual of the awards won by women in this volume is the star on the Hollywood Walk of Fame, for Hedy Lamarr, for her contributions to the motion picture industry, also posthumously inducted into the National Inventors Hall of Fame, for her pioneering work in the field of wireless technology.

A number had later life careers or occupations beyond computing – like Mavis Batey, one of the Bletchley Park codebreakers, who won the Veitch Memorial Medal in 1985 for contributions to the science and practice of horticulture; and Marlyn Meltzer, one of the ENIAC group of women, who devoted her last years to volunteering, including knitting more than 500 chemotherapy hats. Some carried their earlier interests with them throughout their lives, like Ellen Ochoa, a classical flautist and the first Hispanic woman to go into space when she served as a mission specialist on a nine-day mission aboard the Space Shuttle *Discovery* STS-56 – taking her flute with her.

Sage words of advice are included from a number of the subjects in this volume. Jean Bartik's enduring advice to young women contemplating a career in computer science was, 'You should be prepared and work hard – everybody that succeeds must work hard – and open the door when opportunity knocks. Opportunity comes in a lot of different ways. But I do believe that you should enjoy what you do.' Astronaut Ellen Ochoa encouraged young women to set big goals, 'Don't be afraid to reach for the stars. I believe a good education can take you anywhere on Earth and beyond!'

In this book, Professor John Croucher continues his celebrations of the contribution of women scientists in *Women of Science: 100 Inspirational Lives* (Amberley Publishing, 2019) and his biography of one of his ancestors, *Mistress of Science: The Story of the Remarkable Janet Taylor, Pioneer of Sea Navigation* (Amberley Publishing, 2016). Very much a polymath, with four PhDs across a range of disciplines, Professor Croucher brings to this book an abiding curiosity and passion for celebrating the achievements of women over the generations and across the world.

Emeritus Professor Rosalind F. Croucher AM FAAL FRSA FACLM (Hon)

Sarah Allen

Born: 18 January 1968

Sarah Allen (née Lindsley) was born in New York City. Her father's work as a civil engineer and urban planner led the family to live abroad in the West Indies, the Philippines, and El Salvador. She became fluent in Tagalog at the age of eight and in the following year also mastered Spanish. She returned to the US the year after that, and it wasn't until high school that she would realise her fluency in Tagalog had been replaced by Spanish. At which point, she promptly set out to learn German.

Sarah's mother was a teacher, although as a result of the family travelling was unable to return to that occupation when they returned to the US. She became one of the first women to sell Apple computers and, in 1980, she brought one home. On a day off from school, Sarah volunteered to help unpack it and then spent the day teaching herself BASIC from the instruction manual. She later reflected that it seemed like magic to her: 'I could wave my hands, and I could create this pattern in the machine, and then this thing exists that didn't exist before.' Sarah, at age 12, assisted in instructing Boston Public School teachers Logo and Basic, since it was part of the contract that her mother was awarded to supply the school system with computers.

Sarah decided to attend Brown University in Providence, Rhode Island, in part because of its extensive foreign language offerings. She later double-majored in Computer Science and Visual Art, graduating in December 1990. While there, she joined the Brown University Graphics Group as an animator, leading a small team of five students to create 3D animations under the direction of the Dutch-American Professor Andries van Dam.

In mid-1990, Sarah co-founded The Company of Science & Art (CoSA) and for the next two years worked as a software engineer. During this time she developed PACo (a cross-platform synchronised audio/video player) and After Effects 1.0. In 1992 she moved to San Francisco to work as a quality assurance (QA) engineer at Apple on AOCE, the Apple Open Collaboration Environment. The following year she returned to CoSA, which was shortly thereafter acquired by Aldus, that then merged with Adobe. There, she worked on what was later released as Adobe ScreenReady, a software tool that turns vector files into images with anti-aliasing and alpha channel.

For the following eight years, until 2002, Sarah was employed by Macromedia, a small San Francisco-based graphics, multimedia, and web development software company. For the first five years she served as a software engineer, working on a project then code-named 'Shockwave'. She was one of four engineers who designed and implemented the first web-based Shockwave player (cross-platform Mac/Windows) which was one of the first Netscape plugins, as well as one of the first Internet Explorer ActiveX controls.

In 1997 Sarah was appointed as Director of Multiuser Technology, creating the Shockwave Multiuser Server and leading a small team to develop several releases of a new product that allowed Director developers to easily create multi-party applications. Director was a multimedia application authoring platform. In 2002, she joined Jonathan Gay and a group of engineers to add two-way audio/video to Flash. She negotiated the technical aspects of licensing codecs, which was critical to updating the Flash Player to include realtime streaming audio and video. The technology was released as Flash Communication Server (later renamed Flash Media Server) and she led the team from inception through its initial release. She served as Director of Engineering of the group and grew the team from 5 to 30 engineers two years later.

In June 2003 Sarah joined Laszlo Systems, a now-discontinued open-source platform for the development and delivery of rich Internet applications, where she was appointed as the Director of Application Development. Her team created Laszlo Webtop, a mail and calendar system, licensed to Earthlink, Verizon, Alcatel-Lucent, and other telcos and ISPs. They also developed core components for the first open-source JavaScript framework to enable desktop-like interactions on the Web. She also participated in an effective transition from a proprietary closed source solution to an open-source project with an active community.

In January 2009 Sarah joined the founding team at Mightyverse where she later became Chief Technology Officer. They built a global community who exchange words, phrases, and sentences translated from one language to another, including jokes, slang, lyrics, localisms, and technical terms. This is a role she still holds today. In February 2009 she became the founder and CEO of Blazing Cloud, hiring an expert design/development team, developing mobile expertise as needed. She created iOS, Android and cross-platform mobile and web applications for small and large companies, including AOL, McKesson, Adobe, TrueCar, CNN and BET. Before taking a leave of absence, Sarah initiated an acquisition of the Blazing Cloud team by crowd-funding company Indiegogo in 2013.

From June 2013, Sarah spent the following six months as a Presidential Innovation Fellow at the Smithsonian Institution in Washington, DC. There she joined a team developing a crowdsourced transcription platform. Working with eight museums, archives and libraries to launch the platform, they engaged thousands of digital volunteers in just a few months to transcribe and review over 3000 historic and scientific documents. She also organised the first ever Smithsonian 'Hackathon', where participants created interactive museum exhibits showcasing Smithsonian art.

After completing her fellowship, Sarah then took on the role of Innovation Specialist at 18F, an open-source development shop within the US Federal Government. There she transformed US government services with modern software development techniques to create better services at significantly lower cost. Sarah also developed strategic relationships across the federal government to drive software adoption and culture change, leading open-source development of the Open Opportunities platform with almost 40 open source contributors.

In May 2016 Sarah joined Google. She held a variety of roles as a Technical Lead/Manager, eventually leading an engineering team that enabled server-side event-driven programming and security policy across Google Cloud Platform and Firebase.

Concurrently, starting in 2009, Sarah co-founded *RailsBridge*, initiating free programming workshops that increased the San Francisco Ruby community's percentage of women from 3% to 20% in less than six months. The organisation broadened outreach to other underrepresented groups with chapters across the world. It was later renamed Bridge Foundry to reflect inclusion of other programming languages. In 2013, Sarah became Executive Director and Board Chair of the non-profit organisation, which today supports and amplifies the work of thousands of volunteers all over the world. Their vision is to create a tech industry where diversity is the norm. Since 2009, they have used open source and agile approaches to build a community of teachers and students learning from each other.

Sarah remains an enthusiastic programmer whose work has won awards and acclaim. In 1998 she was named one of the Top 25 Women of the Web by San Francisco WebGrrls and was honoured on Ada Lovelace Day (held on the second Tuesday of every October) by the Bay Area Girl Geek Dinners in 2010. She remains passionate about language, the ways people learn, effective teaching methodologies and software design and is currently learning Japanese. Sarah and her husband, Bruce, still live in the same house where they raised their son Jack in San Francisco.

Ruth Leach Amonette

Born: 24 September 1916
Died: 21 June 2004 (aged 87)

Ruth Leach was born in Oakland, California, her only sibling being a sister, Helen. After completing Piedmont High School in Piedmont, California, in 1933 she enrolled at the University of California, Berkeley. While there she played tennis, acted as a camp counsellor and became a life member of Kappa Kappa Gamma into which she was initiated on 3 October 1934. In 1937 she graduated with a Bachelor of Arts degree in political science and then worked for a few years as a dental assistant.

Her next position in February 1939 was as a Systems Service Representative for IBM, with her role at the Golden Gate International Exposition involving the demonstration of IBM typewriters. Her career continued at the company, where she received training in service system work, later becoming manager, and was relocated to their Atlanta Georgia office. In July 1940, aged 23, she became an IBM instructor at the United States Department of Education in Endicott, New York. Three months later she assumed the role of Secretary of Education for IBM, a position that saw her train female employees about their products and selling them across the United States.

Such was her success that on 16 November 1943 Ruth became vice-president of IBM, thanking Thomas J. Watson, the 69-year-old Chairman and CEO of IBM, for his 'vision and foresight' in employing her in such a high-level position. It made her one of the few women in corporate power in the country, as well as one of the youngest, at age 27. According to the IBM board of directors, her promotion was 'in recognition of her ability and of the increasingly important part which women are playing in the operation of the company'.

In the mid-1940s Ruth was diagnosed with tuberculosis and took leave. In 1945 she received several awards, including Outstanding American Woman of the Year, Women's National Press Club and was selected as one of 10 Women of the Year by *Mademoiselle* magazine. The following year she served on the New York State Women's Council and received an Achievement Award from the Women's National Press Club. Back at IBM in 1947, during the following six years she was a board member for the Camp Fire Girls, the New York Public Library, the Professional Women's Club of New York, the American Association of University Women, and other organisations.

Ruth retired in 1953 at the young age of 37 and the next year married Walter Bill Pollock, the couple living near Philadelphia, Pennsylvania. There she became a board member of the Pennsylvania Horticultural Society and in 1956 she and Walter adopted a daughter, Elizabeth. The family relocated to Switzerland and then to California where Walter passed away in 1977. Ruth remarried in 1988 to Wilbur K. Amonette and she became Ruth Amonette, writing a 200-page autobiography, *Among Equals: A Memoir: The Rise of IBM's First Woman Corporate Vice President* that was published by the Creative Arts Book Company in 2000.

On 21 June 2004 Ruth passed away at age 87 in Carmel, California and was survived by her daughter, Elizabeth Pollock Scimone and her sister, Helen Hurst. Ruth was notable across the USA for her work in business and as an outstanding educator, performing in many roles of note, including as a Trustee Emeritus of Community Hospital, serving on the boards of Monterey Peninsula United Way, Monterey County Symphony Association, Monterey Institute of International Studies (including four years as Chairman) and Pebble Beach-Del Monte Forest Foundation. She was a member and president of the Carmel by-the-Sea Garden Club. She received an honorary degree of Master of Science in Business Administration from Bryant College in Providence, Rhode Island.

Kathleen Rita 'Kay' Antonelli

Born: 12 February 1921
Died: 20 April 2006 (aged 85)

Kathleen 'Kay' McNulty was born in Creeslough, County Donegal, Ireland, to father James McNulty (1890-1977) and mother Anne Nelis (1892-1966). There were two other children, Patrick John McNulty (1918-1986) and James Joseph McNulty (1919-2001). On 7 February 1921 her father was with a group of men who blew up a railway bridge, causing a derailment in which fifteen British soldiers were injured. A week later, on the night that Kathleen was born, he was arrested at his home and kept in Derry Jail. In July 1921 he was sentenced to five years penal servitude for having 'alleged seditious documents'. In December 1921 he was one of about a dozen IRA prisoners who attempted to break out of Derry Jail during which two Royal Irish Constabulary guards were killed. On 12 January 1922 he was released from prison with all charges dropped, and the family later relocated to Wyndmoor, Pennsylvania, in the US. Two years later they moved to a larger home at 48 Highland Avenue in Chestnut Hill in the same state.

From the age of six in 1927, Kathleen was educated in the Catholic school system, spending seven years at her first school. She then attended Hallahan High School, an all-girls Catholic school, after which in 1938 she was awarded a scholarship at Chestnut Hill College for Women in Philadelphia. At high school she studied four years of mathematics, four years of English, four years of Latin, three years of French, and a year each of biology and chemistry. She revealed in a later interview the reason that she majored in mathematics: 'I loved it and found it fun and easy to do. I didn't want to teach. I just wanted to do the math puzzles. I took algebra, differential

20

calculus, integral calculus, differential equations, different kinds of geometry, astronomy, and two years of physics.' She had originally intended to minor in physics, but after deciding that she did not want to be a teacher, changed her minor to business administration, enrolling in courses that included business, accounting, money and banking. She graduated from Chestnut Hill College in 1942.

After graduation, Kay answered an advertisement by the Moore School of Engineering for math majors and was subsequently employed as a mathematician, working on preparing firing tables for guns. Desk calculators at that time were mechanical and driven by electric motors and could do only simple arithmetic. She prepared a firing table for each gun, with around 1,800 simple trajectories, the hand-computations for just a single trajectory involved 30 to 40 hours of sitting at a desk with paper and a calculator. Before long, they ran short of young women to do the calculations. Her title on the ballistics project was 'computer' as she not only did arithmetic, but also made decisions on what to do next.

The Second World War was still being fought when one of the first actual computers, the ENIAC (Electronic Numerical Integrator and Computer) was being constructed by John Mauchly and John Eckert in the Moore School of Engineering. Its specific task was to compile tables for the trajectories of bombs and shells, in doing so taking over the manual calculations which Kay and about 75 other women were carrying out. The war ended before the machine came into service, but it was still used for the numerical solution of differential equations as intended.

Kay was one of six women who became operators of the ENIAC, making very substantial contributions to computer science, although it took many years before they received the deserved credit for their pioneering work. The ENIAC was demonstrated to the world on 15 February 1946, causing great excitement in the scientific and business communities, as the potential of such machines was already in evidence. However, no recognition was given to Kay or the other five women who were essential to its success.

On 7 February 1948 Kay married John Mauchly. Her mother objected to the union on the grounds that John was not Irish or Catholic, was 14 years her senior, and was a widower with two children. On their honeymoon, he presented Kay with a cookbook, with the words: 'You are our new cook.' At the time of their wedding, John Mauchly had left the Moore School and was now designing further computers in partnership with John Eckert. John and Kay lived on a farm in Amber, Pennsylvania.

While cooking and raising their seven children, Kay continued, uncredited, to program the ENIAC computer developed by John. He passed away on 7 January 1980 at the age of 72 with the marriage having lasted nearly 22 years. In 1985, the 64-year-old Kay remarried, to a photographer, Severo Antonelli. Although he was nearly eighty years old, the couple had nine years of marriage before he was diagnosed with Alzheimer's disease. Severo passed away on 9 December 1995, just before their tenth wedding anniversary.

In 1997 Kay was inducted into the Women in Technology International Hall of Fame and in the following year was a keynote speaker at the Women In Technology International's East Coast Summit in Boston. She received an honorary doctorate from Chestnut Hill College, and a scholarship in computer science is named in her honour at the Letterkenny Institute of Technology in Ireland. In 2017 a computer science building was renamed in her honour in Dublin City University.

Kay passed away from cancer at age 85 on 20 April 2006 at Keystone Hospice in Wyndmoor, Pennsylvania. Her funeral was held in St Anthony's Roman Catholic Church, Ambler.

Růžena Bajcsy

Born: 28 May 1933

Růžena Bajcsy was born in Bratislava (now in Slovakia) into the Jewish family of Mr and Mrs Kučera. Her mother, a teacher, died when Růžena was three years old, and her father, a civil engineer, remarried to a paediatrician. The family converted to Catholicism in 1938 and her half-sister Marie, who was seven years younger, was born from her father's second marriage. At the time they lived in Zvolen in central Slovakia. Her family was initially spared from Nazi concentration camps due to her father's profession, as he was needed to support their war effort by maintaining the roads. For this they were given a 'presidential exception'.

However, most of Růžena's adult relatives were killed by the Nazis in late 1944, and in autumn that year her parents were arrested by the Gestapo and were killed and buried in a mass grave. Růžena and Marie, who were close, spent the rest of the war in an orphanage supported by the Red Cross, after which they found their aunt who had survived the war in Budapest. Not long after, Růžena returned to the orphanage and later lived in foster care.

Following the loss of her parents, Růžena began studying mathematics, perhaps in part as a distraction from her grief. At the age of twenty, in 1953 she married the 22-year-old scientist and teacher Július Bajcsy and the couple later had two children, Klara (1957) and Peter (1964). Růžena attended Slovak Technical University where she earned a Master's degree in 1957 and PhD in electrical engineering in 1967 with a thesis 'Computer Identification of Textured Visual Scenes' under the supervision of the American computer scientist John McCarthy. She was the first female PhD in Slovakia in electrical engineering.

In 1967 Růžena was invited by McCarthy to study at Stanford University and so she travelled to the US, leaving her family behind. In October that year her husband joined her, but eventually the couple separated, and he returned home. She had also intended to return home after a year, but when the Russians invaded Czechoslovakia in 1968 she decided to remain in the US. She then enrolled for a second PhD at Stanford, completing it in 1972, this time in computer science in the field of computer vision and texture recognition. This involved recognition of visual patterns and repetitive kinds of patterns.

Růžena's involvement in computer science and robotics led to her being hailed as an expert in the field. She and Július divorced and Růžena then married the physicist Professor Sherman Frankel. Her next role was as an Assistant Professor at Penn (the University of Pennsylvania) located in Philadelphia, where she constructed an image processing laboratory that later expanded into a robotics laboratory. In 1968 her 'GRASP Lab' (General Robotics and Active Sensory Perception) was created. In 1997, Růžena was elected a member of the National Academy of Engineering for the development of 'active perception' methods, and for leadership in the community. After Penn, she went for two years to the NSF (National Science Foundation) as Head of CISE (Computer and Information Science and Engineering Directorate), with authority over a $500 million budget. She later returned to Penn where she supervised at least 26 successful PhD students.

At this time Růžena intended to retire but was persuaded to accept the role as Professor of Electrical Engineering and Computer Science at the University of California, Berkeley, where she became the Director Emerita of CITRIS (the Center for Information Technology Research in the Interest of Society), as well as a member of the Neurosciences Institute in the School of Medicine.

In 2001, she received an honorary doctorate from the University of Ljubljana in Slovenia and between 2003 and 2005 was a member of the President's Information Technology Advisory Committee. The November 2002 issue of *Discover* listed her as one of the 50 most important women in science. In 2012, she received honorary doctorate degrees from the University of Pennsylvania and KTH, The Royal Institute of Technology in Sweden.

Růžena has published over 225 articles in journals and conference proceedings, 25 book chapters, and 66 technical reports, as well as serving on many editorial boards. Her current research involves artificial intelligence; biosystems and computational biology; control, intelligent systems, and robotics; graphics and human-computer interaction, computer vision, and security.

Her outstanding research has helped Růžena to gain recognition from The Franklin Institute in Philadelphia. In 2009 she received the Benjamin Franklin Medal in Computer and Cognitive Science for her 'innovations in robotics and computer vision, specifically the development of improved robotic perception and the creation of better methods to analyse medical images'. She also won the 2009 ABIE Award for Technical Leadership from the Anita Borg Institute.

In 2013 Růžena was named by the IEEE Board of Directors the recipient of the IEEE Robotics and Automation Award for her contributions in the field of robotics and automation, 'For contributions to computer vision, the active perception paradigm, and medical robotics'. In her own words: 'During my 50 years of robotics research I have been consistently interested and pursued research in connecting perception and action, motivated by psychology and biology.' She is featured in the *Notable Women in Computing* playing cards set. Her husband Sherman passed away in May 2019 at the age of 96.

Joan Ball

Born: 1934

Joan Ball was born in London to father Johnny Ball and mother Julia Ball (née Anderson) and was the sixth child in a poor working-class family. She was initially an unwanted child and for a short time abandoned by her mother when she was very young. Joan was just five years old when the Second World War began, resulting in her being evacuated to the countryside to escape the aerial bombardments of London three times during the hostilities. When the war was over, she returned to her family in London.

Joan found school difficult as she was dyslexic, struggling with this for most of her life. She was not officially diagnosed until 1973 when she was aged 39. Her home life was also troublesome, with her mother blaming Joan for her failing marriage. In 1949, Joan finished her final year of school and was employed as a shop assistant at The London Co-operative Society. Her dyslexia caused her problems with writing and counting money.

At the age of 19, in 1953 Joan was hired by the department store Bourne & Hollingsworth, but left the following year to work in another store's dress department. Then ensued a variety of jobs in the fashion industry, although she found these unsatisfying because the section she was interested in was design and felt that this role was reserved for men only. However, she did find a position at Berkertex, a leading fashion house in London.

In 1961, when aged 27, she decided to leave Berkertex and found a job at a marriage bureau. It was then that she decided to start her own business to assist people in being connected, founding the Eros Friendship Bureau Ltd in 1962. She found that she had a gift for helping people make connections and her company went on to be successful for a decade.

Joan Ball

In the beginning she had difficulty in advertising as the public were very suspicious of such services. Moreover, there was a view by some that they were really a front for prostitution. Because she could not easily advertise in the print media, Joan instead placed ads with the 'Pop Pirates', the pirate radio stations that operated just off the coast of Britain in the 1960s, sometimes playing rock'n'roll music that the BBC had banned.

Joan focused her company on long-term match-ups and relationships, especially those looking for a marriage partner. These were generally older people who were previously divorced or simply looking to settle down. In 1961, at age 27, she met a man named Ken, although his family name is unknown. He would later become her business and life partner, although they never married.

In 1964 Joan changed the name of her marriage bureau to the St James Computer Dating Service and the bureau ran its first set of computer match-ups in the same year. In doing so she became the first commercially successful computer dating service in either the UK or the US. In the following year she merged her company with another marriage bureau run by a woman and together they formed Com-Pat, or Computer Dating Services Ltd. Soon after, the owner of the other marriage bureau sold her share in the company to Joan, who then became the sole proprietor.

By 1969, Com-Pat was receiving a good response to ads in the *News of the World* newspaper, although Joan still felt there was still a deal of mistrust of services such as hers. Newspapers did not help her cause, as they frequently implied that customers who used such services were lonely, sad or dysfunctional, while she took the view that she was providing a fun and intelligent way to meet people. She then began to advertise in mainstream British newspapers including *The Sunday Express*, *Evening Standard*, and *The Observer*. At this time, she was running both Com-Pat and Eros, but sold Eros to concentrate all her efforts on Com-Pat as she had the foresight to see the immense potential of online dating.

In 1970 Joan launched Com-Pat Two that was now using the most advanced matching system available at the time. This involved changing the whole system for 50,000 members in a single weekend, the system using a questionnaire that listed four of the top matches at the end. Although a success, because of financial and personal issues Joan and Ken parted ways after eight years and she moved into her own flat to gain independence and a sense of security.

Her company ran into trouble when it was discovered that their telephone number and address had been printed incorrectly in one of the major advertisements. It became worse when their actual telephone number was removed from the directory, forcing Joan to get a new number. Meanwhile, her competitor, Dateline, had taken her advertising spaces and placed its own ads in others. Matters were also not helped by the 1971 Post Office strike that lasted eight weeks, during which time Com-Pat Two's business all but evaporated. To add to her woes, there was a miner's strike and the country's economic problems were becoming apparent.

By 1973, when Joan was aged was 39, the recession had worsened and her efforts to keep her company afloat were in vain. In the following year she was so much in debt that she decided to sell the business, contacting John Paterson of Dateline and offering him Com-Pat if he would agree to pay all of the company's debts as part of the purchase deal. Paterson immediately agreed as he saw it as a way of acquiring a monopoly on the computer dating market.

Unfortunately, Joan's personal difficulties continued, and she converted to Buddhism in an attempt to come to terms with her illnesses and setbacks. Joan had been as a successful entrepreneur who was the first person to run a commercially viable computer dating service, even predating Harvard's 'Operation Match' in the US and Dateline in the UK. Joan was very much an early pioneer in the field of computer dating and social networking by computer.

Jean Bartik

Born: 27 December 1924
Died: 23 March 2011 (aged 86)

Betty (Jean) Jennings was born the sixth of seven children in Gentry County, Missouri, USA. Her father, William Smith Jennings (1893-1971) was a schoolteacher as well as a farmer, and her mother was Lula May Spainhower (1887-1988). Jean had three older brothers, William (b. 1915), Robert (b. 1918), and Raymond (b. 1922); two older sisters, Emma (b. 1916) and Lulu (b. 1919), and a younger sister Mable (b. 1928).

Jean commenced her education at a local one-room school and was known in the district for her softball skills. As there was no high school in her town, she lived with her older sister in the neighbouring town where Stanberry High School was located. Despite being aged only 14, she drove to school each day until graduating in 1941 at age 16.

She then enrolled at Northwest Missouri State Teachers College (now Northwest Missouri State University) where she majored in mathematics with a minor in English. She graduated in 1945 with the only mathematics degree in her class, at a time when the US Army was recruiting mathematicians from universities to aid in the war effort. As a result, Jean, known as Betty at the time, decided to become a 'human computer'. Her calculus professor encouraged her to apply for a position at the University of Pennsylvania because they had a differential analyser, a mechanical analogue computer designed to solve differential equations by integration.

At the age of 20, Jean applied to both IBM (who rejected her) and the University of Pennsylvania, which hired her to work for Army Ordnance at Aberdeen Proving Ground, calculating ballistics trajectories by hand. It was here that she met her future husband, William Bartik, who was an engineer working on a Pentagon project at the same university. They married in December 1946.

The Electronic Numeric Integrator and Computer (ENIAC) had been developed for the purpose of calculating ballistic trajectories. Up until then, female 'human computers' like Jean had been doing these by hand, but she applied for and was selected to become a part of the project, eventually becoming one of its first programmers. Without any basic instruction, Jean was asked to formulate problems for the ENIAC to solve. There were five other women in the programming team apart from Jean, namely Betty Holberton, Marlyn Wescoff, Kathleen McNulty, Ruth Teitelbaum, and Frances Spence. Initially, the six-woman team was not allocated space so they could work together, instead being forced to find places to work wherever they could, mostly in abandoned classrooms and fraternity houses.

These six women performed incredible work on the ENIAC, developing subroutines, nesting, and other fundamental programming techniques. They learned to physically modify the machine, moving switches and rerouting cables to perform successful programs. Before long they became operators on the Los Alamos nuclear calculations, expanding the programming capabilities of the computer. Jean's programming partner was Betty Holberton (at the time Betty Snyder) and the pair performed vital trajectory programs for the military.

On 15 February 1946, the ENIAC had its first public demonstration. It was highly anticipated by the scientific community in particular, and its unveiling was a resounding success. The ENIAC proved that it operated faster than the Mark I, a renowned electromechanical machine located at Harvard University. It also showed that calculations, which that would take a 'human computer' 40 hours to complete, could be done in 20 seconds. Jean described the demonstration in her own words:

'The day ENIAC was introduced to the world was one of the most exciting days of my life. The demonstration was fabulous. ENIAC calculated the trajectory faster than it took the bullet to travel. We handed out copies of the calculations as they were run. ENIAC was 1,000 times faster than any machine that existed prior to that time. With its flashing lights, it also was an impressive machine illustrating graphically how fast it was actually computing.'

Unfortunately, the successful public demonstration gave the six women no credit, instead heaping praise on its two engineers, John Mauchly and J. Presper Eckert. However, Jean was later asked to form and lead a group of programmers to convert the ENIAC into a stored program computer, working with the eminent John Von Neumann, Dick Clippinger and Adele Goldstine. Jean assisted them to develop the BINAC and UNIVAC I computers. BINAC was the first computer to use magnetic tape instead of punch cards to store data, the first computer to utilise the twin unit concept, and it was still working well into the mid-1950s.

Jean also had responsibility for designing the UNIVAC's logic circuits among other computer programming and design tasks. Together with Betty Holberton, she co-programmed the first generative programming system

(SORT/MERGE) for a computer. When the Eckert-Mauchly Corporation was sold to Remington Rand, she then trained others on how to program and use the UNIVAC for the first six UNIVACs sold, including the programmers at the United States Census Bureau (the first UNIVAC sold) and Atomic Energy Commission.

Later, when her husband, William ('Bill') took a job with Remington Rand, the couple moved to Philadelphia. As the company policy at the time did not allow husbands and wives to work together, Jean was forced to resign. Consequently, between 1951 and 1954 she mainly undertook freelance programming assignments for John Mauchly, as well as assisting her husband. At some point in the 1950s she began going by the name 'Jean' rather than her birth first name 'Betty', which is what she had been known as during her time with ENIAC, UNIVAC and Remington-Rand.

After the birth of her son John (born 26 March 1954), Jean left the world of computing to concentrate on raising a family, having two more children. In 1967, at age 42, Jean earned a master's degree in English at the University of Pennsylvania. In the same year she joined the Auerbach Corporation, where she wrote and edited technical reports on minicomputers. She remained with Auerbach for eight years, before moving on to a variety of positions in other companies for the rest of her career as a manager, writer, and engineer. Jean and Bill were divorced in 1968 after having two more children together, Jane Helen (born 8 August 1959), and Mary Ruth (born 2 February 1961). Jean retired from the computing industry in 1986 when her final employer, Data Decisions (a publication of Ziff-Davis), was sold. For the next 25 years she was employed as a real estate agent.

In 2002, Jean was awarded an honorary doctorate degree from Northwest Missouri State University. She received many honours during her lifetime, including being an Inductee into the Women in Technology International Hall of Fame (1997), being made a Fellow, Computer History Museum (2008), receiving the IEEE Computer Pioneer Award, IEEE Computer Society (2008), and the Korenman Award from the Multinational Center for Development of Women in Technology (2009). She wrote her autobiography *Pioneer Programmer: Jean Jennings Bartik and the Computer that Changed the World* assisted by her long-time colleagues, Dr. Jon T. Rickman and Kim D. Todd.

Jean passed away at age 86 on 23 March 2011 from congestive heart failure in a Poughkeepsie nursing home, New York. In 2013 her autobiography was published by Truman State Press. Her enduring advice to young women contemplating a career in computer science was 'You should be prepared and work hard – everybody that succeeds must work hard – and open the door when opportunity knocks. Opportunity comes in a lot of different ways. But I do believe that you should enjoy what you do.'

Carol Bartz

Born: 28 August 1948

Carol Bartz was born in Winona, Minnesota, the daughter of Shirley Ann (née Giese) and Virgil Julius Bartz. When Carol was eight years old her mother died. A few years later, Carol and her younger brother, Jim, relocated to the home of their grandmother, Alice, on a dairy farm near Alma, Wisconsin. Carol excelled in mathematics at high school and was also homecoming queen.

Excellent grades in high school earned her a scholarship to William Woods, a prestigious all-girls college in Fulton, Missouri. She later transferred to the University of Wisconsin–Madison, where in 1971 she graduated with a bachelor's degree in computer science. While in college, she worked as a cocktail waitress. In 1972, she found work at the manufacturing company 3M, finding herself the only woman professional in a division of 300 men. In 1976 she resigned after being refused a transfer to headquarters. She then took on several positions in the computer industry, including jobs at Digital Equipment Corporation and then Sun Microsystems where she served as vice president of worldwide field operations and as an executive officer of the company.

By 1992 Carol had become CEO of the software company Autodesk and, according to *Forbes* magazine, 'transformed Autodesk from an aimless maker of PC software into a leader of computer-aided design software, targeting architects and builders'. In this role she instituted and promoted Autodesk's '3F' or 'fail fast-forward' concept – the idea of developing a company to risk failure in some missions, but to be resilient and move on quickly when failure occurs. During her 14-year reign as CEO there was a marked increase in Autodesk's net revenue, rising from US$300 million to US$1.5 billion, with the stock price rising 20 per cent annually.

As well as Autodesk, Carol served on several boards of directors, including those of Intel, Cisco Systems, BEA Systems, Network Appliance, and the Foundation for the National Medals of Science. She was also a member of the United States President's Council of Advisors on Science and Technology. In 2002 she was awarded an Honorary Doctorate of Humane Letters degree from New Jersey Institute of Technology.

In 2006 Carol resigned as CEO of Autodesk and three years later, on 13 January 2009, she assumed the role of CEO of Yahoo! on a reported annual salary of US$1 million. She was also eligible for an annual 400% bonus and received 5,000,000 shares, along with an equity grant of US$18 million of stock (to compensate for the forfeiture of the value of equity grants and post-employment medical coverage from her previous employer). Yahoo! was at the time the Internet services company which operated the fourth most-visited Web domain name in the world.

In the year before her appointment, Yahoo! had experienced significant cuts, including the axing of 1600 staff. Just four months into the role, in May 2009, Reuters reported that Carol had already 'worked through an impressive checklist', restructuring the organisation, replacing executives and cutting costs. This reportedly included the loss of a further 675 jobs, or 5 per cent of the workforce.

Staff were becoming anxious, especially with the secrecy surrounding the developments at Yahoo! and Carol was quoted as saying that she would punish any employee who leaked to the press. In 2010 Carol was named as the 'most overpaid' CEO by proxy voting firm Glass-Lewis when she received US$47.2 million in compensation.

On 6 September 2011, Carol was removed from her role, via a phone call from Yahoo! Chairman, Roy Bostock, with CFO Tim Morse being named as Interim CEO of the company. Although Carol requested to remain on the Board of Directors, three days later she resigned from it.

Carol received a number of awards, including the Ernst & Young Entrepreneur of The Year Award in 2001. In 2005 she was included in *Forbes* magazine's list of The World's 100 Most Powerful Women, remaining on the list for six consecutive years. She also received an Honorary Doctor of Science degree from Worcester Polytechnic Institute and an honorary Doctor of Letters degree from William Woods University. In 2019 she was named as Chairman of the Board of Directors of Caliva, one of the largest vertically integrated cannabis companies in California.

Carol has two half-brothers and two half-sisters, and is married to Bill Marr, a former executive at Data General and Sun Microsystems, and the couple have three children: Bill, Meredith, and Layne. Her hobbies include golf, tennis, and gardening.

'Be open-minded. A lot of times, that means not only open-minded about where the product could go, but open-minded about the kind of people you need at the time. So, the lesson here is you need to be adaptable, adjustable, and smart enough to make some really hard decisions.'

Mavis Batey

Born: 5 May 1921
Died: 12 November 2013 (aged 92)

Mavis Lilian Lever was born in Dulwich, an area of south London, England, to a seamstress mother and postal worker father. She was raised in the suburb of Norbury and attended Coloma Convent Girls' School in Croydon. At the outbreak of the Second World War, she was studying German at University College, London. Mavis later remarked that 'I was concentrating on German romantics, and then I realised the German romantics would soon be overhead and I thought well, I really ought to do something better for the war effort.'

She dropped out of university and applied to be a nurse, before finding employment in London checking the personal columns of *The Times* for coded spy messages. In 1940, she was recruited to work as a codebreaker at Bletchley Park, a British government cryptological establishment in operation during the Second World War. She worked as an assistant to the British scholar and codebreaker Alfred Dillwyn 'Dilly' Knox.

At age 19 in 1940, Mavis commenced work on the Italian Naval Enigma machine, and by late March 1941 she effectively broke into their framework, deciphering a message which read 'Today's the day minus three'. She and her colleagues then worked for three days and nights, finally discovering that the Italians were intending to assault a Royal Navy convoy transporting supplies from Cairo, Egypt, to Greece. Their deciphered messages uncovered a detailed plan of the Italian assault, enabling an Allied force to destroy of much of the Italian naval force off Cape Matapan, situated at the end of the Mani Peninsula in southern Greece. The leader of the Matapan attack, Admiral Andrew Cunningham, later visited Bletchley Park to personally thank Mavis for their role in making his victory possible.

In December 1941 Mavis decoded a message between Belgrade and Berlin that enabled Knox's team to determine the wiring of the Abwehr Enigma, an Enigma machine previously thought to be unbreakable. She also deciphered the GGG, another Abwehr machine, in doing so enabling the British to be able to read its messages. They were able to confirm that the Germans believed the Double-Cross intelligence they were being fed by the double agents who were recruited by Britain as spies. From that point onwards, MI5 knew the Germans believed everything the double agents told them, allowing them to suggest that the allies had an entire army ready to storm the Pas de Calais.

While still working at Bletchley Park, Mavis met a mathematician and fellow codebreaker, Keith Batey, and the couple were married in 1942. At the end of the war in 1945, she spent some time in the Diplomatic Service, as well as raising her family of three children. In the 1960s, Keith was appointed Secretary of the Chest, the chief financial officer of Oxford University, and the couple resided on the university's Nuneham Park estate where the gardens, landscaped in the eighteenth century, had become overgrown.

Mavis published a number of books on garden history, including in 1982 *Oxford Gardens: University's Influence on Garden History* (Ashgate Publishing Limited) and in 1996 *Jane Austen and the English Landscape*, which explored real and fictional settings of Jane Austen's novels. Other works included *Alice's Adventures in Oxford* (Jarrold Publishing) in 1980, *From Bletchley with Love* (Bletchley Park Trust) in 2008 and *The Story of the Privy Garden at Hampton Court*, co-authored with Jan Woudstra in 2006.

In 2009, at age 87 Mavis authored a 256-page biography of Dilly Knox. Titled *Dilly: The Man Who Broke Enigmas* (published by Dialogue). Its description read: 'The highly eccentric Alfred Dillwyn Knox, known as 'Dilly', was one of the leading figures in the British code-breaking successes of the two world wars. Mavis Batey, who worked for Knox at Bletchley Park, reveals the vital part Dilly played in the deception operation that ensured the success of the D-Day landings, altering the course of the Second World War.'

Mavis served as President of the Garden History Society, of which she became Secretary in 1971. In 1985 she was presented with the Veitch Memorial Medal, which is awarded to 'persons of any nationality who have made an outstanding contribution to the advancement and improvement of the science and practice of horticulture'. She was made a Member of the Order of the British Empire (MBE) in 1987 for her work on the conservation of gardens.

In 2005, The Gardens Trust held the first annual Mavis Batey Essay Prize, a competition geared towards international students who are enrolled in a university, institution of higher education or who have recently graduated from one. It is intended to encourage vibrant, scholarly writing and new research, especially by those who have not yet had their work published.

Mavis passed away of natural causes at age 92 on 12 November 2013, survived by her three children, Elizabeth, Christopher and Deborah.

Gwen Bell

Born: 20 July 1934

Gwen Bell was born in Elkader, Iowa, a town which was the most northerly outpost of Spanish settlement in America. She attended the University of Wisconsin, graduating with a Bachelor of Arts in 1957. She then obtained a Master of City and Regional Planning from Harvard University in 1959, and later commenced a PhD in geography at Clark University, a private research university in Worcester, Massachusetts.

In 1966 Gwen was appointed as an associate professor of urban affairs at the University of Pittsburgh's Graduate School of Public and International Affairs. She completed her PhD in the following year and in 1972 was a visiting associate professor at the Harvard Graduate School of Design. Between 1966 and 1977 she was also the editor of the monthly periodical *Ekistics: The Problems and Science of Human Settlement, of Ekistics in Athens, Greece*, and a consultant on planning to the United Nations for Indonesia, the Philippines and Brazil. She served for a short time in 1978 as a social science editor for Pergamon Press.

During the 1970s Gwen authored three books: *Human Identity in the Urban Environment* (Penguin Books, 1972, co-editing with Jacqueline Tyrwhitt), *Urban Environments and Human Behavior: An Annotated Bibliography* (Hutchinson Ross Publishing Company, 1973) and *Strategies for Human Settlements: Habitat And Environment* (University Press of Hawaii. 1976).

While on a Fulbright scholarship in Australia, Gwen was introduced to the English Electric DEUCE, a computer designed after the Pilot ACE of Alan Turing. Returning to Cambridge, Massachusetts, she used the TX-0 at MIT to analyse a redevelopment area of Boston. In doing so she became the first person to develop a 'geographic information system' on a computer, producing a variety of maps. In 1978, the President of Digital Equipment Corporation (DEC), Ken Olsen, asked Gwen to recreate the TX-0 at their Marlboro facility. She accepted, as some years before she had been collecting and exhibiting artifacts relating to the history of computing.

In 1980, Gwen co-founded, along with her husband, the eminent American electrical engineer Chester Gordon, the Computer Museum. She assumed the role of its first president, holding the position until 1996. The couple developed an acquisitions policy for the Museum in which computing materials were classified into Processor, Memory, and Switch categories, known as the PMS classification. The Transducer category was also added to cover input/output devices. In spring 1982, the Museum received non-profit charitable foundation status from the Internal Revenue Service (IRS).

Notable early acquisitions included parts of Whirlwind 1, UNIVAC 1, the TX-0, a CPU from the Burroughs ILLIAC IV, IBM 7030 'Stretch', NASA Apollo Guidance Computer Prototype, a CDC 6600, a CRAY-1, PDP-1, PDP-8, EDSAC Storage Tube, Colossus pulley, and components of the Ferranti Atlas and the Manchester Mark I.

Throughout its history, the Museum had vigorously collected artifacts, and the criteria for inclusion became more selective over time due to lack of storage space. Acquired items ranged in size from a single chip to the multiple components of a mainframe computer. In addition to artifacts, the Museum collected images, film, and video. Gwen decided to expand the Museum relocating it to a new facility in downtown Boston. On 13 November 1984, the Museum officially re-opened to the public at its new 53,000 square-foot location.

The collection of artifacts and films now included 900 catalogued items. Acquisitions in the preceding year included an Apple 1, Burroughs B-500, Digital Equipment Corp. PDP-1, Franklin Ace 100, and IBM SAGE: AN/FSQ-7 components. In 1999, the Computer Museum merged with the Museum of Science, Boston. The Museum finally closed its doors in 2000, with most of its collection being sent to the Computer History Museum in California.

Gwen had been actively collecting since the 1970s and is rightly viewed as the initial inspiration and driving force of the Museum. She also held other important roles in her career, including between 1992 and 1994 as the president of the Association for Computing Machinery (ACM).

Mary Adela Blagg

Born: 17 May 1858
Died: 14 April 1944 (aged 85)

Mary Blagg was born on 17 May 1858 in Cheadle, Staffordshire, England, the daughter of France Caroline (née Foottit) Blagg and the solicitor John Charles Blagg. Although she received her formal education in London at a private boarding school, she trained herself in mathematics by reading her brother's textbooks, while undertaking an assortment of activities to benefit the community. Astronomy became her passion after hearing a lecture by Joseph Hardcastle, the grandson of the eminent astronomer William Herschel, as part of a series on astronomy in 1904–1905. Mary began corresponding with Hardcastle and he arranged publication in 1906 of her analysis of 4,000 star observations in the course of a year.

Hardcastle suggested that there was a need to standardise lunar nomenclature as there were inconsistencies in the way in which formations were being named. To this end, in 1905 the International Association of Academies formed a committee on which Mary was given the task of collating the labels assigned to the formations found on existing lunar maps, two German and one English. With the assistance of Hardcastle and Herbert Hall Turner, the Savilian Professor of Astronomy and Director of the Radcliffe Observatory at Oxford University, Mary eventually published her 1913 book-length table, *Collated List of Lunar Formations*, which contained an index of 4,789 entries. In this volume she proposed a new standard of names for various features of the moon, using telescopes and photographs to find the exact locations. Although she received assistance from her eminent colleagues, this was very much her project.

At the same time, Mary undertook a meticulous analysis of variable stars, ones whose brightness changes, either irregularly or regularly, in which she combined the raw data obtained by her predecessors. To achieve this, Turner had acquired a number of notebooks written by an astronomer who had compared, over time, the brightness of variable stars with those that were 'firmly' lit. Her task was to identify those nearby stars and calculate each variable star's brightness. She established a system to measure a star's brightness, her findings serving as a basis for future astronomers. Part of the mathematical skills she employed involved the calculation of the length of the cycle of brightening and dimming. Previous astronomers had simply graphed the data from what they observed. Without the aid of modern computers, it was an incredible feat.

Her research work led to her writing papers for the Royal Astronomical Society, the most important of which was 'Suggested Substitute for Bode's Law', published in 1913. During the same year, Professor Turner put her name forward for election as a Fellow to the Royal Astronomical Society, a position which had not previously been open to women. Mary was actually elected in 1916.

One of Mary's interesting conclusions was that, in a particular star, *Beta Lyrae*, there was a slowing in the cycle of brightening and dimming. Her assertion was confirmed in 2008 when data from the Center for High Angular Resolution Astronomy (CHARA) Array Inferometer at Georgia State University confirmed that *Beta Lyrae* is a binary star, one which is actually two stars orbiting a common centre of mass. *Beta Lyrae* is located in the constellation of *Lyra*, about 960 light years from the Sun and is one of the brightest and easiest-to-find variable stars in the sky.

The senior scientist and planetary geologist, Dr Chuck Wood, undertook similar work for the National Aeronautics and Space Administration (NASA) in the 1960s when NASA wanted to re-examine the naming designations. Underscoring the incredible work of Mary, he declared 'I can attest that that's very difficult. With even more modern hi-res images, it is still almost impossible sometimes to identify what the maps showed with what the photographs shows was the reality of the moon.'

By 1920, Mary's reputation had grown to the extent that she was appointed to the Lunar Commission of the newly formed International Astronomical Union. This led to her collaborating with Karl Müller, an amateur astronomer and retired government official. (Müller later had a lunar impact crater, 'Müller', located in the highlands near the centre of the Moon, named after him.) Their role was to prepare a definitive list of names which would later become the official authority in 1935, with the release of their joint two-volume work, *Named Lunar Formations*.

Their work remained as the benchmark until 1963–66 when it was replaced by the catalogue *System of Lunar Craters*, that gave a detailed account of all nearside lunar craters with diameters larger than 3.5 km. Its creation was undertaken by the Lunar and Planetary Laboratory, established in 1961 at the University of Arizona. It made additions, deletions and changes to the contents in the Bragg-Müller volumes.

Kevin Kilburn, an astronomer and astronomical historian, Fellow of the Royal Astronomical Society and founder of The Society for The History of Astronomy, is a great admirer of her work:

> Back in Mary Blagg's days, you had to have an analytical turn of mind to take that raw data and make sense of it. That's what made her so unusual at the time. I think the thing that strikes me most is that she wasn't ahead of her time; she was part and parcel of late Victorian astronomy. It was recognised that women were involved in science, they weren't just pressing flowers into books.

Mary Blagg's charitable works extended to caring for Belgian refugee children during the First World War. One of her favourite hobbies was chess. She was honoured with a moon crater named 'Blagg', a lunar impact crater located on the small lunar mare *Sinus Medii*, before she passed away on 14 April 1944 at the age of eighty-five. She never married and despite her fame spent most of her life in Cheadle where she communicated with her astronomical colleagues largely through her writing and correspondence.

Gertrude Blanch

Born: 2 February 1897
Died: 1 January 1996 (aged 98)

Gertrude Blanch was born Gittel Kaimowitz in Koln, formerly a part of Poland, but at the time partitioned off into the Russian Empire. She was youngest of seven children to Dora Blanc. Her father, Wolfe Kaimowitz, emigrated to New York in the US where he was joined in 1907 by Dora, a 10-year-old Gertrude and another daughter.

Attending schools in Brooklyn, New York, Gertrude graduated from Eastern District High School in 1914. When her father died later that year, she decided to find a job to support her family. For the next fourteen years she worked in various clerical positions, putting money aside for her education. In 1921 she became an American citizen and following the death of her mother in 1927 she attended evening classes at Washington Square College, which formed part of New York University.

In 1932, Gertrude graduated summa cum laude from the university with a Bachelor of Science degree in mathematics with a minor in Physics. In the same year, she changed her family name from Kaimowitz to Blanch, an Anglicised version of her mother's name, Blanc. She then enrolled in the PhD program at Cornell University, graduating in 1935 with her thesis in algebraic geometry entitled 'Properties of the Veneroni Transformation in S4'. Her doctoral supervisor was the American mathematician Virgil Snyder who specialised in the field.

As this was the time of the Great Depression, Gertrude could not find employment in her field, instead filling in for a colleague on leave at Hunter College, before taking up a position as a bookkeeper with a firm in Manhattan who were manufacturing cameras for colour photography.

During this time she enrolled in an evening course on relativity at Brooklyn College, and while there her instructor, the physicist Arnold Lowan, invited her to join the Works Progress Administration (WPA) project, where she was assigned as a supervisor.

In February 1938, Gertrude began work on the Mathematical Tables Project of the WPA, for which she was mathematical director and Chair of the Planning Committee. In this role she decided which mathematical functions would be calculated and constructed the plans used by the computers. The committee had charge of 450 'human computers' with varying levels of mathematical ability.

Gertrude's role included the design of algorithms that were carried by the teams under her control. Despite the variable skills of the mathematicians, their output was of sufficient quality to define the standard for transcendental function solutions for decades. The project later became the Computation Laboratory of the National Bureau of Standards. Gertrude also worked as a tutor at Brooklyn College during her last two years at the WPA.

When the WPA was wound up in 1942, the Mathematical Tables Project became an independent organisation, operating as a major computing office for the US government during the Second World War. It performed calculations for the Office of Scientific Research and Development, the Army's map grid, the Navy's LORAN radio navigation system, the Manhattan Project and other institutions. It also performed important calculations for 'Operation Overlord', the codename for the Battle of Normandy in 1944.

Using mathematical models developed by the eminent Polish mathematician and statistician Jerzy Neyman, the group led by Gertrude throughout the war helped evaluate strategies that were designed to bomb the Normandy beaches. Following the war, Gertrude was plagued with suspicions by the FBI that she was secretly a communist. Part of the evidence was that she had not married or had children (she was aged 48 at the end of the war), along with her sister being involved with the Communist party. All charges against Gertrude were resolved in May 1952 and she was able to resume her work, landing a job with the Electrodata Corporation in Pasadena.

A year later she commenced work at the Institute for Numerical Analysis at UCLA until its closure in June 1954, and later that year spent two months as a mathematician for the computer division of Consolidated Engineering in Pasadena, California. She was then hired as a senior mathematician for the Aerospace Research Laboratory at Wright-Patterson Air Force Base in Dayton, Ohio, where she worked on calculations involving turbulence, air flow, and transonic and supersonic flight. In 1962, she was promoted to the position of government senior scientist.

Gertrude was an early member of the Association for Computing Machinery (ACM) that had been founded on 15 September 1947 as the Eastern Association for Computing Machinery at a meeting at Columbia University in New York. She was also a prolific publisher in the fields of functional approximation, numerical analysis and Mathieu functions, with over 30 research articles to her name. She published several papers, most jointly with Arnold Lowan, including 'Tables of Planck's radiation and photon functions' (1940), 'Errors in Hayashi's table of Bessel functions for complex arguments' (1941) and 'On the inversion of the q-series associated with Jacobian elliptic functions' (1942).

In 1963, she was elected a Fellow of the American Association for the Advancement of Science. There were other honours bestowed on Gertrude, including the Air Force Outstanding Performance Award (1958), Air Force Exceptional Service Award (1963), and the Federal Woman's Award from President Lyndon Johnson for exemplary professional service in the United States Government (1964).

In 1967 Gertrude retired at the age of 69 and was honoured with the publication of the 'Blanch anniversary volume' which contained a series of papers by her friends. However, through Ohio State University, she continued to work as a consultant to the Air Force until 1970 when Ohio State cancelled all military-funded contracts. She then relocated to San Diego, California, where she worked on a manuscript involving functional approximations. Although she completed it in 1982, this work was never published.

Gertrude passed away in San Diego on 1 January 1996, just a month before her ninety-ninth birthday. The 'Gertrude Blanch Papers, 1932–1996' may be found at the Charles Babbage Institute, University of Minnesota, Minneapolis. In 2017 she was posthumously inducted into the Portrait Gallery at the National Institution of Standards and Technology.

Sharla Boehm

Born: 4 December 1929

Sharla Perrine was born in Seattle, Washington, with her family moving to Santa Monica in California three years later. She attended Roosevelt Elementary School, followed by Lincoln Middle School and finally Santa Monica High School where she was an outstanding mathematics student. After finishing high school, she enrolled at the University of California Los Angeles (UCLA) where she graduated with a bachelor's degree and a teaching qualification. After this, she accepted a position as a teacher of mathematics and science in Santa Monica schools.

In 1959, at age 29, she left her teaching role and took up a position at RAND Corporation, becoming an integral key partner with the Polish-American engineer Paul Baran, one of the pioneers of computer networks. Here she developed and published material on a switching program in the computer language Fortran. It was at RAND that she met her husband, the renowned American software engineer Barry Boehm, and became Sharla Boehm after their marriage in 1961.

In 1964, together with Paul Baran, Sharla published a paper titled 'On Distributed Communications: II. Digital Simulation of Hot-Potato Routing in a Broadband Distributed Communications Network'. As her name appeared first in the original paper, it indicated that she was the lead author, confirmed by a later RAND report that declared Sharla did most of the work. She was the driving force behind the simulation programmed in Fortran and their research revealed that packet switching (or 'hot-potato routing') was indeed possible.

During her time at RAND, Sharla undertook various simulations under different conditions, demonstrating that the protocol routed traffic efficiently.

Of special interest was her discovery that if half the network was destroyed, the remainder reorganised and began routing again in less than a second. In his 1996 paper 'An Early Application Generator and Other Recollections', the author, her husband Barry, revealed that Sharla, along with Paul Baran, had developed the original packet-switched network simulation, a discovery that led him to become involved in the pioneering ARPAnet Working Group.

Sharla eventually left RAND and raised her two daughters, Romney and Tenley. She also thrust herself into community activities, becoming a Girl Scout Leader, mathematics tutor and serving as a wonderful role model to young women whom she urged to follow their dreams. Her ninetieth birthday on 4 December 2019 was celebrated with a reception held at the Santa Monica Public Library. The Mayor, Gleam Davis, remarked that Sharla had been 'a tremendous role model and a stalwart in this community', in particular serving on the Santa Monica Public Library Board from 1989 to 1998 and holding the role of Treasurer for the Friends of the Santa Monica Public Library for fourteen years.

Barry passed away at age 87 on 20 August 2022, the couple having been married for over 60 years. They had two daughters, Romney and Tenley.

Kathleen Hylda Valerie Booth

Born: 9 July 1922
Died: 29 September 2022 (aged 100)

Kathleen Hylda Valerie Britten was born in Stourbridge, Worcestershire, England. She attended the University of London gaining a Bachelor of Science in mathematics in 1944, after which she became a Junior Scientific Officer at the Royal Aircraft Establishment, a British research organisation, from 1944 to 1946. She then enrolled in the PhD program in Applied Mathematics.

In 1946 Kathleen commenced work as a research assistant at Birkbeck College in Bloomsbury, London, later becoming a lecturer and Research Fellow. She was to stay there in different positions for the next fifteen years. Her next role was as a Research Scientist at the British Rubber Producer's Research Association (BRPRA) and during her time there she met an electrical engineer, Andrew Donald Booth, who was also a physicist and computer scientist.

In 1946 Andrew developed a computer called the Automatic Relay Computer (ARC), an early electro-mechanical computer the relays of which were the precursors to the more efficient transistor. They were basically electric switches used to perform logical operations such as addition, subtraction, multiplication and division. It contained components which involved using an electrical signal to create mechanical movement. As such, the ARC was deemed to be an electro-mechanical computer and was constructed in Welwyn Garden City, close to the BRPRA facility.

After meeting Andrew, Katheen and another research assistant, Xenia Sweeting, worked on the ARC and they were largely responsible for its development and construction. The design used 600 relays and 100 vacuum tubes, the latter controlling the flow of the electric current through the computer.

In 1947, Andrew and Kathleen (as his research assistant), travelled to the US on a six-month tour, assisted by funding from the Rockefeller Foundation at BRPRA. The couple were based at the Institute for Advanced Study in Princeton, New Jersey, and it was here they became acquainted with the eminent mathematician, physicist and computer scientist John Von Neumann. In 1947 the pair published two reports about the ARC2. It included sections that highlighted her outstanding programming skills and which described the possibility of synchronous vs asynchronous operations.

They discussed with Von Neumann his concept of 'Von Neumann architecture' that had been first published in his 30 June 1945 'First Draft of a Report on the EDVAC'. The EDVAC was the first computer to use the Von Neumann architecture, which comprised the following constituents:

A Processing Unit responsible for carrying out the instructions of a computer program.

A Control Unit responsible for coordinating the movement of instructions to the Processing Unit and Memory, as well as the input and output devices.

Memory as mentioned in number two, which stores the data (information) as well as the instructions for that data to be processed by the Processing Unit.

A Mass Storage device to storage a larger amount of persistent data (data that will remain when power is lost to the computer).

An Input and Output mechanism for the transfer of information into, and out of, the computer.

Andrew redesigned the ARC, naming it the ARC2, to incorporate Von Neumann's instructions. In doing so he created the world's first rotating electronic storage device, to store persistent data. It used a cylindrical drum, rather than the circular discs used later. The computer officially came online on 12 May 1948.

More machines followed, with Andrew as the primary builder and Kathleen performing all of the programming. In 1950 Kathleen graduated with her PhD and in the same year she and Andrew were married. The couple later had two children. As well as being an outstanding electrical engineer, physicist and computer scientist, Andrew is also known for 'Booth's multiplication algorithm' that he derived in 1950 while undertaking research on crystallography at Birkbeck College in Bloomsbury, London.

Between 1947 and 1953, Andrew and Kathleen, assisted by a very small team, built two more computers aside from the ARC/ARC2. The first was an experimental fully electronic computer named the Simple Electronic Computer (SEC), a redesign of the ARC2. A fully electronic machine, it required no mechanical moving parts (aside from the drum drive) and relied solely on electricity and electric current. The second, was the APE(X)C (All-Purpose Electronic (X) Computer).

In 1953 the couple published a book, *Automatic Digital Calculators* (Butterworths Scientific Publications, London), which considered various topics, such as an introduction to computing machinery, the mechanical age of computing, the arrival of electronic techniques, and the design of a computing system. It was also in this book that Kathleen explained the Planning and Coding style of programming.

In 1957, Kathleen, Andrew and J.C. Jennings co-founded the School of Computer Science and Information Systems at Birkbeck College. The following year Kathleen taught a programming course and authored one of the first books describing how to program APE(X)C computers. She also wrote the first assembly language and designed the assembler and autocode for the first computer systems at Birkbeck College. In all, she helped design three different machines, including the ARC (Automatic Relay Calculator), SEC (Simple Electronic Computer), and APE(X)C.

Kathleen's research on neural networks led to successful programs simulating ways in which animals recognise patterns and character. During the 1961-2 academic year, Kathleen and Andrew resigned from Birkbeck College and they relocated to Canada, where she became a Research Fellow, Lecturer and Associate Professor at the University of Saskatchewan from 1962 to 1972. She then accepted a position as a Professor of Mathematics at Lakehead University, working there until her retirement in 1978.

In January 1993 she co-authored a paper with her son, Dr. Ian J. M. Booth. Titled 'Using neural nets to identify marine mammals', it outlined an artificial neural network that was created to recognise the calls of individual seals. It was found to perform well with the animals tested.

Andrew passed away on 29 November 2009 at the age of 91, his marriage to Kathleen lasting for 59 years. Kathleen died at age 100 on 29 September 2022. For many years her outstanding achievements were unheralded, but her legacy has paved the way for higher level languages such as FORTRAN and COBOL to develop, making programming more accessible for everyone.

Anita Borg

Born: 17 November 1949
Died: 6 April 2003 (aged 53)

Anita Borg Naffz was born in Chicago, Illinois, her only sibling being a sister Lee Naffz. Her father had several occupations, beginning as a salesman for a family company that sold drafting materials, before selling furniture in Illinois. When she was aged one, Anita's family moved to Palatine Cook County, then just outside Chicago. It was a small village of farmers and commuters and had the feel of country living. They later moved to Washington where her father learned how to build houses, including the one they lived in. While in Illinois, her mother, Beverly, had been a housewife, but in Washington she worked for Boeing for a short time. It was she who inspired Anita to have fun solving problems, especially in mathematics.

In 1967 Anita enrolled at the University of Washington in Seattle, initially not declaring a major as she was unsure of the direction she wanted to take. As a default position she took advanced mathematics classes and in 1969 she landed her first programming job, although originally it was not her intention to go into computer science. She had taught herself to program while working at a small insurance company. She later enrolled in the PhD program at New York University, graduating in 1981 with a thesis on the synchronisation efficiency in operating systems. Her supervisors were Gerald Belpaire and the computer scientist and academic Robert Dewar.

For the first four years after graduation, Anita built a fault-tolerant Unix-based operating system, first for Auragen Systems Corp. of New Jersey, and then with Nixdorf Computer in Germany. In 1986 she joined Digital Equipment Corporation (DEC) where she spent the next twelve years, starting with Western Research Laboratory, developing and patenting a method for generating complete address traces for analysing and designing high-speed memory systems.

In 1987 Anita attended the Symposium on Operating Systems Principles (SOSP) and was dismayed to see so few women present. A group of around twelve women who were at the conference later met for lunch where the idea for a 'Systers mailing list', a private, safe online forum for women involved in technical aspects of computing, was formulated. This encouraged her to work in email communication. Systers occasionally also confronted issues that it felt stereotyped women. For example, in 1992, Mattel Inc. sold a Barbie doll that complained 'math class is tough.' The protest, led by Systers, succeeded in getting Mattel to remove that phrase from Barbie's microchip.

While a consultant engineer in the Network Systems Laboratory, Anita developed MECCA, an email and Web-based system for communicating in virtual communities. In 1994 she founded the 'Grace Hopper Celebration of Women in Computing', a series of conferences designed to highlight the research and career interests of women in computing. Her goal was to have 50% representation for women in computing by 2020, and the first of these conferences was held in Washington DC in June 1994, bringing together 500 women in technology. Anita supervised Systers until 2000, and today it is the world's largest body of women in computing.

In 1997, Anita left DEC and took on the role of a researcher in the Office of the Chief Technology Officer at Xerox PARC, soon after created the Institute for Women and Technology, a social enterprise that aimed to recruit, retain, and advance women in technology.

Anita has been honoured for her outstanding achievements, not only as a computer scientist, but for her work on behalf of women in computing. In 1995 she received the Augusta Ada Lovelace Award from the Association for Women in Computing. In the following year she was inducted as a Fellow of the Association for Computing Machinery. In 1999 she was appointed by President Bill Clinton to the Presidential Commission on the Advancement of Women and Minorities in Science, Engineering, and Technology. Her role was to recommend strategies for increasing the breadth of participation fields for women.

In 1999 Anita was diagnosed with a brain tumour, although she continued to lead the Institute for Women and Technology until 2002. In this year she was awarded the 8th Annual Heinz Award for Technology, the Economy and Employment, along with an Honorary Doctor of Science and Technology degree from Carnegie Mellon University

Other recognitions for Anita included the EFF Pioneer Award from the Electronic Frontier Foundation, recognition by the Girl Scouts of the USA, as well being named on the list of *Open Computing* magazine's Top 100 Women in Computing. She was also a member of the board of directors of the Computing Research Association and served as a member of the National Research Council's Committee on Women in Science and Engineering.

Anita passed away 6 April 2003 at age 53 of brain cancer, in Sonoma, California. She was survived by her husband, Winfried Wilcke, her mother, Beverly Naffz and her sister, Lee Naffz.

In 2003, the Institute for Women and Technology was renamed the Anita Borg Institute for Women and Technology, in her honour. In 2004, Google established the Google Anita Borg Memorial Scholarship, changing its name in 2017 to the Women Techmakers Scholars Program. In Sydney, Australia, the University of NSW School of Computer Science and Engineering has established the annual Anita Borg Prize for 'For contribution to the promotion or enhancement of the benefits of computing to society, including encouraging or facilitating the participation of women in computing and meritorious academic performance'.

In a 1999 interview with Girl Geeks, Anita shared her philosophy: 'Being in technology is hard, but in the bigger picture, anything that is really worth doing in our lives is – stick with it. See if you can find ways to combine your vocation and your avocation, your intellect and your passion!'

Ellen Broad

Born: 14 October 1987

Ellen Marie Broad was born in Perth, Western Australia, to Clare Agnes (Scammell) Broad, a primary school teacher and Richard Burgess Broad, a bank manager. She has two older brothers (Stephen and Ross), and a younger sister (Katherine).

Despite excelling in mathematics and science until she reached her teens, Ellen never thought she would go into a computing career. Her earliest memory of maths in school is being twelve and representing Western Australia in the mathematics component of the Tournament of Minds competition, where her team built a millennium time machine. By the end of high school, however, Ellen had drifted away from maths and science, recalling that her teachers pulled her out of the classroom to reprimand her for her terrible grades. She also remembers telling her mother that she wanted to be a librarian because they got to work with books all day, only for her mother to say she should expect more than that. By the end of high school, Ellen was focused on starting a double degree in law and arts at the University of Western Australia, and saving up enough money to move to Paris.

Ellen took a gap year from her law degree and moved to Paris for a year at age nineteen, working the day shift in a jazz café in the Latin Quarter while living in a sixth-floor 12m x 2m attic in Montmartre. Returning to Perth, Ellen worked for the multinational law firm Mallesons Stephens Jaques (now King & Wood Mallesons) as a paralegal in Applied Legal Technology. She was, by her own admission, a terrible law student and completed her law degree with rejections from every law firm and government department to which she applied.

Ellen fell into computing by accident, taking up a role with the Australian Digital Alliance, a national copyright non-profit organisation focused on emerging technologies as its Executive Officer. This turned out to be a wonderful way into computing for someone curious about the impact of new technologies in the world, and with an insatiable need to understand exactly how everything technically worked.

In 2013 at age 24, Ellen was approached to join the International Federation of Library Associations & Institutions in The Hague, The Netherlands, where she spent a year providing technology policy advocacy and training to organisations and governments in Europe, South America, North America and Southeast Asia. She worked on a copyright treaty for libraries and archives, and supporting the Marrakesh Treaty for the Visually Impaired, at the World Intellectual Property Organisation in Geneva. Then, determined to switch from technology policy to making and implementing technological solutions, Ellen moved to the Open Data Institute (founded by Sir Tim Berners Lee and Sir Nigel Shadbolt) headquartered in London.

It was here that Ellen began researching and producing tools to help people understand how to use data safely. It was at the Open Data Institute that Ellen co-designed the board game, Datopolis, with ODI CEO Jeni Tennison, that ended up being sold in nineteen countries. She also created the Data Ethics Canvas, one of the earliest data ethics tools to come out of the AI wave of the early twenty-first century. This was later translated into Spanish, German and French and became the most visited page on the ODI website.

Returning to Australia in 2016, Ellen was one of the first to call on Australian governments and organisations to take data ethics seriously as they increasingly rolled out automated decision-making tools affecting citizens. A lecture for the ABC's Big Ideas program became the basis of a book after then-CEO Louise Adler heard Ellen on Radio National. Ellen published *Made by Humans: the AI Condition* (Melbourne University Publishing, 2018), the first Australian study for mainstream audiences to seriously engage with the complexities and errors of AI systems. In 2019 Ellen was named one of the inaugural '100 Women in AI Ethics' worldwide.

Between 2017–2019, Ellen stood up the engineering program for CSIRO's Data61 designing API standards and software validation tools for Australians sharing their own banking data, a 'nation building' effort to produce data infrastructure that would support more flexible and empowering financial products for consumers. Then she moved to the Australian National University to join renowned technologist and anthropologist, Distinguished Professor Genevieve Bell AO's institute, the 3A Institute, as an academic exploring what new approaches to trustworthy, responsible AI engineering should look like.

In August 2022, Ellen took leave from ANU to join the office of the Minister of Industry and Science, Ed Husic, as his senior adviser on Science and Technology. She has two children, Jean and Nico, with her husband Aaron.

Joy Buolamwini

Born: 1989/90

Joy Buolamwini was born in Edmonton, Alberta, to Ghanaian parents, her mother being an artist and her father completing his PhD in pharmaceutical sciences at the University of Alberta. She spent her early childhood in Ghana, coming to the United States at the age of four when her father accepted a post at the University of Mississippi. Joy was then raised in Mississippi where she attended Cordova High School. At age nine she was inspired by 'Kismet', the MIT robot head made there in the late 1990s by the American roboticist and entrepreneur Dr. Cynthia Breazeal as an experiment in affective computing; a machine that could recognise and simulate emotions. Joy taught herself the markup language XHTML, along with the computer languages JavaScript and PHP.

Joy enrolled in a computer science degree at Georgia Institute of Technology, where she researched health informatics. In 2011 she collaborated with the Trachoma program at Carter Center. The center trains and equips local health workers to surgically correct eyelids deformed by trachomatous trichiasis (TT), the scarring that results from multiple trachoma infections. Joy developed an Android-based assessment system for Ethiopia and assisted in the drive to eradicate the disease worldwide. In the following year she graduated as a Stamps President's Scholar and was the youngest finalist of the Georgia Tech InVenture Prize in 2009, at age 20.

In addition, Joy was a Rhodes Scholar, enabling her to study technology at Jesus College, Oxford. During her time there she took part in the Rhodes Service Year, working on community-focused projects, including the launch of Code4Rights, a technology education initiative. As a Fulbright Fellow, she developed the idea of empowering Zambian youth to become creators of technology. She was also an Anita Borg Institute scholar, an award for women studying computing at university at undergraduate and postgraduate level. They are funded and administered by Google in memory of the renowned American computer scientist Anita Borg.

On 14 September 2016 Joy attended the White House summit on Computer Science on artificial intelligence (AI). In the same year she founded the Algorithmic Justice League (AJL) that sought to acquire equitable and accountable AI. The AJL combines art and research to illuminate the societal implications and harms of AI, with the mission 'to raise public awareness about the impacts of AI, equip society with research, give a voice to the most vulnerable communities, and galvanise the tech industry and Congress'. It operates on four guiding principles: affirmative consent, meaningful transparency, continuous oversight and accountability, and actionable critique. AJL aims to highlight the bias in code that can lead to discrimination against underrepresented groups.

In 2017 Joy graduated from MIT with a master's degree, her research supervised by Ethan Zuckerman who was the director of the MIT Center for Civic Media. Part of her investigations included showing facial recognition systems 1,000 faces and asked them to identify whether faces were female or male. She concluded that software found it difficult to identify dark-skinned women.

Her project, Gender Shades, gained media attention and formed part of her MIT thesis. In 2018 she co-authored, with Timnit Gebru, the paper 'Gender Shades: Intersectional Accuracy Disparities in Commercial Gender Classification' that appeared in the 2018 Proceedings of Machine Learning Research. Her findings prompted IBM and Microsoft to improve their software.

Joy also created the 'Aspire Mirror', a device that lets you see a reflection of yourself based on what inspires you. She has created two films, *Code4Rights* and *Algorithmic Justice League: Unmasking Bias*, the latter highlighting 'the stories of people who have been impacted by harmful technology and shows pioneering women sounding the alarm about the threats artificial intelligence poses to civil rights'. The documentary premiered at the Sundance Film Festival in January 2020.

In 2017, Joy was awarded the grand prize in the professional category in the 'Search for Hidden Figures' competition that was related to the release of the film *Hidden Figures* in December 2016. The contest, which attracted 7,300 submissions from young women across the US, was sponsored by PepsiCo and 21st Century Fox. Its aim was 'help uncover the next generation of female leaders in science, technology, engineering and math'.

In 2018 Joy appeared on TED Radio Hour and was featured on Amy Poehler's 'Smart Girls'. In the same year she was listed by *Fast Company* magazine as one of four 'design heroes who are defending democracy online' as well as being included as one of BBC's *100 Women*. She was included in *Fortune* magazine's 2019 list of the World's Greatest Leaders, being described as 'the conscience of the AI revolution'. In 2019 she was part of the inaugural

Time 100 Next list and in 2020 featured in a Levi's woman empowerment campaign for 8 March International Women's Day.

The 86-minute 2020 movie *Coded Bias* is a documentary film, directed by Shalini Kantayya, that follows Joy's research into AI inaccuracies in facial recognition technology and automated assessment software. The documentary has so far won three awards, including winner of the best international biography at the Calgary International Film Festival (2020), the New York Women in Film & Television Award at Hamptons International Film Festival (2020) and Grand Reportage at the International Film Festival and Forum on Human Rights (2021).

Joy currently serves on the Global Tech Panel convened by the vice president of the European Commission to advise world leaders and technology executives on ways to reduce the harms of AI. She is currently a researcher at the MIT Media Lab, where she identifies bias in algorithms and develops practices for accountability during their design, as well as Chief Technology Officer for Techturized Inc, a haircare technology company.

Alice Burks

Born: 20 August 1920
Died: 21 November 2017 (aged 97)

Alice Rowe was born and raised in East Cleveland, Ohio, along with her three brothers, Bus, Bill and Fred, who was her twin. She was an exceptional student at Lakewood High School in Lakewood, Ohio, and was valedictorian. She won a competitive mathematics scholarship that enabled her to attend Oberlin College in Ohio, but after two-and-a-half years she ran out of money and asked her mathematics professor to help her find a job. He had a friend in Aberdeeen in Brown County, Ohio, and so Alice decided to spend a month there before returning to Oberlin.

Her plans changed in July 1942 when she met her future husband, Arthur Burks, whom she married the following year. She was told of a project at the University of Pennsylvania in Philadelphia and immediately applied to go there, then being employed as a 'human computer'. This involved calculating artillery trajectories for the war effort at their Moore School of Electrical Engineering. She graduated with a Bachelor of Arts in mathematics in 1944.

Alice retired from full-time work after marrying Arthur, who was a mathematician employed as one of the principal engineers in the construction of the ENIAC, the world's first general-purpose electronic digital computer. It was constructed at the Moore School between 1943 and 1946 and, although there were a number of other female human computers, Alice did not work directly with the ENIAC.

In 1946, the couple moved to Ann Arbor, Michigan, where Arthur joined the faculty of the University of Michigan and was part of the team who founded the computer science department. Alice furthered her education by earning a Master of Science degree in educational psychology in 1957 from the university.

Alice became embroiled in an interesting court case. Honeywell, Inc. v. Sperry Rand Corp., et al. led to a landmark ruling. The US federal court ruled in October 1973 that the 1964 patent for the ENIAC was invalid. The result was that the invention of the electronic digital computer came into the public domain. Alice and Arthur publicly backed John Vincent Atanasoff, a largely unknown Iowa State College physics professor, whom the court had ruled invented the first electronic digital computer that was named the Atanasoff–Berry Computer in the 1930s and from which the ENIAC was ruled to be derived.

In 1989, Alice and Arthur co-authored the 400-page *The First Electronic Computer: The Atanasoff Story* (University of Michigan Press), which examined the Atanasoff computer and its influence on the ENIAC, along with other computers. It also provided a technical foundation as well as a narrative involving human interest and won the 1989 University of Michigan Press Award.

In 2003 Alice was the sole author of the 415-page book, *Who Invented the Computer? The Legal Battle That Changed Computing History* (Prometheus), a volume that centred on the court case and declared that the Judge Larson had indeed made the correct decision, even though many in the computing community have never accepted Atanasoff as the legitimate inventor of the electronic computer.

Alice's forthright stance pitted her in a very acrimonious controversy against the exponents of the ENIAC inventors, John Mauchly and J. Presper Eckert. In the ensuing years, and still in Ann Arbor, Alice assisted Arthur with writing his memoirs and preparing his papers for university donation. Arthur died on 14 May 2008 after 65 years of marriage. Alice served as a critic and editor of his many publications while raising their three children, Edward, Nancy and Douglas. Alice and her family enjoyed frequent travel in the US, Europe and Asia, with a sabbatical leave in India providing a great deal of material for her own writing. She had authored a young person's novel, *Leela and the Leopard Hunt* (Methuen, London), in 1983.

Alice passed away peacefully of natural causes aged 97 on 21 November 2017. She was survived by her three children, her three brothers had pre-deceased her. Throughout her life, she was involved in many charitable activities, especially those devoted to her values of peace, fairness, and community. Living out her final five years at Huron Woods senior community, Alice enjoyed art, music, and playing cards late into the night. In recognition of her achievements, she received the Old Gold Medal from DePauw University, a highly ranked national liberal arts university in Indiana, in 2000.

Margaret Burnett

Born: 3 June 1949

Margaret Burnett was born and raised in Springfield, Illinois, in the US, and while growing up worked at the family's department store on vacations and Christmas holidays. It was a job she enjoyed, some years serving as a gift wrapper or in sales. She later attended Miami University in Oxford, Ohio, between 1967 and 1970, attracted by their newly established program in computer science. However, she majored in mathematics with a computer science minor in her Bachelor of Arts degree, graduating Cum Laude and Phi Beta Kappa. Following this, at age 21 she landed a role as a software engineer for Procter & Gamble in their Ivorydale factory and research centre in Cincinnati, Ohio. She was the first women to be hired in a management position but did not stay long, as she followed her husband, Bob, to Santa Fe, New Mexico. It was here that she started her own business before again relocating to Lawrence, Kansas, where Bob had been hired by the U.S. Geological Survey.

In 1979 Margaret enrolled in the computer science program at the University of Kansas, graduating with a Master of Science in 1981. The following year she founded a group for the professional women of Lawrence, Kansas, to enable them to network with each other. Known as the 'Lawrence Women's Network', it is still active today, providing 'an outlet for women in the Lawrence business community to get together and share their career experiences'.

She then worked in a small independent consulting business with William G. Bulgren, a professor at the university. By 1987 she decided to return to university studies, enrolling in the PhD program, which she completed in 1991 with honours. Her thesis, 'Abstraction in the

Demand-Driven, Temporal-Assignment, Visual Language Model' examined visual programming languages and was supervised by Allen L. Ambler. In April 1993, Margaret and Ambler published their joint paper, 'Visual programming languages from an object-oriented perspective' in the journal ACM SIGPLAN OOPS Messenger, Volume 4, Issue 2.

Following her doctorate, Margaret joined the faculty of Computer Science department at Michigan Technological University. Two years later, in 1993, she resigned to take up an appointment in the Computer Science Department at Oregon State University, becoming one of the first two women (along with Cherri M. Pancake, an ethnographer and computer scientist) to be given a tenure-track position there. In 1994 she received the National Science Foundation's Young Investigator Award and in 2000 Oregon State University's Elizabeth P. Ritchie Distinguished Professor Award, the University's highest teaching award.

By the early 2000s Margaret had developed techniques for software engineers to monitor whether their software was gender-inclusive. This became her field of expertise, and she delivered a number of keynote addresses on this topic, leading the team that created 'GenderMag', a software inspection process that 'helps software developers and usability professionals find and fix software features with such gender-inclusiveness "bugs"'. For the following four years from 2012 she was on the Editorial Board of ACM Transactions on Interactive Intelligent Systems.

In 2016, Margaret was made a Distinguished Professor at Oregon State University (OSU), as well as being named to the CHI Academy. In the following year she was elected as a Fellow of the Association for Computing Machinery 'for contributions to end-user software engineering, understanding gender biases in software, and broadening participation in computing'. In 2018-2019 she was a Guest Editor for a Special Issue of ACM TiiS.

Margaret is an ACM Fellow and currently serves on three editorial boards, along with the Academic Alliance Advisory Board of the National Center for Women in Technology (NCWIT) and on over 50 conference organisation and program committee roles. Her honours include being a recipient of OSU College of Engineering's Research Collaboration Award (2005), IBM's International Faculty Award (2007, 2008), the OSU College of Engineering's Research Award (2009), and OSU's Excellence in Graduate Mentoring Award (2010).

In January 2020 she was honoured with an iGIANT ('impact of Gender/ Sex on Innovation and Novel Technologies') Champion Award, and in 2021 received ACM IUI's ('Intelligent User Interfaces') Highest Impact Award, for her 2015 IUI paper 'Principles of Explanatory Debugging to Personalize Interactive Machine Learning', co-authored with Todd Kulesza, Weng-Keen Wong, and Simone Stumpf.

Margaret is still undertaking outstanding teaching and research. In March 2023 she joined ACM TOSEM's Editorial Board. She reveals that she has spent most of her time recently 'taking a serious look at software engineering aspects of end-user programming. The objective is to improve the dependability of software produced by end-user programming languages.'

Karen Catlin

Born: 1963

Karen was born and raised in the small town of Westerly in Rhode Island, USA, the same place where her father and paternal grandfather also grew up. While she was in high school, her father advised her that as she loved crafting and making things, was good at maths, and enjoyed solving puzzles, maybe she could combine them and major in this new field called 'computer science'. He had discovered an article in *Money* magazine that dealt with how women with computer science degrees were making substantial amounts of it!

Karen graduated from high school in 1981 at a time when computers were rising in popularity. It was the year that the PC came to market, and three years later the Apple Macintosh appeared. Although she had not touched or even seen a computer, she took her father's advice and decided that this was the field for her. To this end, she applied to the best school in an 80-kilometre radius, Brown University located in Providence, Rhode Island, and she was accepted.

In her last summer before graduating, Karen continued her interest in applied research with a job at IRIS, a new group at Brown that focused on hypertext and combining object-oriented programming with modern user interface technology. She later said that 'This was long before today's browsers, and it makes me happy that our work had an influence on HTML and the Internet that followed.'

In 1985 she earned her bachelor's degree with a major in computer science. It was during her time at university that she met her husband, Tim, someone she describes as fortunately being more adventurous than her. Happy to be coding for a living, she signed on full-time with IRIS after graduating and stayed with the organisation for five years until 1990.

At this time, the couple moved to England, just outside of London, where Karen obtained a position at Hitachi Europe Limited, undertaking similar research to that during her time at Brown. However, she became dissatisfied with her role and the pair relocated to the San Francisco Bay Area, living among a community of software engineers and she soon became one of them, joining a startup company called GO Corp, which was developing an early tablet computer. She later moved into their project management team, but the company, like many others of its type at the time, was not a success and so she left.

Her next role saw her spending the following twelve years at the graphics, multimedia, and web development software company Macromedia that had started in 1992, and that later made well-known products including Flash and Dreamweaver. Here she rose to an executive level, as well as starting her family. In December 2005 Macromedia was acquired by its rival, the multinational computer software company Adobe, and it was with them that Karen started Adobe's women's initiative to provide career development opportunities and support to women across the company. She was an executive at Adobe Systems between 2006 and 2012 where she was responsible for shared engineering services.

In 2012 she commenced her organisation Karen Catlin Consulting in which she serves as a leadership coach for women and helps them in motivational speaking, imparting knowledge on how to make it in the world of computing. She is a frequent speaker at technology events and in 2014 started the Twitter handle @betterallies to share simple, actionable steps that anyone could take to make their workplace more inclusive.

Karen has published three books: *Present! A Techie's Guide to Public Speaking* (co-authored with Poornima Vijayashanker) (2015), *Better Allies: Everyday Actions to Create Inclusive, Engaging Workplaces* (2019), and *The Better Allies Approach to Hiring* (2020).

Today she is a highly sought-after and engaging presenter and is determined to bring more diversity to speaker lineups at tech industry events. In 2014 Karene spoke at TEDx at the College Of William And Mary with the event theme being 'Forward'. Her topic was on women in the software industry, and how they are missing from the force shaping the future of technology

Beatrice Mabel Cave-Browne-Cave

Born: 30 May 1874
Died: 9 July 1947 (aged 73)

Beatrice Cave-Browne-Cave was born in Streatham and raised in the 'Burnage', Streatham Common in North London, the daughter of Sir Thomas Cave-Browne-Cave and Blanche Matilda Mary Ann (née Milton). She was one of six siblings. Beatrice was educated at home, and in 1895 attended, along with her younger sister Frances, Girton College, Cambridge.

In 1898, Beatrice graduated with a second-class honours degree in the first part of the mathematical tripos, a prestigious course taught in the faculty of mathematics. In the following year, she passed Part II of the mathematical tripos with third-class honours. As there were few options for female mathematicians at the time, Beatrice spent the next eleven years teaching mathematics to girls at a high school in Clapham in south-west London, as well as undertaking computing work at home.

In 1913, an opening appeared in the Galton Laboratory at University College, London, Beatrice worked under the eminent mathematician and statistician Professor Karl Pearson. She was among six researchers, including her sister Frances, who collaborated on a large child development study led by Pearson. Initially she performed work in statistics, but as the Great War progressed she took the opportunity to supplement her income by working at the Admiralty, performing aircraft tail loading analysis and studying aircraft oscillations. Pearson was reportedly not happy with her taking on outside work.

The project undertaken by Pearson was an attempt to establish evidence of the inheritance of attributes by collecting physical and mental data from 4000 children and their parents. Beatrice assisted in the collection and processing of data, as well as performing relevant analysis. She co-authored with Pearson two articles in *Biometrika*, a journal of statistics in which emphasis is placed on papers containing original theoretical contributions of direct or potential value in applications. One of these papers was 'Numerical Illustrations of the Variate Difference Method' (Vol. 10, No. 2/3, 340-365) in 1914, the other was 'On The Distribution of the Correlation Coefficient In Small Samples. Appendix Ii to the Papers Of 'Student' And R. A. Fisher. A Cooperative Study', co-authored with Pearson, H.E. Soper, A.W. Young and A. Lee. It appeared in *Biometrika* Vol. 11, No. 4, May 1917, 328–413.

In 1916, Beatrice carried out original research for the government on the mathematics of aeronautics and aircraft design, the project remaining classified under the Official Secrets Act for fifty years. Her work involved an examination of the effects of loads on different areas of planes during flight, and her research helped to improve aircraft stability and propeller efficiency.

Beatrice carried out other research at the Galton Laboratory, including computations on bomb trajectories, terminal velocities, timber tests, and detonators for the Admiralty Air Department and Ministry of Munitions. Some of her output, including correspondence and work, is held in the University of London College (UCL) archives.

In 1917 she created a set of correlation tables showing amount of pigment, connecting old and new processes of determining amount of pigmentation, mother and son pigmentation percentages, grandparents and grandchildren, and father and son amount of pigment in mice. They were based on a series of mice breeding experiments conducted by Raphael Weldon, who was a colleague of Pearson's.

Beatrice was elected an Associate Fellow of the Royal Aeronautical Society in 1919 and in the following year was awarded an MBE 'for services in connection with the War'. In 1922 she was an assistant to Sir Leonard Bairstow, the Zaharoff Professor of Aviation at Imperial College, where she worked on fluid motion. In the same year her results on aircraft oscillations were published in an Advisory Committee for Aeronautics technical report, her name also appearing alongside Bairstow in his 1922 and 1923 published reports on fluid mechanics.

In 1937, Beatrice retired, continuing to live in Streatham, passing away at age 73 on 9 July 1947. In 2012, her 100-page biography *Beatrice Mabel Cave-Browne-Cave* was authored by Eldon A. Mainyu and published by Aud Publishing.

Edith Clarke

Born: 10 February 1883
Died: 29 October 1959 (aged 76)

One of nine children, Edith Clarke was born on 10 February 1883 in Ellicott City, Howard County, Maryland, US, into a prosperous family. Her mother was Susan Dorsey (Owings) Clarke and father, John Ridgely Clarke. Edith's father died when she was seven and her mother when Edith was twelve years old. Edith's uncle became her legal guardian. Her upbringing was typical for girls of the day with her status, the emphasis being on proper grooming in preparation for marriage and motherhood. To this end, Edith attended Briarley Hall, a boarding school for girls in Montgomery County. Here she studied Latin, History and English literature, along with receiving a rigorous training in arithmetic, algebra, and geometry, which laid the groundwork for her future profession.

Inheriting money from her parents' estate at the age of eighteen, Edith enrolled to study mathematics and astronomy at Vassar College in New York, from which she graduated in 1908 and was invited to join Phi Beta Kappa, America's oldest academic honour society. From there she taught mathematics and physics at a private school in San Francisco and Marshall College in Huntingdon. Edith also developed a passion for engineering and decided to pursue formal qualifications in the field. In 1911, she enrolled in the civil engineering program at the University of Wisconsin-Madison, but at the end of her first year took up a summer position as a computer assistant to an AT & T research engineer, Dr George Campbell, whose research included the application of mathematical methods to the problems of long-distance electrical transmissions. One of her first assigned computational tasks was to calculate the first seven terms of an infinite series that represented a probability function.

Edith eventually became the manager of a group of women 'computers' who made calculations for the Transmission and Protection Engineering Department during the First World War. At this time she also studied radio at Hunter College, and electrical engineering at Columbia University. She left her role at AT & T in 1918 to study electrical engineering at the Massachusetts Institute of Technology in Boston, earning a master's degree in 1919, the first electrical engineering degree ever awarded to a woman at that institution. Her thesis, supervised by the Irish-American electrical engineer, Arthur Edwin Kennelly, was titled 'Behavior of a lumpy artificial transmission line as the frequency is indefinitely increased'.

Not being able to find employment as an engineer, Edith accepted a role at General Electric as a supervisor of computers in the Turbine Engineering Department. In 1921, while employed at General Electric, she invented the 'Clarke calculator', a simple graphical device that solved equations involving electric current, voltage and impedance in power transmission lines. It could solve line equations involving hyperbolic functions ten times faster than previous methods. She filed a patent for the device in 1921, which was granted in 1925. Still unable to obtain a position as an engineer, Edith left General Electric to teach physics at the Constantinople Women's College in Turkey for the following two years.

On her return, she was re-hired by General Electric, now as an electrical engineer in the Central Station Engineering Department. Between 1923 and 1945, Edith published eighteen technical papers and in doing so, became an authority on the manipulation of hyperbolic functions, equivalent circuits, and graphical analysis. In 1926, she became the first woman to present a paper before the American Institute of Electrical Engineers. Titled 'Steady-state stability in transmission systems', it described a mathematical technique to model a power system and its behaviour, allowing engineers to analyse the longer transmission lines then becoming more common.

Another of her papers, which she co-authored in 1941, was published in the *Transactions of the American Institute of Electrical Engineers*, receiving the National First Paper Prize of the Year award. It was reported as 'the first published mathematical examination of transmission lines over 300 miles long, and the first published use of the network analyser to obtain data'. Her book, *Circuit Analysis of A–C Power Systems*, based on the notes for her lectures to General Electric engineers, and published in 1943, soon became the main textbook for new engineers. A second volume appeared in 1950.

In 1945, at age sixty-two and after twenty-six years of service, Edith retired from General Electric. Two years later, however, Edith was appointed a full professor at the University of Texas, becoming the first female professor of electrical engineering in the country. In 1948, she became the first woman elected as a Fellow of the American Institute of Electrical Engineers (now known as the Institute for Electrical and Electronics Engineers). In an interview in the *Daily Texan* on 4 March that year, she remarked, 'There is no demand for women engineers, as such, as there are for women doctors; but there's always a demand for anyone who can do a good piece of work.'

In 1954, Edith received the Society of Women Engineers Achievement Award 'in recognition of her many original contributions to stability theory and circuit analysis'. Three years later she retired from her academic position in Texas and was the first female engineer to achieve professional standing in Tau Beta Pi, the oldest engineering honour society in the US.

Edith Clarke passed away in hospital in Olney, Maryland on 29 October 1959 at the age of seventy-six. She never married. In 2015, she was posthumously inducted into the National Inventors Hall of Fame.

In 1985, a leader in the engineering industry, Dr James E Brittain, wrote of Edith:

Edith Clarke's engineering career had as its central theme the development and dissemination of mathematical methods that tended to simplify and reduce the time spent in laborious calculations in solving problems in the design and operation of electrical power systems. She translated what many engineers found to be esoteric mathematical methods into graphs or simpler forms during a time when power systems were becoming more complex and when the initial efforts were being made to develop electromechanical aids to problem solving. As a woman who worked in an environment traditionally dominated by men, she demonstrated effectively that women could perform at least as well as men if given the opportunity. Her outstanding achievements provided an inspiring example for the next generation of women with aspirations to become career engineers.

Mary Clem

Born: 19 October 1905
Died: January 1979 (aged 73)

Mary McLaughlin was born the daughter of Michael McLaughlin and Lucy A. Wheelock in the small town of Nevada, Story County, in western Iowa. She was the second of seven children, with siblings James (b. 1904), Bertha (b. 1907), Florence (b. 1910), Michael (b. 1917), Lucy (b. 1920) and Dorothy (b. 1924). After completing high school, she was employed for six years with the Iowa State Highway Commission and Iowa State College as a computing clerk, auditing clerk, and bookkeeper.

In 1931, at age 26, Mary joined the Mathematics Statistical Service of the Mathematics Department of Iowa State College as its only staff member with primary responsibilities in computing. In 1936 she worked in a group of mainly women as a 'human computer' under the supervision of the prominent American mathematician and statistician George Snedecor. Although mathematics was her poorest subject in high school, she was fascinated with numbers and data, soon becoming quite adept when working with them. Much of her efforts involved dealing with punch cards, both creating formulas and cards, and running accuracy checks on them.

While working in Snedecor's laboratory, Mary invented the term and method 'zero check', which is a sum that should equal zero if all other numbers had been correctly calculated. These sums helped check for errors in computing algorithms and she felt that her lack of training as a mathematician is what made her notice these sums, which had often been overlooked by others. When the American statistician and founder of the department of Experimental Statistics at North Carolina State University, Gertrude Cox, left in 1940, Mary was promoted to the rank of technician and chief statistical clerk in charge of the Computing Service of the Statistical

Laboratory. During her time there she performed hundreds of thousands of mathematical calculations and her computing lab became one of the most powerful computing facilities of the time.

In 1946, Mary accompanied the 2nd Allied Mission to Greece as a junior statistician, and while there observed the elections held on 31 March that year. The result was a victory for the United Alignment of Nationalists. In 1947 she published, along with co-authors Paul G. Homeyer and Walter T. Federer, her only research paper, entitled 'Punched card and calculating machine methods for analyzing lattice experiments including lattice squares and the cubic lattice'. It appeared in the *Iowa Agriculture and Home Economics Experiment Station Research Bulletin*, Vol. 28, No. 347, Article 1.

In 1952 Mary served as a statistical consultant to the Atomic Bomb Casualty Commission in Hiroshima, Japan, and in 1962 she transferred to the new Computation Center at Iowa State University. She passed away in 1979 at age 74.

On 1 July 1996 Iowa State University laid a paving stone, No. 45, in their Plaza of heroines, for eight women, the with the inscription 'Statistics Dept. & Lab.'. Mary Clem is one of them.

Lynn Ann Conway

Born: 2 January 1938

Lynn Conway was born in Mount Vernon, New York and raised in White Plains, New York. He later adopted the pseudonym 'Robert Sanders' to protect his parents, a schoolteacher and a chemical engineer, from unwelcome attention. From an early age he exhibited a high IQ, as well as being shy and experiencing gender dysphoria. While still young, he developed a fascination with astronomy, one summer building a 150 mm reflector telescope. At high school he excelled in mathematics and science, enabling him in 1955 to enrol at MIT as a 17-year-old. However, after a failed attempt at gender transition in 1957-58, he left and worked for the next few years as an electronics technician.

Robert resumed his education in the School of Engineering and Applied Science at Columbia University, graduating with a Bachelor of Science in 1962 and Master of Science in Electrical Engineering in 1963. The following year he was recruited by IBM Research in Yorktown Heights, New York, and was chosen to join the architecture team designing an advanced supercomputer. He joined others on the Advanced Computing Systems (ACS) project that was responsible for the invention of generalised dynamic instruction handling.

The ACS was a key advance used in out-of-order execution, used by most modern computer processors to improve performance. It is described by the Computer History Museum as appearing to have been 'the first superscalar design, a computer architectural paradigm widely exploited in modern high-performance microprocessors.'

In the late 1960s Robert became aware of the pioneering research of Harry Benjamin in treating transsexual women. As he had struggled to cope with life in a male role, Robert contacted him and became his patient, agreeing to undertake counselling and take prescribed hormones. And so he began a gender transition. At the time he was married to a woman and had two children. IBM fired him in 1968 after he revealed his intention to transition, something for which the company in 2020 apologised.

Then adopting the new name 'Lynn Conway' and identity, under the legal constraints of the time, she was denied access to her children after transitioning, restarting her career in 1968 in what she called 'stealth-mode' as a contract programmer at Computer Applications, Inc. Between 1969 and 1972 Lynn worked as a digital system designer and computer architect at Memorex, a company founded in 1961 that started by selling computer tapes before later adding other media including disk packs.

In 1973, Xerox recruited Lynn to work at the company's new research center at Xerox PARC where she led the 'LSI Systems' group under Bert Sutherland where she founded the 'multiproject wafers' (MPW). This new technology not only made it possible to pack multiple circuit designs from various sources into a single chip, but it also increased production and decreased costs.

In 1978, Lynn was appointed as a visiting associate professor of electrical engineering and computer science at MIT. In 1980 she co-authored, with Carver Mead, the 396-page volume *Introduction to VLSI Systems* (Addison-Wesley), a groundbreaking work that would soon become a standard textbook in chip design. The course she lectured validated the new design methods and by 1983 their book had been used in nearly 120 universities with sales of over 70,000 copies.

With the new integration of her MPC79/MOSIS innovations, the Mead and Conway revolution became part of VLSI design that spread quickly through the research universities and computing industries during the 1980s. This was the forerunner of an emerging electronic design automation industry, spawning the modern 'foundry' infrastructure for chip design and production. It was also the catalyst for an avalanche of impactful high-tech startups in the 1980s and 1990s.

In the early 1980s, Lynn left Xerox for the Defense Advanced Research Projects Agency (DARPA), a research and development agency of the United States Department of Defense. Here she was a key architect of the Defense Department's Strategic Computing Initiative, a research program studying high-performance computing, autonomous systems technology, and intelligent weapons technology.

Lynn's other contributions to the development of computing included the invention of dimensionless, scalable design rules that greatly simplified chip design and design tools. It also helped develop a new form of internet-based infrastructure for rapid prototyping and short-run fabrication of large numbers of chip designs, known in 1981 as the Metal Oxide Semiconductor Implementation Service (MOSIS) system. Two years later, Lynn and Mead received *Electronics* magazine's annual award for achievement. Since that time, MOSIS has fabricated more than 50,000 circuit designs for commercial firms, government agencies, and research and educational institutions around the world.

Lynn was appointed as a professor of electrical engineering and computer science at the University of Michigan in 1985, also being the associate dean of engineering. In 1987, Lynn met her future husband Charles Rogers, a professional engineer who shared her interest in outdoor activities, including whitewater canoeing and motocross. They purchased a 24-acre (9.7-hectare) property in rural Michigan in 1994 and the couple were married on 13 August 2002. In 2012, the IEEE published a special issue of the IEEE Journal of Solid-State Circuits devoted to outlining Lynn's career.

In 2020, the National Academy of Engineers, President John L. Anderson, remarked that 'Lynn Conway is not only a revolutionary pioneer in the design of VLSI systems ... But just as important, Lynn has been very brave in telling her own story, and her perseverance has been a reminder to society that it should not be blind to the innovations of women, people of color, or others who don't fit long outdated – but unfortunately, persistent – perceptions of what an engineer looks like.'

Lynn has received many honours for her achievements, which include the Electronics Award for Achievement with Carver Mead (1981), the Harold Pender Award of the Moore School, University of Pennsylvania, with Carver Mead (1984), and the IEEE EAB Major Educational Innovation Award (1984). Lynn was made a Fellow of the IEEE 'for contributions to VLSI technology' (1985), received the John Price Wetherill Medal of the Franklin Institute, with Carver Mead (1985), received the Secretary of Defense Meritorious Civilian Service Award (1985), was made a Member of the National Academy of Engineering (1989), won the National Achievement Award, Society of Women Engineers (1990), received an Honorary Doctorate from Trinity College, Cambridge (1998), was elected to the Electronic Design Hall of Fame (2002), won the Computer Pioneer Award, IEEE Computer Society (2009) and received Honorary Doctorates from the Illinois Institute of Technology (2014), the University of Victoria (2016) and the University of Michigan, Ann Arbor (2018). In 2019 she received the Pioneer in Tech Award, National Center for Women in Technology (NCWIT) and in 2020 the Lifetime Achievement Award, IBM Corporation.

Joëlle Coutaz

Born: 1946

Joëlle Coutaz received her university education from Université Joseph Fourier, in the city of Grenoble, France and now part of Université Grenoble Alpes. In 1970 she earned her doctorate in computer science with a doctoral thesis examining operating systems. She then worked as a software engineer for the French National Centre for Scientific Research (CNRS) where she developed her research interests in operating systems and computer networks. Among other things, in 1972, Joëlle explored the use of packet switching for interconnecting computers.

From 1983 to 1984, she worked as a visiting scientist at Carnegie Mellon University where her research interests shifted to the problem of human–computer interaction, inspired in part by attendance at the second Computer Human Interaction (CHI) conference in 1983.

After her return to France in 1985 she focused her research on problems related to software architecture modeling for interactive systems, including multimodal interaction, augmented reality, and user interface plasticity, in an effort to establish sound software engineering methods for building human-computer interaction (HCI) systems.

In 1987, Joëlle invented the presentation-abstraction-control (PAC) software architecture model for interactive systems, resolving a number of problems with the recently published Model View Controller (MVC) architecture model. Many of the innovations proposed in PAC have since been incorporated into modern forms of MVC in what should properly be called PAC-MVC. In 1988, Joelle earned her Thèse d'Etat (state thesis) in human-computer interaction from Université Joseph Fourier in Grenoble, qualifying her for appointment as a university professor. Her thesis manuscript, in French, was published as a textbook, and has served as a foundational text for the development of the French research community on human–computer interaction.

Between 1989 and 1995, she participated in the European Multi-disciplinary AMODEUS project, a basic research action funded by the European Commission ESPRIT program. AMODEUS brought together researchers from cognitive science, mathematics and computer science to develop the foundations for the design and implementation of interactive systems.

In 1993, Joëlle collaborated with her former doctoral student and now colleague Laurence Nigay to combine the PAC model with ARCH, a model designed for the implementation of multimodal user interfaces. In 1998 she served as program co-chair of ACM CHI conference in Los Angeles.

From 2001 to 2004 she participated in the European FAME collaborative project (Facilitating Agent in Multicultural Exchange), exploring creation of intelligent agents that could facilitate communication between people of different cultures when solving common problems. Within FAME, her architectural models were used to develop new techniques for multimodal interaction, including vision, speech and object manipulation to create and manipulate new information based on context. From 2001 to 2003, she participated in the European GLOSS collaborative project (Global Smart Spaces) that investigated computational models for ambient systems. In particular, she proposed a software framework for multi-surface interaction.

In 2007, Joëlle was awarded membership to SIGCHI (Special Interest Group on Computer–Human Interaction). She was an appointed member of the editorial board of ACM Transactions on Computer–Human Interaction (TOCHI). In the following year, Joëlle coordinated a group working on ambient intelligence for the Ministry of Higher Education, Research and Innovation, the aim being to solve the problems of society in novel ways. She helped to create a system that intersects information and communication technologies, along with social and human sciences.

Between 2012 and 2015, Joëlle participated in the French AppsGate project that developed a smart home control system to empower ordinary people to configure and program smart home services.

In 2013 she received several prestigious awards, including the title of IFIP TC13 Pioneer by the International Federation for Information Processing, in recognition of her 'outstanding contributions to the educational, theoretical, technical, commercial aspects of analysis, design, construction, evaluation and use of interactive systems.' On 8 March 2013, Joëlle was awarded the Legion of Honour by the Republic of France for her pioneering contributions to Human-Computer Interaction. In 2020, she was named an IFIP Fellow of the first cohort recognised by IFIP (International Federation for Information Processing) for substantial and enduring contributions.

Joëlle is a prolific author with over 130 papers to her credit. She has also authored two books, *Interfaces homme-ordinateur: conception et realisation* (1990) and *Developing Software for the User Interface* (Addison Wesley) in 1991 with Len Bass. She has also contributed numerous book chapters. Today, Joëlle is researching end-user software engineering for smart homes in the field of ubiquitous computing. Since 2012 she has been a professor emeritus at the Université Grenoble Alpes. Her advice to young researchers is: 'You need to do what you feel is right, and not follow the path comfortably paved by mainstream research areas.'

Kate Crawford

Born: 1976

Kate Crawford was raised in Canberra, Australia. She was co-founder of the Sydney-based Deluxe Mood Recordings record label and is a member of the Clan Analogue music collective, an Australian record label which started in 1992 as a co-operative interested and active in electronic music.

In 1994, at age 18 Kate joined the composer and writer Nicole Skeltys to create B(if)tek, an Australian electronic music duo. They released three albums, *Sub-Vocal Theme Park* (1996), *2020* (2000) and *Frequencies Will Move Together* (2003). They disbanded in 2003. Kate graduated with a PhD from the University of Sydney and in 2007 she published a book based on her dissertation, *Adult Themes – Rewriting the Rules of Adulthood* (Pan Macmillan) that won the individual category of the Manning Clark National Cultural Award. In 2008 she won the biennial medal for outstanding scholarship from the Australian Academy of the Humanities.

Along with writing articles for *The Sydney Morning Herald* and *Foreign Policy*, Kate was a Fellow of the Centre for Policy Development. In March 2008 she was selected as one of 1000 Australians to attend the Australia 2020 Summit in Canberra on 19–20 April 2008. The summit was announced by then Australian Prime Minister Kevin Rudd with the aim 'to help shape a long-term strategy for the nation's future'.

Among Kate's keynote presentations were those at the 2013 O'Reilly Strata Conference and in the same year the DataEDGE conference hosted by the University of California School of Information. In 2014 she co-authored with Chris Chesher, Anne Dunn, and Scott Shaner *Understanding the Internet: Language, Technology, Media, and Power* (Palgrave Macmillan).

Kate has held a number of key positions, including as a principal researcher at Microsoft Research (Social Media Collective), a senior fellow at the Information Law Institute at New York University, an associate professor in the Journalism and Media Research Centre at the University of New South Wales, and a visiting professor at the MIT Center for Civic Media. She is also the co-founder, with Meredith Whittaker, and director of research at the AI Now Institute that had its origins in 2017 after a symposium hosted by the White House under President Barack Obama.

She is also a member of the World Economic Forum's Global Agenda Council on Data-Driven Development, having published on cultures of technology use and the way media histories have led to the present day. Her research examines social change and media technologies, especially those involving the intersection of humans, mobile devices, and social networks. In 2018, Kate was awarded the Richard von Weizsäcker Fellowship, a program of the Robert Bosch Academy in Germany.

In 2019 Kate was the inaugural holder of the AI & Justice visiting chair at École Normale Supérieure in Paris, in partnership with Foundation Abeona. In the same year, her project 'Anatomy of an AI System' with Vladan Joler won the Beazley Design of the Year Award and is in the permanent collection of the Museum of Modern Art in New York and the V&A Museum in London. It is an anatomical case study in the form of a large-scale map and essay of the Amazon Echo as an artificial intelligence system made of human labour, data and planetary resources.

Kate's research has been published in leading academic journals such as *Nature, New Media & Society, Science, Technology & Human Values and Information*, and *Communication & Society*. Her career has concentrated on understanding large-scale data systems, machine learning and AI in the wider contexts of history, politics, labour, and the environment. In 2022 she published the book *Atlas of AI: Power, Politics, and the Planetary Costs of Artificial Intelligence* (Yale University Press). She is a member of the feminist collective 'Deep Lab', a group of female artists, researchers, writers, engineers, and cultural producers involved in critical assessments of contemporary digital culture. Kate also serves on France's 3IA scientific advisory jury.

Klára Dán von Neumann

Born: 18 August 1911
Died: 10 November 1963 (aged 52)

Klára Dán was born in Budapest, Hungary, into a wealthy Jewish family with father Károly Dán and Kamilla Stadler. There was an older daughter, Erzsébet 'Böske' Deg (Dán), who was born on 17 October 1908. Károly had previously served in the Austro-Hungarian Army as an officer during the First World War, and the family relocated to Vienna to escape the Hungarian Soviet Republic of Béla Kun, the Hungarian communist politician. After the regime was overthrown, the family moved back to Budapest.

After the war, Klára attended an English boarding school and at age 14 became a national figure skating champion in 1925. She graduated from her high school, Veres Pálné Secondary Grammar School, a prestigious Hungarian public grammar school in Budapest, in 1929. In 1938 she married her third husband, the eminent Hungarian mathematician John von Neumann.

Following the wedding, the couple emigrated to the United States where he held a professorship at Princeton University. Despite only having a high school education in algebra and trigonometry, her interest in numbers led her to securing a wartime position with Princeton's Office of Population Research investigating population trends. In 1943, John moved to Los Alamos National Laboratory in New Mexico to work on the Manhattan Project that produced the first nuclear weapons. Klára remained at Princeton until 1946 where she worked at the university's Office of Population Research.

After the war, Klára joined her husband in New Mexico to program the MANIAC I (Mathematical Analyzer, Numerical Integrator, and Computer, or, Mathematical Analyzer, Numerator, Integrator, and Computer) machine, which could store data, designed by John and the American computer engineer Julian Bigelow. The MANIAC ran successfully in March 1952 and was shut down on 15 July 1958 after being succeeded by MANIAC II in 1957. She and John then worked together on the ENIAC (Electronic Numerical Integrator and Computer) to produce the first successful meteorological forecast on a computer.

The ENIAC was moved to Maryland in 1947, where it became one of the first stored-program computers. This meant the complicated sets of instructions telling the computer to perform various tasks could be stored in binary code on a memory device, instead of being entered and re-entered manually. To install this new system, Klára trained five people who had worked on the Manhattan Project to program the ENIAC. Up until then, no one but the von Neumanns and the young Greek-American physicist Nick Metropolis understood the workings of the computer.

For 32 consecutive days they installed the new control system, checked the code, and ran the ENIAC day and night. John remarked that Klára was 'very run-down after the siege in Aberdeen, lost 15 pounds (7 kilograms), and [had] a general physical check-up at the Princeton Hospital.'

In February 1957 John died from cancer at age 53 and Klára wrote the preface to his Silliman Lectures that were published in the following year, later editing and having them published by Yale University Press as *The Computer and the Brain*. In 1958 she married her fourth husband, the oceanographer and physicist Carl Eckart, and the couple relocated to La Jolla, California.

Klára passed away at age 52 on 10 November 1963 when she drove from her home in La Jolla to the beach and walked into the surf and drowned. The San Diego coroner's office listed her death as a suicide.

Eleanor Dodson

Born: c.1940

Eleanor McPherson was born in rural Australia, the daughter of farmers of Scottish descent. In 1958, she graduated with a degree in mathematics and philosophy from the University of Melbourne. While on a visit to the UK, Eleanor replied to an advertisement for a technical assistant in the University of Oxford laboratory of the late Dorothy Hodgkin. She was one of several women who joined the laboratory of the physicist John Desmond Bernal in the 1930s, and with him she took the first X-ray photographs of crystalline proteins. In 1964, her solutions of the structures of penicillin and vitamin B12 won her the Nobel Prize in Chemistry.

Eleanor's role was as a technician, leading her to work alongside the New Zealand-born scientist Guy Dodson. She had only three weeks before Guy's arrival and became responsible for much of the computing. They married in 1965, in doing so setting a precedent for married couples working together on the insulin project. They had four children, Richard, Philip, Victoria and Thomas. Eleanor was responsible for the computation and active in developing software for macromolecular crystallography in the project. In 1976 Guy was offered a lectureship in chemistry at the University of York where he had responsibility for teaching biochemistry. The couple moved there, and Guy developed, along with Rod Hubbard and Keith Wilson, the York Structural Biology Laboratory (YSBL).

At that time was that there were no agreed standards and very few programs for the computers to use. Eleanor had become the driving force in for these developments, and in 1974 she and others founded a computing cooperative. At York in 1979 it became CCP4, standing for collaborative computing project number 4. The CCP4 computing project currently shares more than 250 software tools with protein crystallographers worldwide. Today it is one of the UK's most successful technology transfer stories, generating over £1m per year in partnership agreements with companies across the globe. The key to its and Eleanor's success has been to turn half described ideas and ill-defined theories into practical programs that work everywhere for everyone.

As well as her contribution to CCP4, Eleanor has contributed to the theory and practice of methods used to determine the atomic structures of macromolecules, including molecular replacement, phasing and refinement. Without her work, there would be no CCP4, and far fewer breakthroughs in crystallography. She has been outstanding in her field, forming the foundation of protein crystallography that has largely stood for thirty years. In 2001 she was awarded an Honorary Degree of Doctor of Science from the University of Uppsala in Sweden.

Eleanor's reputation for excellence has led to many other crystallographers requesting to work with her at the University of York. In 1998 she was awarded The Fankuchen Memorial Award, which recognises crystallographers for both research and effective teaching of crystallography. She was elected as a Fellow of the Royal Society in 2003 and is one of only just over a hundred female fellows and the first woman elected from York University. In 2006 she was awarded the 2nd Max Perutz ECA Prize by the European Crystallographic Association 'for developing, implementing, teaching and applying the best tools available to produce macromolecular structures of highest quality'.

Eleanor has lectured generations of scientists, and her fame has spread globally. Students, colleagues and researchers constantly seek her advice on the crystallography bulletin board. In 2010 she was awarded the Honorary Degree of Doctor of Science *honoris causa* by the University of St Andrews in Scotland.

In 2012 her husband Guy passed away in York at age 75. Eleanor still holds a chair in the Department of Chemistry at the University of York and, although she does not hold a PhD, has illustrated that one can achieve greatness in science without one.

Elizabeth Feinler

Born: 2 March 1931

Elizabeth Jocelyn 'Jake' Feinler was born and raised in Wheeling, West Virginia, where she enrolled as an undergraduate at West Liberty State College. She was the first from her family to attend college and later graduated with a Bachelor of Science, majoring in chemistry. She then undertook a PhD in biochemistry at Purdue University in Indiana under the supervision of Dr. Roy Whistler who later became the Hillenbrand Distinguished Professor of Biochemistry.

During her study for a doctorate in biochemistry, she decided to earn some money by working for one or two years before commencing work on writing her thesis. She secured a position at the Chemical Abstracts Service in Columbus, Ohio, where she landed the role of assistant editor on a huge project to index the world's chemical compounds. Elizabeth found the task so intriguing and challenging that she never returned to biochemistry.

When the project was completed, she joined the Shuman Chemical Company where she analysed nutritional supplements for sufferers of phenylketonuria, a birth defect that causes the amino acid phenylalanine to build up in the body. In 1958, at age 27, she joined Chemical Abstracts Service in Columbus, Ohio, as Assistant Editor for several sections of the Chemical Abstracts 5th Decennial Index.

In 1960, Elizabeth relocated to California and joined the Information Research Department at the Stanford Research Institute (now SRI International) where she helped to develop the *Handbook of Psychopharmacology* and the *Chemical Process Economics Handbook*. In 1972 she became becoming a member of the Augmentation Research Center (ARC) that was conducted by the American engineer and inventor

Dr Douglas Engelbart. It was here that she began her work on the Internet, initially on Host 2, where she pioneered and managed first the ARPNET, and then the Defense Data Network (DDN), Network Information Centers (NIC) under contract to the Department of Defense (DoD). These early networks were the forerunners of the Internet we have today.

From 1974 she assumed the role of Principal Investigator for the NIC project, and between 1985 and 1989 as the Director for the Network Information Systems Center at SRI International. Elizabeth's team developed the first Internet 'yellow-page' and 'white-page' servers as well as the first query-based network host name and address (WHOIS) server. They also managed the Host Naming Registry for the Internet between 1972 and 1989. Among their many achievements, her group developed the top-level domain naming scheme of .com, .edu, .gov, .mil, .org, and .net, these still being in use today. She retired from SRI at age 58.

Elizabeth was also the editor-in-chief for several Internet reference publications, including the DoD Protocol Handbook, the Arpanet/DDN Directory, the Arpanet/DDN Resource Handbook, and the DoD Protocol Implementation and Vendors Guide. Following her time at SRI, she worked for Sterling Software Corp. as a contractor for NASA Ames Research Center in Mountain View, California. Here she was a Network Requirements Manager helping to bring networking to the large NSF and NASA telescope sites. At Ames she also was active in setting up the NASA Science Internet and Globe NICs, as well as assisting with guidelines for the development and management of the NASA World Wide Web.

She was appointed as 'Delegate at Large' to the White House Conference on Libraries and Information Centers and has been a member of ACM, ASIS, and IEEE. She was also a founding member of the Internet Engineering Task Force, a past chair of the IFIP Working Group 6.5 on User Requirements for Electronic Mail, and founder of the Using working group, that later became the IETF Users working group. In 2000 she was inducted into the SRI Alumni Hall of Fame and in 2012 was also inducted into the Internet Hall of Fame by the Internet Society. In July the following year Elizabeth received the annual Jonathan B. Postel Service Award 'for her contributions to the early development and administration of the Internet through her leadership of the Network Information Center (NIC) for the ARPANET'.

In her retirement, Elizabeth has been active as a volunteer for the Computer History Museum in Mountain View where she donated, organised, and described over 350 boxes of archives from the Engelbart and NIC projects.

Christiane Floyd

Born: 26 April 1943

Christiane Floyd (née Riedl) was born in Vienna, Austria, and after completing high school enrolled at the University of Vienna where she studied mathematics and astronomy. In 1966 she completed her PhD, supervised by Wilfried Nöbauer, with her thesis 'Radikale für Fastmoduln, Fastringe und Kompositionsringe' (Radicals for fast modules, fast rings and composition rings). For the two years following graduation she was employed as a systems programmer using an ALGOL 60 compiler at Siemens in Munich. Between 1968 and 1973, she worked as a research associate and part-time lecturer in the computer science department of Stanford University in US.

In 1973, Christiane joined the Munich software development company Softlab, where she worked as a senior consultant, a role that involved the development and demonstration of Maestro I, the first integrated development environment for software. In 1978, she became a full professor of software engineering at the Technical University (TU) of Berlin, making her the first woman in Germany to be a professor in the field of computer science.

Christiane and her group produced one of the first conceptual contributions to participatory design methods with the STEPS process model (Software Technology for Evolutionary Participatory Systems development). In a January 2021 interview with Bettina Klotz in TU Berlin's Alumni newsletter, Christiane commented on gaining her professorial position:

> At that time, the discipline was only about ten years old and was very much in development as a core subject. It was a major challenge for me to establish research and teaching in this area. My main difficulties as a

woman were due to the little consideration I received for the fact that I was a single parent with two children.

Christiane was a pioneer of evolutionary participatory software design, a precursor to open-source software development. In 1985 she co-edited with Hartmut Ehrig, Maurice Nivat and James Thatcher the 440-page volume *Mathematical Foundations of Software Development. Proceedings of the International Joint Conference on Theory and Practice of Software Development ... (Lecture Notes in Computer Science, 185)* (Springer).

Christiane formally retired at age 65 in 2008, becoming a professor emerita at Hamburg. She then became involved with the Vienna University of Technology WIT project (Wissenschaftlerinnenkolleg Internettechnologien; Women's Postgraduate College for Internet Technologies). The program offers a specialised PhD program for women in the computer science field. In January 2012 she was awarded an honorary professorship at TU Wien (Technical University of Vienna).

Currently she is involved in an IT development project which she devised with the universities of Linz and Addis Ababa. Its goal is to improve access to the health system for (sometimes illiterate) women and children in rural areas, with an emphasis on pregnancy, giving birth, postpartum care and infant care. While there, Christiane has developed IT systems for three target groups: an app for mothers providing basic information about relevant topics; an information and planning system for female health workers in the field; and a system for supporting working and communication processes in health centres. These have all been very well received in pilot projects and are now used in several locations.

In 2017 Christiane was awarded an honorary doctorate from Paderborn University, a public research university in the state of North Rhine-Westphalia in Germany. She also received the Klaus Tschira Medal in 2020 for her contribution to the advancement of science and research.

Christiane was married to the eminent computer scientist Robert W. Floyd who passed away at age 65 in September 2001. She later married a prominent Danish computer scientist, Peter Naur, who passed away at age 87 in January 2016. Both husbands were winners of the prestigious A.M. Turing Award, the highest honour in computer science.

Sally Jean Floyd

Born: 20 May 1950
Died: 25 August 2019 (aged 69)

Sally Jean Floyd was born in Charlottesville, Virginia, in the USA. Her father, Edwin, was a mathematician at the University of Virginia and her mother, Marguerite (Stahl) Floyd, was an operating room nurse. Sally enrolled at the University of Michigan, Ann Arbor, later transferring to the University of California, Berkeley, in 1969. Here she received a bachelor's degree in sociology in 1971, along with a minor in mathematics.

Following graduation, Sally enrolled in a two-year course in electronics at Merritt College, a community college in Oakland, California. In 1975 she became a computer systems engineer for the Bay Area Rapid Transit, BART. It was while working there that she became attracted to theoretical computer science and returned to Berkeley, where she graduated in 1987 with a Master of Science in Computer Science and in 1989 completed her PhD under the supervision of the American computer scientist and computational theorist, Richard M. Karp. Her thesis was titled 'On Space-Bounded Learning and the Vapnik-Chervonenkis Dimension'.

With the rapid growth of the internet capturing her attention, in 1990 she joined the Network Research Group at Lawrence Berkeley National Laboratory. Together with the computer science academic Vern Paxson, Sally identified the lack of knowledge of network topology as major stumbling block in understanding how the Internet works. In 1993 the pair published their paper 'Random Early Detection Gateways for Congestion Avoidance' that appeared in the August issue of *IEEE/ACM Transactions on Networking*. That paper has now been cited an astonishing 10,000 times.

In 1997 they also jointly wrote a paper 'Why We Don't Know How to Simulate the Internet' that was published in the *Proceedings of the*

1997 Winter Simulation Conference. In 2001 it was republished as 'Difficulties in Simulating the Internet' in *IEEE/ACM Transactions on Networking*, Vol. 9, No. 4, August. It was so highly regarded that it won the IEEE Communication Society's William R. Bennett Prize Paper Award.

Sally's major research was in the field of congestion control, and she was the inventor of Random Early Detection (RED) active queue management scheme. This led to the new field of Active Queue Management (AQM) that she founded with the renowned US computer scientist Van Jacobson. Sally developed the method of adding delay jitter to message timers to avoid synchronisation, and today almost all Internet routers use RED or something developed from it to cope with network congestion.

In 2005 she received the IEEE Internet Award and in 2007 the prestigious ACM SIGCOMM Award for her contributions to congestion control. She has been involved in the Internet Architecture Board, and in 2007 was one of the top-ten most cited researchers in computer science. Sally is also a co-author on the standard for TCP Selective acknowledgement (SACK), Explicit Congestion Notification (ECN), the Datagram Congestion Control Protocol (DCCP) and TCP Friendly Rate Control (TFRC). She retired in 2009, two years after she was diagnosed with multiple sclerosis.

Sally passed away at age 69, surrounded by her family at Ashgate Hospice on 25 August 2019. She had developed gallbladder cancer that had metastasized. She was survived by her partner Carole Leita, a reference librarian whom she had met in 2003 and married in 2013. Sally was also survived by her sister Judith Floyd.

A professor of computer science at Harvard University, Eddie Kohler, had worked with Sally at ICS and remarked that while her focus on congestion control was important, she was beyond that regarded with a great deal of affection. He said: 'She knew herself so well, down to bedrock. She was filled with love. She loved her backyard, her wife, her life. It was hard to spend time with her and not come out of it happier.'

Alexandra 'Sandra' Winifred Illmer Forsythe

Born: 20 May 1918
Died: 2 January 1980 (aged 61)

Alexandra 'Sandra' Winifred Illmer was born in Newton, Massachusetts, to father Louis Illmer Jr (1877–1958) and mother Lillian Winifred 'Win' Illmer (née Rogers) (1880–1953), who was a Quaker. Sandra was raised in Cortland, New York, and because of her mother's religious beliefs was not baptised until age seven. She had an older sibling, Gustav H. Illmer, who was born in 1907 but passed away at age 17 in 1925.

While attending Swarthmore College, a private liberal arts college in Swarthmore, Pennsylvania, Sandra met her future husband George Elmer Forsythe who would later be the founder and head of Stanford University's Computer Science Department. Sandra later graduated from Swarthmore with a bachelor's degree majoring in mathematics.

Sandra and George were both accepted into the PhD program in mathematics at Brown University, a private Ivy League research university in Providence. Although an outstanding student, Sandra was unable to continue in the program because the Dean did not approve of female mathematicians and cut her fellowship support. She eventually left Brown and completed her master's degree at Vassar College in 1941 while serving as an instructor. On 14 June that same year, Sandra and George were married in Providence, Rhode Island, at a Quaker Meeting. This was the same day that George received his PhD in mathematics.

The next year Sandra obtained employment as a mathematics engineer at Douglas Aircraft Company in Santa Monica. The couple had a son, Warren, and daughter, Diana Elizabeth Forsythe. From 1960 for about 12 years

Alexandra 'Sandra' Winifred Illmer Forsythe

Sandra taught high school mathematics in Palo Alto in California. Her most famous student was Grace Slick, who soon afterwards became the lead singer for the rock band Jefferson Airplane.

In the 1960s and 1970s Sandra co-authored a number of college textbooks in computer science. The most prominent of these was published in 1969, *Computer Science: A First Course* (Wiley & Sons, New York). This was the first computer science textbook ever published. Her books have now been translated into 15 languages including Chinese. The following year she published the first edition of *Computer Science: BASIC Language* (New York: Wiley) with co-authors Thomas Keenan, Elliott Organick, and Warren Stenberg. She also helped to establish the computer science program at Stanford University.

Sandra was a member of Phi Beta Kappa, Sigma Xi and many professional societies, including playing an active role in the Audubon Society and the Sierra Club, and lecturing for Stanford University's Jasper Ridge biological preserve. On 9 April 1972 her husband George passed away at the age of 55. In 1975 a second edition of *Computer Science: A First Course* was published, and in 1978 she co-authored with Elliott Irving Organick *Programming Language Structures* (2nd ed.) published by Academic Press.

Sandra passed away in Santa Clara County, California, at age 61 years on 2 January 1980. She was survived by her son Warren (1944–2017), who was an adjunct professor of botany at the University of Utah, her daughter Diana who was an anthropologist and her sister Elizabeth Ticknor of Cortland, New York. She is buried at the Quaker Center in Ben Lomond in Santa Cruz County, California.

Margaret R. Fox

Born: 19 May 1916
Died: 27 August 2006 (aged 90)

Margaret R. Fox graduated from Wisconsin State College in 1940 where she majored in English, although she studied a great deal of mathematics and physics subjects. Following her graduation she taught at high school, but eventually decided to join the U.S. Naval Reserve in 1943 and was stationed at the Naval Research Station in Washington, assuming the role of electronic engineer in radar. After being discharged in 1946, she continued to work there as an electronics engineer in radar and on 10 September 1951 joined the National Bureau of Standards as a member of the technical staff of the Electronic Computer Laboratory. She found it fascinating.

The field of radar formed the basis of her background in computing, although it was largely analogue rather than digital. She later joined the Research Information Center and Advisory Service on Information Processing (RICASIP) where she was involved in producing reviews and bibliographies. Between 1966 and 1975 she served as Chief of the Office of Computer Information in the NBS Institute for Computer Science and Technology.

Margaret was involved with many professional groups, including the Association for Computing Machinery (ACM). Her participation in the National Joint Computer Committee led to her to become in 1966 the founder and first secretary of the American Federation for Information Processing Societies (AFIPS), an organisation that played a role in the

International Information Processing Conference in Paris in 1959. She served in that role for six years.

In 1966 she was appointed Chief of the Office of Computer Information, part of the Institute for Computer Science and Technology of the National Bureau of Standards (now the National Institute of Standards and Technology). In the same year she began preparation, along with Samuel N. Alexander, of a series of college computer courses. Alexander was an American computer pioneer who developed SEAC, one of the earliest computers.

In 1973 Margaret chaired the Technical Program Committee and became representative of the Bureau's Center for Computer Sciences and Technology. She passed away in Argyle, Wisconsin, at age 90 on 27 August 2006.

Timnit Gebru

Born: 1983

Timnit Gebru was born in Addis Ababa, Ethiopia, one of three daughters. Her father, an electrical engineer, passed away when Timnit was five years old, and she was then raised solely by her mother. They eventually received political asylum in the United States where Timnit attended high school in Massachusetts. She then enrolled at Stanford University from which she graduated with both a bachelor's and master's degree in electrical engineering.

Between June 2004 and September 2004, Timnit worked as an Audio Hardware Intern at Apple in Cupertino, a city in California's Silicon Valley, being involved in projects relating to the audio quality of Apple's computers. Examples of her projects included noise cancellation techniques to improve the quality of speech recognition and to limit fan noise heard by the internal microphone of the computer.

In July 2005 Timnit took the role of Audio Systems Engineer at Apple, designing the audio circuitry of Apple TV, iMacs, MacBooks and MacBook Pros as well as other Apple products including the iPad. She also assisted vendors to develop chips such as CODECs and created specifications for audio hardware. She researched new technologies that could potentially improve the audio quality of Apple's next generation products, as well as debugging problems with the audio hardware circuitry of Apple's computers.

In June 2007 she changed her position at Apple to an Audio Software & Hardware Engineer, now concentrating on several audio-related projects surrounding digital signal processing. In one instance, she was involved in the design, simulation and implementation of a 4th order delta sigma modulator and various noise shaped clock generation circuits for iPads and iPhones.

In August 2011, Timnit left Apple and became co-founder, along with Andrew Chen, of MotionThink, a design thinking framework under the structure of Eric Schmidt's Innovation Endeavors runway program to identify deep needs in the small business space and develop solutions. Located in Palo Alto, California. Schmidt had been the CEO of Google between 2001 and 2011, and then its executive chairman until 2015. MotionThink did not turn out to be a successful venture and it ceased operations in April 2012 after only eight months.

In 2017 Timnit was awarded a PhD from the Stanford Artificial Intelligence Laboratory, under the supervision of the computer scientist Fei-Fei Li. Her thesis related to using large-scale publicly available images to gain sociological insight and working on computer vision problems that arise as a result.

In particular, Timnit used Google Street View to estimate the demographics of neighbourhoods in the US, revealing that socioeconomic attributes such as voting patterns, income, race, and education can be inferred from observations of cars. For example, If the number of pickup trucks (a light-duty truck that has an enclosed cabin and an open cargo) outnumbers the number of sedans, the community is more likely to vote for the Republican party. In the project she analysed over 15 million images from the 200 most populated cities in the US.

After receiving her PhD, Timnit joined Microsoft as a postdoctoral researcher in the Fairness, Accountability, Transparency and Ethics in AI (FATE) lab. When she attended an artificial intelligence (AI) conference in 2016, she was aware that she was the only black woman out of 8,500 delegates. And so, together with her colleague Rediet Abebe, she founded 'Black in AI', a community of black researchers working in artificial intelligence.

She entered her research in the 2017 LDV Capital Vision Summit competition, one in which computer vision scientists present their work to members of industry and venture capitalists. She was the winner, resulting in a series of collaborations with other entrepreneurs and investors. In 2017 Timnit also gave presentations at the Fairness and Transparency conference, where she was interviewed by *MIT Technology Review* regarding biases that exist in AI systems.

Timnit explained how adding diversity in AI teams can address the issue of biases that exist in the software developers. For example, a study conducted by MIT researchers revealed that Amazon's facial recognition system had more difficulty identifying darker-skinned females than any other technology company's facial recognition software.

Google later employed Timnit as a co-leader, along with Margaret Mitchell, on a team working on the ethics of artificial intelligence. They studied the implications of AI, seeking ways to improve the ability of technology to help society. Collaborating with the MIT research group 'Gender Shades', Timnit worked with Joy Buolamwini to investigate facial recognition software, revealing that black women were 35% less likely to be recognised than white men.

An issue for Timnit arose with the publication of a paper involving several authors, including Timnit, Emily Bender, Margaret Mitchell (named as Shmargaret Shmitchell as an author), and Angelina McMillan-Major, titled 'On the Dangers of Stochastic Parrots: Can Language Models Be Too Big?'. It can be found in the *Proceedings of the 2021 ACM Conference on Fairness, Accountability, and Transparency*, 610-623. In the introduction, the authors indicate '...we discuss how large datasets based on texts from the Internet overrepresent hegemonic viewpoints and encode biases potentially damaging to marginalized populations ... most language technology is built to serve the needs of those who already have the most privilege in society.' Although some mystery still surrounds the exact details, Jeff Dean, the then head of Google AI, informed colleagues in an internal email that the paper 'didn't meet our bar for publication' and that Timnit had said she would resign unless Google met a number of conditions, to which they were unwilling to agree. As a result, both Timnit and Margaret Mitchell were fired, or said to have resigned, from their leadership roles in Google's Ethical AI group. It was claimed by Google that the paper ignored recent research that showed methods of mitigating the bias in those systems.

Timnit's departure from Google caused public controversy, following which Google CEO Sundar Pichai issued an apology without admitting wrongdoing. A letter was signed by close to 2700 Google employees and more than 4300 academics and civil society supporters, condemning Timnit's and Margaret's alleged sackings. Nine members of Congress sent a letter to Google asking it to clarify the circumstances around Timnit's leaving.

Timnit, along with Joy Buolamwini and Inioluwa Deborah Raji, won VentureBeat's 2019 AI Innovations Award in the category 'AI for Good' for their research into issues of bias in facial recognition. In June 2021, Timnit announced that she was raising money to 'launch an independent research institute modelled on her work on Google's Ethical AI team and her experience in Black in AI'. In the same year she was named one of the world's 50 greatest leaders by *Fortune*. Both of Timnit's sisters are electrical engineers.

Adele Goldberg

Born: 22 July 1945

Adele Goldberg was one of twin sisters born in Cleveland, Ohio, residing in Cleveland Hill until the age of eleven where she attended public schools. Her father was an industrial engineer and her mother, who had a college degree in mathematics, worked as a secretary in a school as there were no teaching positions available. In 1956 the family, now with three daughters, moved to Chicago, Illinois, where their father had obtained a position.

In 1963 Adele attended the University of Michigan in Ann Arbor, staying there for three years before taking six months' leave from her studies to travel around Europe before returning to complete her bachelor's degree in mathematics. She then attended the University of Chicago, obtaining a master's degree in information science, and in 1973 completing her PhD there, also in information science, with her dissertation 'Computer-Assisted Instruction: The Application of Theorem-proving to Adaptive Response Analysis'.

After her PhD, in 1973 Adele found a position as a laboratory and research assistant at Xerox PARC (Palo Alto Research Center), later reaching the rank of manager of the System Concepts Laboratory. It was here that she, along with the American computer scientist Alan Kay and others, developed 'Smalltalk-80'. This program developed the object-oriented approach of Simula 67, a simulation programming language, as well as introducing a programming environment of overlapping windows on graphic display screens.

With its innovative format, Smalltalk was simpler to use, along with being adaptable so that objects could be easily transferred among applications. Adele and Kay also developed design templates that were the forerunners of the patterns often used in software design. Smalltalk was used to prototype the WIMP (windows, icons, menus, pointers) interface at Xerox Parc, the foundation of today's graphical user interfaces. It also had a large influence on many later languages, including Java, Objective-C, and Python.

In 1977 Adele and Kay co-wrote the influential article 'Personal Dynamic Media' (*Computer*, Volume: 10, Issue: 3, March) which correctly predicted that in the future members of the public would use notebook computers to exchange, modify, and redistribute personal media. This paper outlined the vision for the Dynabook, a portable computer concept.

Between 1984 and 1986 Adele was president of the Association for Computing Machinery (ACM), and, along with Kay and computer programmer Dan Ingalls, received the ACM Software Systems Award in 1987. She was also included in *Forbes*'s 'Twenty Who Matter' and in 1994 was inducted as a Fellow of the Association for Computing Machinery. In 1996 she received *PC Magazine*'s Lifetime Achievement Award.

In 1988, Adele left PARC to co-found, along with several ex-Xerox employees, ParcPlace Systems Inc. She served as chairwoman and CEO until its merger with Digitalk in 1995. ParcPlace introduced its initial product in the form of 'ObjectWorks\Smalltalk', renaming it 'VisualWorks for UNIX workstations' in the same year.

In 1999, Adele co-founded Neometron Inc., an Internet support provider in Palo Alto, California. She continues her interest in computer science education by conducting courses at community colleges in the United States and at overseas schools. Adele is a board member and adviser at Cognito Learning Media, a provider of multimedia software for science education. The Computer History Museum houses a collection of her working documents, reports, publications and videotapes related to her work on the development of Smalltalk. In 2010 Adele was inducted into the Women in Technology Hall of Fame. In 2022, along with Dan Ingalls, Adele was made a Fellow of the CHM for 'promoting and codeveloping the Smalltalk programming environment and contributions advancing use of computers in education'.

She currently works at Bullitics, an organisation that was created to 'enhance existing polling methods and to build a grassroots polling community that better reflects society at large while empowering people to participate at all levels'.

Adele Goldstine

Born: 21 December 1920
Died: 1 November 1964 (aged 43)

Adele Goldstine (née Katz) was born in New York City to Yiddish-speaking Jewish parents, her father having emigrated from Pandėlys, Lithuania (then part of the Russian Empire) in 1902. She attended Hunter College High School, then Hunter College in New York where she received a Bachelor of Arts degree. She then enrolled at the University of Michigan, earning a master's degree in mathematics. This was where she met her future husband Herman Heine Goldstine, the military liaison and administrator for the construction of the ENIAC. The couple were married in 1941 when Adele was aged 20, and later had a daughter, Madlen, and a son, Jonathan.

Adele worked as an instructor of mathematics for the female 'human computers' at the Moore School of Electrical Engineering, including training some of the six women who were the original programmers of the ENIAC to manually calculate ballistic missile trajectories. Their roles were considered critical to the war effort, since women were viewed as more capable, faster and more accurate than men in performing calculations. Moreover, men were in short supply due to their involvement in the fighting. From 1943 until the end of the war, all these human computers were women, as were their immediate supervisors.

The six main human computers were Kay McNulty, Betty Jean Jennings, Betty Snyder, Marlyn Wescoff, Fran Bilas and Ruth Lichterman. Adele wrote the Operators Manual for the ENIAC and the women were then able to train themselves to 'program' it using its logical and electrical block diagrams. They were able to reconfigure the machine to solve a different problem by physically plugging and unplugging wires on the machine. At this time the word 'programming' was not used, but rather the process was simply referred to as 'setting up'. It is reported that these women received a sub-professional rating from the Army and were paid around US$2,000 per year.

Following the war, in 1946 Adele joined programming sessions with an ENIAC programmer Jean Bartik and Dick Clippinger, a computing laboratory staff member at the Aberdeen Proving Ground, Maryland, who had converted the ENIAC to a stored-program computer using its read-only hand-set function tables. Adele was hired to help implement Clippinger's stored program modification to the ENIAC under the watchful eye of the eminent mathematician John von Neumann.

The group were able to solve the problem of the programmers having to unplug and replug patch cables for every program the machine was to run. Instead, the program was entered on the three function tables, which had previously been used only for storage of a trajectory's drag function. Their system provided a 51-order vocabulary. Jean Bartik referred to Adele as one of her 'three perfect programming partners', the others being Betty Holberton and Art Gehring, and they worked together to implement the Taub program (named after Professor A.H. Taub) for the ENIAC.

Adele continued her programming work with von Neumann at Los Alamos National Laboratory, devising problems for ENIAC to process. In 1962 she was diagnosed with cancer, passing away two years later at the age of 43 on 1 November 1964. Her husband Herman died at age 90 on 16 June 2004.

Adele's daughter, Madlen Goldstine Simon, Associate Dean for academic affairs and outreach, University of Maryland School of Architecture, Planning and Preservation, said of her mother, 'She radiated warmth. She was a tremendous teacher, always teaching us math and music. She played the violin well and taught it to me. There was always music in the house.'

Von Neumann's daughter Marina Whitman, professor emerita of business administration and public policy, University of Michigan, recalled:

> Adele spent quite a bit of time at our Princeton house, working with my father on the project of transforming the ENIAC. It was clear that he regarded her as a significant participant in the project. She sometimes carried the infant Mady in her arms, and as I was a high-school girl, gave me my first example of a young woman enthusiastically embracing new motherhood and carrying on with her professional career at the same time. She gave me confidence to do the same when my time came.

Shafi Goldwasser

Born: 14 November 1959

Shafi Goldwasser was born in New York City to Israeli parents, resulting in Shafi having dual American/Israeli citizenship. Shortly after her birth, the family returned to Israel where she attended schools in Tel Aviv. After completing high school, Shafi returned to the United States, where she graduated in 1979 with a Bachelor of Science, majoring in mathematics and science, at Carnegie Mellon University in Pittsburgh.

During her undergraduate studies, Shafi became attracted to the field of computer science and enrolled in a master's degree in the Department of Electrical Engineering and Computer Science at the University of California, Berkeley. After obtaining her degree in 1981, she then enrolled in the PhD program, graduating in 1984. Her thesis, 'Probabilistic Encryption: Theory and Applications' was supervised by the eminent Venezuelan-American computer scientist Manuel Blum. By now her interests had changed more towards theoretical computer science and cryptography.

In 1983 Shafi joined MIT, and by 1993 had a concurrent position as professor at Israel's Weizmann Institute of Science. In 1997 she became the first RSA professor of Electrical Engineering and Computer Science at MIT. Her research interests include computational complexity theory, cryptography and computational number theory. She also has several inventions to her name, including being the co-inventor with Silvio Micali of probabilistic encryption that uses randomness in an encryption algorithm, so that when encrypting the same message several times it will, in general, yield different ciphertexts. This sets the standard for security for data encryption.

Shafi is also the co-inventor, along with Silvio Micali and Charles Rackoff, of 'zero-knowledge proofs'. These probabilistically and interactively demonstrate the validity of an assertion without conveying any additional knowledge and are a key tool in the design of cryptographic protocols. Shafi's research in complexity theory includes the classification of approximation problems, showing that some problems in NP (nondeterministic polynomial time) remain hard even when only an approximate solution is needed. Along with Joe Killan, she invented primality proving using elliptic curves. In 2012 Shafi was a co-recipient, with Silio Micali, of the prestigious Turing Award for 'transformative work that laid the complexity-theoretic foundations for the science of cryptography and in the process pioneered new methods for efficient verification of mathematical proofs in complexity theory'.

Since November 2016, Shafi has been the chief scientist and co-founder, along with Vinod Vaikuntanathan and Kurt Rohloff, of Duality Technologies, a US-based start-up which offers secure data analytics using advanced cryptographic techniques. She is also a scientific adviser for several technology startups in the area of security, including QED-it, specialising in the Zero Knowledge Blockchain. In this method, one party (Prover) can prove that a specific statement is true to the other party (Verifier) without disclosing any additional information. She is also an adviser to Algorand, a Blockchain network that aims to build a borderless economy using a decentralised, unregulated public Blockchain.

On 1 January 2018, Shafi was appointed the director of the interdisciplinary Simons Institute for the Theory of Computing at the University of California, Berkeley. She was also on the Mathematical Sciences jury for the Infosys Prize in 2020 and is currently a member of the theory of computation group at MIT Computer Science and Artificial Intelligence Laboratory.

Shafi has received many honours, including the ACM Grace Murray Hopper Award (1996) for outstanding young computer professional of the year, and the RSA Award for Excellence in Mathematics (1998) for outstanding mathematical contributions to cryptography. In 2001 she was elected to the American Academy of Arts and Sciences and in 2004 was elected to the National Academy of Science. In 2005 she was elected to the National Academy of Engineering and selected as an IACR Fellow in 2007.

Shafi received the 2008-2009 Athena Lecturer Award of the Association for Computing Machinery's Committee on Women in Computing and in 2010 won The Franklin Institute's Benjamin Franklin Medal in Computer and Cognitive Science. In the following year she received the IEEE Emanuel R. Piore Award. She is featured in the Notable Women in Computing cards and in 2016 won the Suffrage Science award. She was elected as an ACM Fellow in 2017.

In 2018 Shafi was the co-winner, along with the mathematicians Silio Micali, Ronald Rivest and Adi Shamir, of the Frontier of Knowledge award. In the same year she was awarded an honorary degree by her alma mater, Carnegie Mellon University. On 26 June 2019 she was awarded an honorary Doctor of Science by the University of Oxford and in 2020 served on the Mathematical Sciences jury for the Infosys Prize.

Evelyn Boyd Granville

Born: 1 May 1924

Evelyn Boyd was born in Washington, D.C., USA. Her father, William Boyd, worked at various jobs including as a janitor, chauffeur, and messenger. Her mother, Julia Boyd, had been a secretary before her marriage but gave up work to raise her family. In 1929, when Evelyn was aged five, the Great Depression arrived and the unemployment rate in US stood at 25%. William sold vegetables from a lorry during this time and, although the family were poor, they had a home and always managed to have a meal on the table.

When Evelyn was still young, her parents separated and, together with her sister Doris, who was about eighteen months older, she was raised in the African American community in Washington, D.C. by her mother. She attended elementary school, junior high school, and Dunbar High School. The Dunbar school was for black students and aimed to send their pupils to top universities. As her results were outstanding, Evelyn was strongly encouraged to further her education, selecting Smith College, a high-ranking private liberal arts women's college in Northampton, Massachusetts as her chosen destination. However, she was aware that her mother could not afford to send her there, and for the first year her aunt gave her $500 to assist with her expenses.

Evelyn lived in a co-op there and did so well that after her first year she was awarded scholarships, meaning she was no longer reliant on her family for financial support. Moreover, she also worked during the summer breaks at the National Bureau of Standards. Looking back, she said that she saw well-dressed black women teaching school, leading her to want to be one of them. She added that she was not really aware of any other profession.

As an undergraduate, Evelyn majored in mathematics and physics, as well as taking a keen interest in astronomy. She was elected to Phi Beta Kappa and to Sigma Xi, and in 1945 graduated summa cum laude. The Smith Student Aid Society of Smith College awarded her a graduate scholarship, and she was accepted into the graduate programs in mathematics of both Yale University and the University of Michigan. She selected Yale as it offered financial assistance. As part of her PhD program, Evelyn studied functional analysis under the supervision of the American mathematician Einar Hille, completing her doctorate in 1949. Her dissertation was titled 'On Laguerre Series in the Complex Domain'. She was reportedly only the second African-American woman to receive a PhD in mathematics from an American University.

After completing her PhD, Evelyn found a role in teaching and research at the New York University Institute for Mathematics. The following year she took up a teaching position at Fisk University, a college for black students located in Nashville, Tennessee. In 1952 she resigned, returning to Washington where she was employed at a research facility, Diamond Ordnance Fuze Laboratories. When IBM received a NASA contract, in January 1956 Evelyn moved there as a computer programmer at the Vanguard Computing Center in Washington, D.C.

In 1957 she moved from Washington to New York City and in 1961, following her marriage to the Reverend Gamaliele Mansfield Collins, Evelyn went to Los Angeles. There she was employed by the U.S. Space Technology Laboratories, later renamed in 1962 as the North American Aviation Space and Information Systems Division. Her role involved several projects for the Apollo program, involving celestial mechanics, trajectory computation, and digital computing.

In 1967 Evelyn and Collins divorced and in 1970 she married realtor Edward V. Granville. From 1967 she served as a full professor of mathematics at California State University, Los Angeles, retiring 17 years later at age 60 in 1984. In the same year she began lecturing at Texas College in Tyler, before in 1990 taking the position of the Sam A. Lindsey Professor of mathematics at the University of Texas. Officially retiring from her academic roles in 1997, she has always been a strong proponent of women's education in technology and in this new role she devised elementary school enrichment programs in mathematics.

Evelyn is the recipient of a number of awards, including being the first African-American woman mathematician to receive an honorary doctorate from an American institution, Smith College. Among her other honours are her appointment to the Sam A. Lindsey Chair of the University of Texas at Tyler (1990-1991). She was honoured by the National Academy of Engineering (1998) and inducted into the Portrait Collection of African-Americans in Science of the National Academy of Engineering

In 2000, Evelyn was awarded the Wilbur Lucius Cross Medal, the highest honour of the Yale Graduate School Alumni Association, and in 2006 received an honorary degree from Spelman College, a private women's liberal arts college in Atlanta, Georgia. She was named as one of 'four giants of women's contributions to science and technology' in 2016 in the technology organisation New Relic's 'Mount Codemore'. In 2019 she became a Black History Month Honoree on 'Mathematically Gifted & Black', a website that features the accomplishments of black scholars in mathematical sciences.

During a lecture at Yale University in 2000, Evelyn revealed her views on the teaching of mathematics:

I believe that math is in grave danger of joining Latin and Greek on the heap of subjects which were once deemed essential but are now, at least in America, regarded as relics of an obsolete, intellectual tradition ... math must not be taught as a series of disconnected, meaningless technical procedures from dull and empty textbooks.

We teach that there is only one way to solve a problem, but we should let children explore various techniques ... But we're not training teachers to provide this new approach ... children end up crippled in mathematics at an early age. Then, when they get to the college level, they are unable to handle college classes. It's tragic because almost every academic area requires some exposure to mathematics.

Make children learn how to add, subtract, multiply, and divide, and they won't need calculators. How do you teach the beauty of mathematics, how do teach them to ... solve problems [and] acquaint them with various strategies of problem solving so they can take these skills into any level of mathematics? That's the dilemma we face.

Evelyn has always been a staunch supporter of STEM education and, after her retirement, travelled around the US stressing the importance of mathematics and learning.

Irene Greif

Born: *c.*1947

Irene Gloria Greif was born in New York City where she attended Hunter College High School, graduating in 1965. She had planned to become a schoolteacher as her mother, an accountant, told her it was good to be a teacher 'because you just worked the hours your kids were in school and you could come home.' Moreover, she liked mathematics, especially problems in logic. Irene was exposed to computers during high school, enrolling in a computing course in the college next door. It was here that she used an IBM 1401 main frame computer that involved punch cards and introduced her to machine language.

In 1965 she commenced a degree in engineering at MIT, Massachusetts, as one of only 30 women in a class of a thousand. Irene received her Bachelor of Science with a major in mathematics, after which she completed a Master of Science and PhD in Electrical Engineering and Computer Science, graduating with her doctorate in 1975. In doing so she became the first woman to earn a PhD in computer science from the university. Her supervisor was the US computer scientist Carl Hewitt and her thesis title was 'Semantics of Communicating Parallel Processes'.

Irene's first job was at the University of Washington, Seattle, where it soon became apparent that her interests did not lie in teaching, but rather in research. As a result, Irene returned to MIT where, after two years, she concentrated solely on research. During the next ten years she gravitated to more people-oriented work such as office automation and human-computer interfaces. In the 1980s she devised a research field in computer-supported cooperative work (CSCW) in which people come together across disciplines, looking at social systems and computer systems at the same time. She then spent much of her life determining techniques to build better systems for humans to work together.

When she left MIT in 1987, Irene went to Lotus Development Corporation where her team developed the Version Manager for 1-2-3, a feature that launched the group-enabling of all Lotus products, including InterNotes Web Publisher (a precursor to the Domino program), the first Palm Pilot conduit for Notes mail and the Sametime system, their real-time communications product, including a design vision for reinventing email.

In 1995 Lotus was acquired by IBM where she had once worked as a summer intern. It was now that she started interacting with their research division and attending strategy meetings. She served as director of collaborative user experience in IBM's Thomas J. Watson Research Center and became a Fellow of the American Academy of Arts and Sciences (AAAS) and the Association for Computing Machinery (ACM). A member of the National Academy of Engineering, her other awards include in 2000 being inducted into the Women in Technology International Hall of Fame, the Women Entrepreneurs in Science and Technology Leadership Award in 2008 and ABIE Award for Technical Leadership from the Anita Borg Institute in 2012.

Irene retired from IBM in 2013, holding the company's highest honour as an IBM Fellow and declaring that 'You can have a family or whatever else you want to mix into your life. You make trade-offs. I can't say I always got it right, but I can say that I thought it through.' She is featured in the Notable Women in Computing cards and is married to Albert R. Meyer, who is Emeritus Professor of Computer Science at MIT. They have a son Eli and daughter Julia, as well as two step-children, Naomi and John.

Margaret Elaine Heafield Hamilton

Born: 17 August 1936

Margaret Elaine Heafield was born in Paoli, Indiana, the eldest of three children to parents Kenneth Heafield and Ruth Esther Heafield (née Partington). After the family moved to Michigan, Margaret attended Hancock High School from which she graduated in 1954. In following year she commenced studies in mathematics at the University of Michigan, later transferring to Earlham College, a private liberal arts college in Richmond, Indiana. In 1958 she completed a Bachelor of Arts degree with a major in mathematics and a minor in philosophy.

It was during her time at Earlham that Margaret met her first husband, James Cox Hamilton, who was a chemistry major. They were married on 15 June 1958, when she was aged 21. For a short time Margaret taught high school mathematics and French at a public school in Boston, Indiana, after which the couple then moved to Boston, Massachusetts. On 10 November 1959 their daughter, Lauren, was born, and in the same year Margaret commenced work for the eminent mathematician and meteorologist Edward Norton Lorenz in the meteorology department at MIT.

While at MIT, she worked on Marvin Minsky's Project MAC, which undertook groundbreaking research in operating systems, artificial intelligence (AI), and the theory of computation. Margaret developed software for predicting weather, as well as programming both the LGP-30 and PDP-1 computers. She also made contributions to the notable publications by Lorenz on chaos theory, as well as performing essential numerical calculations. Margaret left the project in 1961, hiring and training the computer scientist Ellen Fetter to replace her.

Margaret's next role, commencing in 1961, was a programmer on the Semi-Automatic Ground Environment (SAGE) Project at the MIT Lincoln Lab, this being an extension of Project Whirlwind, designed to create a computer system to forecast weather systems and track their movements using simulators. For the next two years she wrote software for the prototype AN/FSQ-7 computer (the XD-1) which was used by the U.S. Air Force to detect enemy aircraft. In 1967 Margaret and James divorced and in 1969 she married the aerospace engineer and programmer Dan Lickly.

Her outstanding contributions to the SAGE project led her to a position as director of the Software Engineering Division of the MIT Instrumentation Laboratory, and at NASA as the lead developer of on-board flight software for the Apollo program. In 1976 she co-founded with the software designer Saydean Zeldin the software technology company Higher Order Software, which developed ideas about error prevention and fault tolerance emerging from their time working on the Apollo program. They created a product called USE.IT, based on the HOS methodology they developed at MIT.

In 1986 Margaret founded Hamilton Technologies, also located in Cambridge, Massachusetts. Its stated aim is 'to provide products and services to modernize the planning, system engineering and software development process in order to maximize reliability, lower cost and accelerate time to market'. Margaret became the CEO, being responsible for creating the Universal Systems Language (USL) and its automation, the 001 Tool Suite.

Margaret is a prolific researcher with over 130 papers to her name, either in journals or conference proceedings. She has been credited with over sixty projects and, along with several others, the term 'software engineering' is ascribed to her when working on the Apollo program. She is the recipient of numerous prizes, including the Augusta Ada Lovelace Award by the Association for Women in Computing (1986), the NASA Exceptional Space Act Award for scientific and technical contributions (2003) and the Outstanding Alumni Award by Earlham College (2009).

In 2016 Margaret received the Presidential Medal of Freedom from Barack Obama and in the following year the Computer History Museum Fellow Award, which 'honours exceptional men and women whose computing ideas have changed the world'. The Polytechnic University of Catalonia awarded her an honorary doctorate in 2018, as did Bard College, a private liberal arts college in Annandale-on-Hudson, New York, in 2019.

Also in 2019, Margaret received the Intrepid Lifetime Achievement Award, along with the Washington Award, an annual engineering prize given for 'accomplishments which promote the happiness, comfort, and well-being of humanity'. In the same year, to celebrate 50 years since the first Apollo landing, Google configured the mirrors at the Ivanpah plant to create a picture in the moonlight of Margaret and Apollo 11.

Mary K. Hawes

Mary K. Hawes was a computer scientist who was one of the pioneers in the development of a common business language in accounting. In 1959 Mary was senior product planning analyst for the Electro Data Division of Burroughs Corporation. On 8 April 1959, Mary called a meeting of representatives from academia, computer users, and manufacturers at the University of Pennsylvania to organise a formal meeting on common business languages. She had the idea of writing code that would resemble ordinary English and approached Grace Hopper with the proposal. Grace suggested that they ask the U.S. Department of Defense (DoD) for funding and they were successful.

In May 1959 around 40 representatives of computer users and computer manufacturers met and formed the Short-Range Committee of the Conference on Data Systems Languages. Mary served as Chair of the committee, her team being initially tasked with identifying problems with the current business compilers.

Her research led to the development of COBOL (Common Business Oriented Language) that was designed to run on different brands of computers and perform advanced accounting calculations, including those required for payroll. In May 1959 Mary co-authored, with James P. Fry and others, the 385-page volume *A survey of generalized database management systems* (Association for Computing Machinery, New York, NY).

In September 1971 Mary was one of the many authors of *Feature analysis of generalized database management systems: CODASYL Systems Committee*. In the same year she co-authored a research paper, with C.G. Woods, *Optimized code generation from extended-entry decision tables* that outlined optimised algorithms that had been developed for the processing of extended-entry decision tables.

COBOL developed further during the 1960s and by 1970 it became the most widely used programming language in the world. Even more features were being added to COBOL throughout the 1970s, such as file organisations, the DELETE statement, and the segmentation module while removing the EXAMINE statement (replacing it with INSPECT). By 1978 the main users of COBOL were business, finance, and administrative systems for companies and governments. However, more changes were necessary, and by 1985 over 60 features were changed or deprecated. The United States of America Standards Institute (ANSI), which had been a committee working on COBOL separate from CODASYL since 1962, adopted the new standard, now known as COBOL 85. Further amendments were made in 1989 and 1993.

By 1997, it was estimated that over 200 billion lines of COBOL were in existence that ran 80% of all business programs, although by then COBOL was already nearly 40 years old. The next iteration of COBOL was 'object-oriented', in that it enabled a system to be modelled as a set of objects containing data and code which could be controlled and manipulated in a modular manner. In 2002 the next iteration of COBOL was released but it was not well supported, partly since no compilers completely supported the standard. Moreover, there was increasing competition from newer programming languages, leading to COBOL losing its importance.

Nevertheless, between 2006 and 2012, sixty per cent of organisations in the US still used COBOL, although many had begun to replace it with the more modern C++ and Visual Basic.NET. However, COBOL's data structures influenced subsequent programming languages, in particular its record and file structure influenced both PL/I and Pascal.

Little is known about the personal life Mary K. Hawes, but she holds a much-deserved place among those women who were pioneers of the development of computer languages.

Grete Hermann

Born: 2 March 1901
Died: 15 April 1984 (aged 83)

Grete Hermann was born in Bremen, in the German Empire, to devout Protestant Christian parents. She attended the University of Göttingen where she enrolled in the PhD program, supervised by the eminent mathematician Emmy Noether along with Edmund Landau. In 1926 she received her PhD with the thesis 'Die Frage der endlich vielen Schritte in der Theorie der Polynomideale' (The Question of Finitely Many Steps in Polynomial Ideal Theory). It was published in *Mathematische Annalen* (*Mathematical Annals*) in June 1926, 95, 736–788, and became the foundational paper for computer algebra as it was the first to introduce the existence of algorithms for many of the basic problems of abstract algebra, including ideal membership for polynomial rings. Her algorithm for primary decomposition is still in use today.

For two years following her doctorate, Grete worked as assistant to the German mathematician and critical philosopher, Leonard Nelson. In 1932, after Nelson's death in 1927, she and Minna Specht, an educator and socialist, combined as editors to publish his work 'System der philosophischen Ethik und Pädagogik' (*System of Philosophical Ethics and Pedagogy*). One of Grete's interests was the philosophy surrounding the foundation of physics.

In 1934 Grete visited the town of Leipzig in the German state of Saxony, as she said 'for the express purpose of reconciling a neo-Kantian conception of causality with the new quantum mechanics'. It was in Leipzig that Grete collaborated with other philosophers of the time, including Carl Friedrich von Weizsäcker, and Werner Heisenberg, leading her to research the distinction between predictability and causality.

In 1935 Grete published her seminal paper 'Die naturphilosophischen Grundlagen der Quantenmechanik' (The natural philosophical foundations of quantum mechanics), described by Heisenberg as 'one of the earliest and best philosophical treatments of the new quantum mechanics' in his 1935 paper 'Ist eine deterministische Ergänzung der Quantenmechanik möglich?' (Is a Deterministic Addition to Quantum Mechanics Possible?). In her work, Grete states that 'Quantum mechanics has therefore not contradicted the law of causality at all but has clarified it and has removed from it other principles which are not necessarily connected to it.'

Also in 1935, Grete published a critique of the mathematician John von Neumann's 1932 proof which purported to demonstrate that a hidden variable theory of quantum mechanics was impossible. It went largely unnoticed for over thirty years, until it was published in 1966 by John Stewart Bell, a physicist from Northern Ireland, and her other discoveries were uncovered in 1974 by Max Jammer, an Israeli physicist and philosopher of physics.

In June 1936 Grete was the joint winner, along with Eduard May and Thilo Vogel, of the Richard Avenarius prize, named after the German-Swiss philosopher. In the same year she relocated to Denmark and later to France and England. In March 1938, at age 37, Grete married Edward Henry and published some of her works under the name Grete Henry-Hermann. After the war, in 1946 Grete returned to Germany to continue her interests in combining mathematics, physics and political philosophy.

Grete was appointed as a professor for philosophy and physics at the Pädagogische Hochschule (Teacher Training College) at the University of Bremen and played a prominent role in the *Gewerkschaft Erziehung und Wissenschaft*, a trade union for the education sector. Between 1961 and 1978, she was the Association Chair of the *Philosophisch-Politische Akademie* (Philosophical-Political Academy), a non-profit association that commemorates the work and further development of the work of Leonard Nelson.

Grete is today considered as a person of some significance in the foundations of quantum mechanics, and who dedicated the second half of her career to reconstructing the educational system in Germany following the war. Her dissertation is credited with being the forerunner of the theory of computer algebra. She passed away at age 83 on 15 April 1984. Fourteen years after her death, in 1998 a translation of her 1926 article 'The Question of Finitely Many Steps in the Theory of Polynomial Ideals' appeared in *Communications in Computer Algebra*, 32(3), 8–30.

Susan M. Hockey

Born: 1946

Susan Petty was born in Halifax, West Yorkshire, England, and attended Princess Mary High School in Halifax. After graduation she attended Lady Margaret Hall, Oxford, where she obtained a Bachelor of Arts with 1st Class Honours in Oriental Studies (Egyptian with Akkadian) in 1969.

That year she joined the Atlas Computer Laboratory at Chilton in Oxfordshire and became a founding member of the Association for Literary and Linguistic Computing (ALLC) in 1973. In 1975 she joined Oxford University Computing Services where she undertook various roles, including as Project Director for the Oxford Concordance Program (OCP) for which she also wrote the user manual, and Project Director for the first version of the manuscript collation program 'Collate'. In 1975 she graduated with a Master of Arts from Oxford and was elected to a Fellowship by Special Election of St Cross College in 1979. In the same year she commenced a term as Editor of *ALLC Bulletin*, completing it in 1983. In 1980 she published *A Guide to Computer Applications in the Humanities* (Duckworth and Johns Hopkins).

While at Atlas, Susan developed software for the display of non-Western characters, and at Oxford played a vital role in the development of the Oxford Concordance Program from COCOA, an early piece of software used in humanities computing. Today, these have become standard tools of the digital humanities in both the United States and UK. She has lectured on Text Analysis and the Computer, and SNOBOL Programming for the Humanities. She was also the First Director of the Computers in Teaching Initiative Centre for Textual Studies and directed the Office for Humanities

Susan M. Hockey

Communication between 1989 and 1991. In 1986 she published *Snobol Programming for the Humanities* (Oxford University Press).

In 1987 Susan became a member of the Executive Committee of the Text Encoding Initiative and has twice served as chair of that committee. From 1991 to 1997 she served as director of the Center for Electronic Texts in the Humanities at Rutgers and Princeton Universities in New Jersey. Between 1997 and 1999 she was Professor and Director of the Canadian Institute for Research Computing in Arts at the University of Alberta in Edmonton. In 2000 she joined University College London (UCL) as Professor of Library and Information Studies, and from 2001 was Director of the School of Library, Archive and Information Studies at UCL. Also in 2000, she published *Electronic Texts in the Humanities: Principles and Practice* (Oxford University Press).

Susan retired in 2004 and became an Emerita Professor of Library and Information Studies at University College London. She has written about the history of digital humanities, the development of text analysis applications, electronic textual mark-up, teaching computing in the humanities, and the role of libraries in managing digital resources.

In 2004, Susan was awarded the Alliance of Digital Humanities Organisations' Roberto Busa Prize in recognition of 'outstanding lifetime achievements in the application of information and communications technologies to humanities research'. In 2014, the University College of London created a Digital Humanities lecture series in her honour.

Susan is married to Martin Hockey whom she met at university. He was an accountant in a large firm dealing with corporate and business tax advice, spending the latter part of his career helping Americans do business in the UK. In their retirement, the couple travel to places they did not have time to go to when they worked.

Dorothy Crowfoot Hodgkin

Born: 12 May 1910
Died: 29 July 1994 (aged 84)

The eldest of four daughters, Dorothy Mary Crowfoot was born on 12 May 1910 in Cairo, Egypt, to Grace Mary (Hood) Crowfoot (known as Molly), an expert in ancient textiles, and John Winter Crowfoot, who worked for the country's Ministry of Education. During the hot seasons in Egypt, the family returned to England. They were in England when the First World War began in August 1914 and Molly left her three daughters – Dorothy, aged four, Joan aged two and Elisabeth aged two months – behind and returned to Cairo with John where she gave birth to her fourth daughter, Diana.

On occasions, Dorothy visited her parents on archaeology sites in the Sudan and developed an interest in science, particularly chemistry, from a young age. Her passion was fuelled by her mother who was an eminent botanist. In 1920 the family settled in Beccles, Suffolk. Dorothy's biographer, Georgina Ferry, wrote that she began her scientific career 'in a small private class for the children of parents of modest means and independent views' run by the Parents' National Educational Union (PNEU), whose motto was 'I am, I can, I ought, I will', as an alternative to the other local schools. It trained young women to be governesses for primary school-aged children, with a set syllabus, including courses in physics and chemistry at a time when 'nature study' was the limit of most primary school teachers. At ten years old, Dorothy briefly attended a small class taught by a Miss Fletcher, who had been trained by the PNEU and introduced the subject of chemistry to her young students. Historian Georgina Ferry described how

The progressive educators who designed the course had grasped the importance of practical demonstrations in catching the imagination of the young. Dorothy and her fellow students made solutions of alum and copper sulphate from which to grow crystals. Over the days that followed they watched as the solutions slowly evaporated. Gradually the crystals appeared, faceted like jewels, twinkling in the light. Dorothy was enchanted. 'I was captured for life,' she later wrote, 'by chemistry and by crystals.'

In 1921, when she was eleven, Dorothy attended a state secondary school, the Sir John Leman School in Beccles, Suffolk. It is reported that she fought to be allowed to participate in the chemistry classes, normally reserved for boys, despite the fact that the chemistry teacher, Criss Deeley, was a woman. Dorothy's mother fostered her daughter's interest in chemistry, giving her the published Royal Institution Christmas lectures of Sir William Henry Bragg in 1923 and 1925, especially prepared for children. It was here that Dorothy learned of X-ray techniques to see the arrangement of atoms in crystals.

Dorothy was also encouraged by geologists and the chemist A.F. Joseph, a friend of the family, who also worked on the sites. At age thirteen, Dorothy found a mysterious mineral on the ground and with the aid of her chemistry set correctly identified it as ilmenite crystal. This triggered a love of crystallography, along with a desire to analyse atomic and molecular structures.

While Dorothy achieved outstanding results in her leaving certificate exams in 1927, she needed Latin for entry into the University of Oxford or Cambridge. The headmaster of Sir John Leman School gave her private tuition, which enabled her to pass the entrance examination to Oxford, where, in 1928 and aged eighteen, she began studying chemistry at Somerville College, named after Mary Somerville. Dorothy was soon recognised as an exceptional student. Her laboratory work included analysing samples of ancient coloured glass that her parents sent her from their archaeological digs. Dorothy was also a keen illustrator and developed her own interest in archaeology by completing a detailed illustration of a Byzantine mosaic for one of her father's publications. For her honours year in her bachelor's degree, Dorothy used X-rays to study the structures of certain salts. At the time, X-ray crystallography was a groundbreaking method of examining the structure of molecules – a process that would usually take years of observation using complex mathematics.

In 1932, Dorothy was awarded a first-class honours degree, only the third woman to achieve this distinction in chemistry at Oxford. She then enrolled in the Department of Mineralogy at Cambridge University as a PhD student in the laboratory of John Desmond Bernal. Bernal had trained with Sir William Bragg and now headed the X-ray crystallography laboratory, which was in great demand, pioneering the use of the technique to study biological molecules. Bernal was often away, so Dorothy was very busy. Not long after she had gone to Cambridge, Somerville College offered her a research fellowship. Dorothy was hesitant to leave the exciting environment of Bernal's laboratory, but Somerville was happy for her to remain there for the first year of her fellowship. So she returned to Oxford in 1934 to continue her doctoral work under the supervision of Herbert 'Tiny' Powell. In 1934, Dorothy experienced pain in her hands, which was diagnosed as rheumatoid arthritis. This became progressively more debilitating over time, ultimately leading to deformities in her hands and feet. In her final years she would spend much of her time in a wheelchair, although she nevertheless remained active in research. In 1936, she completed her Cambridge PhD, an X-ray diffraction analysis of sterols and related hydrocarbons. That same year she was awarded a permanent fellowship at Somerville College. Her research during this time included mapping the architecture of cholesterol and examining the structure of penicillin that had been discovered in 1928. This was essential to create synthetic versions of it.

In 1937, Sir William Bragg invited Dorothy to use the exceptional X-ray equipment at the Royal Institution to obtain higher quality photographs of her insulin crystals. While in London she stayed with Margery Fry, the former principal of Somerville. Staying in the house at the same time was Margery's cousin, Thomas Lionel Hodgkin, a graduate in history who had been Dorothy's exact contemporary at Oxford. He had recently lost his job as personal secretary to the British High Commissioner in Palestine through his vociferous support of the Arabs, had become a communist, and was now reluctantly training as a schoolteacher. It is said that at this time, Dorothy was in love with Bernal, who was married. However, after only one or two further meetings, she and Thomas agreed to marry. By the time of their wedding on 16 December 1937, Thomas had found a new career in adult education and was teaching history to unemployed miners in Cumberland. Dorothy, with the support of both families, retained her fellowship at Somerville, which had by this time been made permanent, and continued her research. They had three children: Luke (born 1938), Elizabeth (born 1941) and Toby (born 1946). However, she continued to publish as 'Dorothy Crowfoot' until 1949 when, it was said, she 'bowed to social pressure' and added her married name to write as Dorothy Crowfoot Hodgkin.

During the Second World War, Dorothy received a large grant from the Rockefeller Foundation to continue her work on the structure of insulin, taking over equipment evacuated from Bernal's lab and two of his research assistants, Harry Carlisle and Käthe Schiff. With Carlisle, Dorothy solved the complete three-dimensional structure of cholesterol iodide – the first crystallographic study she was able to undertake completely, and the first anywhere of such a complex organic molecule. Dorothy's research into the structure of penicillin also intensified, in collaboration with Oxford scientists, leading to the first major publication on its structure. Howard Florey and Ernst Chain demonstrated the efficacy of penicillin against bacterial infections in animals and humans during 1940 and 1941, but its chemical formula was unknown.

Dorothy Crowfoot Hodgkin

In 1944, Dorothy was shortlisted by Oxford for the readership in chemical crystallography, but the post went to her former supervisor, Powell. Two years later she was appointed to the lesser post of university demonstrator, which nevertheless doubled her income from her college fellowship. In 1947 Dorothy was elected as a Fellow of the Royal Society, at the relatively early age of thirty-six.

Her work on penicillin led to many industrial contacts. In 1948, Lester Smith of the British pharmaceutical company Glaxo gave Dorothy some dark red crystals of the anti-pernicious anaemia factor, vitamin B_{12}. She researched the structure of the vitamin. Dorothy chaired the committee to advise on Oxford's first computer purchase, insisting in 1952 that the Cambridge and Manchester machines did not have enough memory for her needs While she had been actively encouraging Oxford to establish computing facilities, an offer from the University of California, Los Angeles, provided the assistance she needed to solve the full structure of vitamin B_{12} by 1957. The fact she succeeded moved Lawrence Bragg (the son of Sir William Bragg, whose lectures had inspired young Dorothy) to describe her achievement as 'breaking the sound barrier'.

From the late 1950s onwards, Dorothy's research focused on the structure of insulin, which she had photographed in 1935. She encouraged and fostered a group of researchers working on insulin in her laboratory. Between the 1950s and 1970s she established lasting relationships with fellow international scientists at the Institute of Crystallography in Moscow, in India and in China, and with those working in Beijing and Shanghai on the structure of insulin. In fact, after her initial visit to China in 1959, she travelled there seven more times over the following 25 years. In 1958, the American Academy of Arts and Sciences elected her a 'Foreign Honorary Member'. Dorothy spent the early 1960s in Africa at the University of Ghana where her husband was the Director of the Institute of African Studies.

In 1969, working with Guy Dodson and Mamannamana Vijayan, Dorothy finally built the first model of the insulin molecule, working almost non-stop over a single weekend. Dodson recalled the moment vividly: 'It was a triumphant occasion in which Dorothy, though suffering from swelling ankles and forced into wearing slippers, worked with concentration and wonderful spirits.' Dorothy's biographer, Ferry, wrote that, in the case of each of the three projects for which she is best known – penicillin, vitamin B12, and insulin – 'Dorothy pushed the boundaries of what was possible with the techniques available. Her distinction lay not in developing new approaches, but in a remarkable ability to envisage possibilities in three-dimensional structures, grounded in a profound understanding of the underlying chemistry.' She was, in the words of former colleague Lord Phillips, not just a scientist's scientist but 'a crystallographer's crystallographer'.

In 1964, having been proposed twice before, Dorothy won the Nobel Prize for chemistry for 'her determinations by X-ray techniques of the structures of important biochemical substances'. She was only the third woman to have won a Nobel prize for chemistry after Marie Curie and her daughter Irène Joliot-Curie, and the fifth woman to win any science Nobel prize. At the time of writing, she was the only British woman scientist to have been awarded a Nobel Prize in any of the three sciences it recognises. In 1965, Dorothy was the second woman in sixty years, after Florence Nightingale, to be appointed to the Order of Merit (OM) by a British monarch. Although she is said to have disliked titles and had reportedly told her husband that she would refuse the title of Dame Commander of the British Empire (DBE) if offered one, she regarded the OM as 'rather different really'. Established in 1902 by King Edward VII to recognise distinguished service, admission into the order remains the personal gift of the Sovereign, and is restricted to a maximum of twenty-four living recipients from the Commonwealth. She also accepted the first 'freedom of Beccles', an honour 'hastily invented for her by the town in which she spent her schooldays'.

Between 1972 and 1975, Dorothy was the President of the International Union of Crystallography and from 1970 to 1988 served as the Chancellor of the University of Bristol. In 1976 she won the prestigious Copley Medal which, since 1731, has been presented by the Royal Society for exceptional achievements in research in any branch of science. Her award was 'in recognition of her outstanding work on the structures of complex molecules, particularly Penicillin, vitamin B_{12} and insulin'. As at 2019, she was still the only woman to receive this award. Between 1977 and 1983, Dorothy was a Fellow of Wolfson College at Oxford and in 1977 she was conferred the title of Professor Emerita by Oxford University. In addition to her scientific work, Dorothy remained actively dedicated to the cause of world peace throughout her life, her political sensibilities encouraged from an early age by her mother. In 1957, she was a founder of the Pugwash Conference on Science and World Affairs, an international organisation bringing together scholars and public figures to work toward reducing the danger of armed conflict and to seek solutions to global security threats.

On 29 July 1994, Dorothy Crowfoot Hodgkin passed away following a stroke, aged eighty-four, at her home at Shipston-on-Stour in Warwickshire, England. Her husband Thomas had passed away on 25 March 1982. She was honoured posthumously in August 1996 as one of five 'Women of Achievement' selected to appear on a set of British postage stamps. All but Dorothy were DBEs. Of a set of stamps issued in 2010 to celebrate the 350th anniversary of the Royal Society, she was the only woman included.

There is an asteroid, 'Hodgkin', named as a tribute to her and the Royal Society awards the Dorothy Hodgkin Fellowship in her honour for outstanding scientists at an early stage of their research. There are also buildings at the University of York, Bristol University and Keele University named after her, along with the science block at her former school, John Leman High School. Since 1999, the Oxford International Women's Festival has presented an annual memorial lecture, usually in March, to celebrate her extraordinary achievements. Marking the fiftieth anniversary of her winning the Nobel Prize, 2014 was designated the 'International Year of Crystallography'.

In his obituary of Dorothy, molecular biologist, Nobel laureate and Copley Medal winner, Max Perutz wrote:

She pursued her crystallographic studies, not for the sake of honours, but because that was what she liked to do. There was a magic about her person. She had no enemies, not even among those whose scientific theories she demolished or whose political view she opposed. Just as her X-ray cameras bared the intrinsic beauty beneath the rough surface of things, so the warmth and gentleness of her approach to people uncovered in everyone, even the most hardened scientific crook, some hidden kernel of goodness.

Frances Elizabeth 'Betty' Snyder Holberton

Born: 7 March 1917
Died: 8 December 2001 (aged 84)

Frances Elizabeth (Betty) Snyder was born in Philadelphia, Pennsylvania, the third of eight children to John Amos Snyder and Frances J. Morrow. She attended the University of Pennsylvania where she studied journalism, one of the few professions open to women at the time and one that also allowed her to travel. It was reported that on the first day of lectures, her mathematics professor told her to stop wasting her time attempting a mathematics degree and instead to stay home and raise children. The advice was not well received by Betty.

During her twenties, Betty saw that women were being hired by the U.S. Army to calculate ballistic trajectories. Women were required as many men were away fighting, and the work had to be done. The Moore School of Engineering at the University of Pennsylvania selected 80 women to become 'human computers' and the calculations they were asked to perform to track these trajectories were quite complex. Some of the equations involved took more than 30 hours to solve.

In early 1943, under the direction of the mathematician and computer scientist, Herman Goldstine, the U.S. Army developed the first programmable general-purpose electronic digital computer, the ENIAC (Electronic Numerical Integrator and Computer). By 1945 the Army was ready to try an experimental project and six of the eighty women were selected to be its first programmers. One of these was Betty, the other five being Kay McNulty, Marlyn Wescoff, Ruth Lichterman, Betty Jean Jennings, and Fran Bilas. Their task was to program the ENIAC to perform calculations to estimate ballistics trajectories electronically on behalf of the Ballistic Research Laboratory (BRL) of the Army.

Initially their work on the ENIAC was classified and so the six women were forced to work only with blueprints and wiring diagrams, making their programming role even more challenging. When the ENIAC was finally presented to the public on 15 February 1946, the cost had spiralled to US$487,000, which is equivalent to over $7 million today. Unfortunately, at the time, the six women received almost no credit for their work in making the project a resounding success.

Following the war, Betty was employed by Remington Rand and later at the National Bureau of Standards. In 1953 she was appointed as the supervisor of advanced programming in a part of the Navy's Applied Mathematics laboratory in Maryland. She worked there with the physicist John William Mauchly to develop the C-10 instruction set for BINAC, widely regarded as the prototype of all modern programming languages. She was also involved in the development of early standards for the COBOL (COmmon Business-Oriented Language) and several initial revisions of the FORTRAN programming language (Fortran 77 and Fortran 90) with Grace Hopper.

The David Taylor Model Basin test facilities for the development of ship designs one of the largest in the world and was one of the first to adopt computers. It became a hub for computer technology. In 1959 Betty was appointed the Chief of the Programming Research Branch, Applied Mathematics Laboratory, and was instrumental in the development of the UNIVAC which became the first general-purpose electronic digital computer designed for business. She designed control panels that placed the numeric keypad next to the keyboard and wrote the first generative programming system (SORT/MERGE).

In 1997, Betty was the only one of the original six programmers of the ENIAC to receive the prestigious Augusta Ada Lovelace Award, the highest award given by the Association of Women in Computing. In the same year, she, along with the other five human computers, were inducted into the Women in Technology International Hall of Fame. Also in 1997, she received the IEEE Computer Pioneer Award from the IEEE Computer Society for developing the sort-merge generator, which 'inspired the first ideas about compilation'.

Betty passed away at age 84 on 8 December 2001 at the Kingshire Manor assisted-living community in Rockville, Maryland. The cause of death was reported as heart disease, diabetes, and complications from a stroke she had suffered several years before. Her burial place is Saint Paul's Cemetery, Ivy, Albemarle County, Virginia. She was survived by her husband of 51 years, John Vaughn Holberton, who passed away two years later at age 92, and their daughters Pamela and Priscilla.

In her later years, Betty said that she had few regrets: 'I have had a fantastic life. Everything I did was the beginning of something new.' In 2015 Holberton School, a project-based school for software engineers based in San Francisco, was founded in her honour.

Erna Schneider Hoover

Born: 19 June 1926

Erna Schneider was born on 19 June 1926, in Irvington, New Jersey, the eldest child of her dentist father and mother who was a former teacher. She had a younger brother who died of polio when he was five. Erna and her younger siblings were raised in South Orange where she attended public school. In her youth she enjoyed swimming, sailing and canoeing in the Adirondacks. Developing a keen interest in science at an early age, her inspiration the biography of Marie Curie, which argued that despite the prevailing views of the time about gender roles, women could succeed.

Erna attended the prestigious Wellesley College in Massachusetts from which she graduated with honours and a Bachelor of Arts in medieval history in 1948. She was a member of Phi Beta Kappa, the oldest academic honour society in the US, as well as a Durant Scholar, a recognition of Wellesley's highest achieving students. In this period, most female university graduates studied education, English or foreign languages, but Erna attended Yale University where she enrolled for a PhD in the philosophy and foundations of mathematics. Her dissertation, a study of logic, was titled 'An Analysis of Contrary-to-Fact Conditional Sentences' and, in 1951, she became one of the five per cent of PhDs in mathematics in the US that were awarded to women at that time.

Erna's first teaching role after graduation was as a professor in philosophy and logic at the private liberal arts institution, Swarthmore College in Pennsylvania, in 1951. In 1953, Erna married Charles Wilson Hoover Jr who encouraged her in her academic career, but she was unable to obtain tenure as a married woman. In 1954, she resigned to relocate to New Jersey when Charles found employment there. It was then that Erna immediately took a role as a senior technical associate for Bell Laboratories, which had just begun investigating the development of electronic switching systems. These were for use not only by the public telephone systems but also for private business exchange systems and their aim was to improve the ability to take a greater number of calls. Call centres had a particular problem if they received a large number of calls in a short amount of time, overloading the unreliable electronic relays, causing the entire system to come to a halt.

Promoted in 1956, the following year Erna enrolled in Bell Laboratories internal training program, considered to be the equivalent of a master's degree in computer science. The symbolic logic included in her dissertation had applications in switching circuit design and her knowledge of feedback theory and analysing traffic and pattern statistics enabled her to design the stored program control. Using computer programming, she was able to apply her theory to eliminate the danger of overload in processing calls and to facilitate more effective service during peak calling times. As she said in an interview in 2008, 'To my mind it was kind of common sense ... I designed the executive program for handling situations when there are too many calls, to keep it operating efficiently without hanging up on itself. Basically, it was designed to keep the machine from throwing up its hands and going berserk.'

After applying in 1967, in 1971 she became one of the first women in the US to receive a software patent when she was issued Patent No. 3,623,007 for a computerised telephone switching system, 'Feedback Control Monitor for Stored Program Data Processing System'. Prior to her work, most businesses relied on hardwired or mechanical switching systems that could not cope with many simultaneous incoming calls.

Erna's revolutionary switching system was the first reliable device to use a computer, including transistor circuits and memory-stored control. She reportedly developed the initial design while she was in hospital around the birth of her second child. The company's lawyers who were managing the patent application had to go to her home so that she could sign the papers while she was on maternity leave. During her time at Bell Laboratories, Erna also developed computer programs designed to ensure that outdoor telephone lines remained in good working order. In addition, her research into radar control programs of the Safeguard Anti-Ballistic Missile System, as designed to intercept intercontinental ballistic missile warheads, was a factor in the ending of the Cold War. In 1978, she was the first woman promoted to the role of Technical Department Head at Bell Laboratories. Her group applied AI techniques, large databases, and transaction systems to support telephone operations using computer software. The first stored program control system was installed in a private business in 1963, and by 1983 1,800 of the switching systems were serving fifty-three million subscriber lines. She was heavily involved in a number of high-level applications, including AI methods, large databases, and transactional software to support large telephone networks.

In 1987, at the age of sixty-one, Erna retired from Bell Laboratories and began promoting the importance of K–12 education and highlighting the lack of females in teaching science disciplines. She developed the first 'Conference for Expanding Your Horizons' program, with the American Association of University Women and Girl Scouts of America. In 1990, Erna received the Wellesley College Alumni Achievement Award, recognising her as a 'champion of affordable, quality public education'. From 1980, she served as chairperson of the Trenton State College Board of Trustees. The president of the College described Erna as 'a tenacious, energetic leader' and credited her with much of the College's progress, particularly in the area of attracting and supporting female professors and staff. In 2008, she was inducted into the National Inventors Hall of Fame, which recognises 'the enduring legacies of exceptional US patent holders', whose influence 'can inspire the future and motivate the next great innovator to transform our world'.

By any measure, Erna Schneider Hoover was an inspiring pioneer for women in the field of computer technology. On 19 June 2022, she turned ninety-six. Her husband Charles passed away at age 91 on 21 April 2017.

Grace Brewster Murray Hopper

Born: 9 December 1906
Died: 1 January 1992 (aged 85)

Grace Brewster Murray was born the eldest of three children on 9 December 1906 in New York City. Her father Walter Fletcher Murray and mother Mary Campbell (Van Horne) Murray, were of Scottish and Dutch descent. Grace's great-grandfather, Alexander Wilson Russell, was an admiral in the US Navy and fought in the Battle of Mobile Bay during the American Civil War.

Grace's preparatory school education was at Plainfield, New Jersey. Her mother, Mary, had developed an interest in mathematics as a young woman, but was unable to study anything beyond geometry as it was not considered appropriate for a woman of her day. As a result, she encouraged Grace not to limit her horizons based simply on her gender. In this she was supported by Walter who gave an equal education to their two daughters (Grace and Mary) and son (Roger). Grace was initially rejected for early admission to Vassar College at age sixteen as her test scores in Latin were not high enough. However, she was admitted the following year, graduating in 1928 with a bachelor's degree in mathematics and physics and admitted to Phi Beta Kappa, the oldest US academic honour society. In 1930, she earned a master's degree in mathematics at Yale University and, in the same year, she married New York University professor, Vincent Foster Hopper. In 1931, Grace began teaching mathematics at Vassar and in 1934 she obtained her PhD under the supervision of the Norwegian mathematician Øystein Ore. Her dissertation, 'New Types of Irreducibility Criteria', was published the same year.

Grace tried to enlist in the US Navy early in the Second World War, but was rejected as, at age thirty-four, she was considered too old. Moreover, her weight to height ratio was too low. Her job as a mathematician and mathematics professor at Vassar College was also valuable to the war effort. In 1941, she was promoted to the rank of associate professor. In 1943, she obtained leave from Vassar and joined the Navy Reserve to serve in the all-female division, 'Women Accepted for Volunteer Emergency Service' (WAVES), that had been formed in 1942. After obtaining an exemption to enlist, as she was 6.8 kg (15 lbs) below the Navy minimum weight of 54 kg (120 lbs), she trained at the Naval Reserve Midshipmen's School at Smith College in Northampton, Massachusetts.

In 1944, Grace topped her class and was assigned as a lieutenant, junior grade, to the Bureau of Ships Computation Project at Harvard University, where she served on the programming staff of the Mark I computer. Also known as the 'Automatic Sequence Controlled Calculator', it weighed over 4,500 kg and was the first large-scale automatic calculator and a precursor of electronic computers. The team was led by American physicist and computing pioneer Howard H. Aiken, with whom Grace co-wrote three papers. After a moth got into the circuits of Mark I, Grace coined the term 'bug' to refer to unexplained computer failures. (The remains of the moth have been retained in the group's log book at the Smithsonian Institution's National Museum of American History in Washington, D.C.)

At the end of the Second World War, Grace and Vincent divorced. She then requested a transfer to the regular Navy, but was denied due to her age, as she was now thirty-eight. She continued to serve in the Navy Reserve and remained at the Harvard Computation Lab until 1949, turning down a full professorship at Vassar in favour of working as a research fellow at Harvard under a Navy contract.

Grace became one of the first programmers in computing history, believing that programming languages should be as easily understood as English. Consequently, she was highly influential on the development of one of the first programming languages, COBOL (COmmon Business-Oriented Language), which became one of the most widespread languages in business.

In 1949, Grace joined the Eckert-Mauchly Computer Corporation where she designed an improved compiler that translated a programmer's instructions into computer codes. She remained working there when it was taken over by Remington Rand in 1951 and by Sperry Rand Corporation in 1955. During 1957, her division developed 'Flow-Matic', the first English-language data-processing compiler.

In 1964, Grace was awarded the Society of Women Engineers Achievement Award, the Society's highest honour, 'In recognition of her significant contributions to the burgeoning computer industry as an engineering manager and originator of automatic programming systems'.

On 31 December 1966, at age sixty, Grace retired from the Navy with the rank of Commander but was recalled to active duty in August the following year to help standardise the navy's computer languages. She retired again in 1971, but was again recalled to active duty in 1972, attaining the rank of Captain in August 1973 and Commodore in December 1983. On 8 November 1985, at the age of seventy-eight, she was made a Rear Admiral (lower half). By age seventy-nine she was the oldest officer on active US naval duty when she retired for the final time on 31 August 1986.

Throughout her illustrious career Grace won many awards, including the inaugural Data Processing Management Association Man of the Year award (now called the Distinguished Information Sciences Award). In 1969, the annual Grace Murray Hopper Award for Outstanding Young Computer Professionals was established by the Association for Computing Machinery in her honour.

In 1973, she became the first American and the first woman of any nationality to be made a Distinguished Fellow of the British Computer Society and, in 1986, upon her retirement, she was the first woman to be awarded the Defense Distinguished Service Medal.

On 1 January 1992, Grace Hopper passed away in Arlington, Virginia, at the age of 85. She never remarried after her divorce in 1945, nor did she have any children. In 1994, the Grace Hopper celebration of women in computing was founded, and has since been organised annually by the Anita Borg Institute for Women and Technology and the Association for Computing Machinery.

In 1996 the USS *Hopper* (DDG-70) was launched, nicknamed 'Amazing Grace', one of the very few US military vessels named after women. The Department of Energy's National Energy Research Scientific Computing Center named its flagship system 'Hopper' in 2009, the same year that the Office of Naval Intelligence created the Grace Hopper Information Services Center. On 22 November 2016, she was posthumously awarded a Presidential Medal of Freedom for her accomplishments in the field of computer science and, in 2017, Hopper College at Yale University was named in her honour. During her lifetime she was awarded over thirty honorary degrees from universities worldwide.

Grace Hopper left us memorable quotes:

> The most important thing I've accomplished, other than building the compiler, is training young people. They come to me, you know, and say, 'Do you think we can do this?' I say, 'Try it.' And I back 'em up. They need that. I keep track of them as they get older and I stir 'em up at intervals so they don't forget to take chances... A ship in port is safe; but that is not what ships are built for. Sail out to sea and do new things.

Grace Hopper was one of the outstanding pioneers of computing and left a legacy that stands to this day and her nickname of 'Amazing Grace' is a testament to the way she improved technology and brought the world of computers to such great heights.

Mary Jane Irwin

Born: *c*.1949

Mary Jane ('Janie') Irwin was raised in Memphis, Tennessee, USA. Her father was a university professor at Memphis State (now University of Memphis) and her mother was an elementary school teacher. In a later interview she remarked: 'All along I was a daddy's girl, and wanted to be a university professor, although I had no idea what they did.' She was awarded an internship in 7th-grade mathematics that would set her on a path in that field. While a senior at high school, Janie accepted a Deanship in the Tennessee community college system.

In 1966, while an undergraduate at Memphis State University, Janie married and the couple had a son, John, who later became a computer scientist. In 1971 she graduated with a Bachelor of Mathematics. As her husband found a position in Indiana, her choice of graduate schools was limited. She selected and only applied to the University of Illinois at Urbana-Champaign, receiving her Master of Science in 1975 and PhD in computer science under the supervision of Dr. James Robertson in 1977. She was only the second female to do so. Her thesis was on the topic of computer arithmetic. Dr. Robertson was renowned for his work developing SRT Division (he was the 'R' in SRT), used to resolve the Pentium Divider Bug.

Working with Robertson, Janie developed an interest in chip design while working on ILLIAC II (the first computer to incorporate Speed-Independent Circuitry) and ILLIAC III (a fine-grained SIMD pattern recognition computer that was initially used for image processing of bubble chamber experiments used to detect nuclear particles). As part of her PhD, she also built hardware that involved signal processing and systolic arrays, as well as developing design tools as they did not exist back then. This led her to explore the field of Electronic Design Automation (EDA).

After gaining her doctorate Janie obtained a tenured position at Penn State University, where she would stay until her retirement some forty years later. She was awarded a grant to build hardware using the newly developed CMOS architecture Those were the early days of CMOS. Her work included the creation of EDA tools. Her research involved application-specific architectures, such as the implementation and field-testing of various board level designs; the Arithmetic Cube, the MGAP and SPARTA. She co-developed along with her student Robert M. Owens a suite of architecture, logic and circuit design tools, including ARTIST, PERFLEX, LOGICIAN, and DECOMPOSER.

In 1989 Janie was promoted to the rank of full professor and in 1993 examined resource constrained systems design, examples including embedded systems with limited battery life and/or memory space, and sensor network systems. She was one of the authors of the architectural level power simulator, SimplePower, used to measure the power on a 5-stage pipeline architecture.

Apart from her research, Janie was very active in her field, serving on a number of important committees, including the Board on Army Science and Technology, the Association for Computing Machinery (ACM's) Fellows Selection Committee, Microsoft Research's External Research Advisory Board, and the National Academy of Engineering (NAE's) Committee on Membership. She was also a founding Co-Editor-in-Chief of ACM's *Journal on Emerging Technologies in Computing Systems*, an elected member of the Computing Research Association (CRA's) Board of Directors, of the IEEE Computer Society's Board of Governors, of ACM's Council, and Vice President of ACM.

Throughout her illustrious career, Janie has been awarded many honours, including her election as IEEE Fellow (1994) and ACM Fellow (1996). She was inducted into the NAE (2003) and in 2004 won the Marie R. Pistilli Women in Electronic Design Automation Award, an 'annual honor that recognises individuals who have visibly helped to advance women in electronic design', and the ACM Distinguished Service Award that 'recognises outstanding service contributions to the computing community as a whole' in the following year. In 2007 she was the winner of the CRA Distinguished Service Award and in 2007 the Anita Borg Technical Leadership Award, given annually by the institute to 'a woman who has inspired the women's technology community through outstanding technological and social contributions'.

Janie was elected as a Fellow of the American Association for the Advancement of Science (AAAS Fellow) in 2009 and received the prestigious ACM Athena Lecturer Award in 2010. The ASP-DAC Ten-Year Retrospective

Most Influential Paper Award was presented to her in 2012 and she also received an Honorary Doctorate from Chalmers University, Sweden. In 2019 she received the Kaufmann Award, the first woman to receive EDA's highest honour.

Janie retired in 2017 with her official title at Penn State University being 'Evan Pugh Professor and A. Robert Noll Chair Emeritus in Engineering in the Department of Computer Science and Engineering'. She devotes much of her time now to helping women achieve the recognition they deserve through awards, promotions and gaining tenure.

Mary Lou Jepsen

Born: 5 April 1965

Mary Lou Jepsen was born in Windsor, Connecticut, USA, to Donald Allen and Jane Anne (Barry) Jepsen. She attended Brown University, Providence, graduating with a Bachelor in Studio Art, as well as a Bachelor of Science in Electrical Engineering in 1987. For the next two years she enrolled at the Massachusetts Institute of Technology (MIT) in Cambridge, Massachusetts, where she earned a Master of Science in Media Technology in 1989 by being involved in the world's first fully computer-generated holographic video system.

In 1989 Mary Lou spent a year at the University of California, San Diego, as a San Diego Fellow studying diffractive/refractive solutions for free space optical interconnects for optical computing. In 1990 she was appointed an Assistant Professor of Computer Science at RMIT in Melbourne, Victoria, where her research involved huge computer-generated holograms, some that filled beach coves, and other small ones that were used on the Australian paper (plastic) currency. She also examined 'straight' 3D computer graphics on flat screens.

In 1991 she travelled to Kunsthochschule für Medien Köln in Germany, a higher education institution located in North Rhine, Westphalia. Here she constructed a massive computer-generated hologram that filled a city block and could only be seen 10 minutes a day for 55 days a year if the weather was not cloudy. In 1992 she returned to the US, now enrolling in a PhD at Brown University. In 1993 she worked as a research scientist for Advanced Environmental Research Group, Providence. In 1993–4 she was a National Aeronautics and Space Administration (NASA) Fellow in the Rhode Island Space Grant Program, and in 1994–5 served as technical director at Brown's

Multimedia laboratory. In 1995 she received a diagnosis of a pituitary gland tumour that had gone undetected for five years, and had it removed. She overcame the disease, although from that time had to take a twice-daily regimen of hormone replacement to keep her hormone output stable.

Mary Lou graduated with a PhD in Optics in 1996, her thesis researching liquid crystal displays that work without polarised light, with liquid crystal filled holographic diffractive structures. As a side project, she created Moon-TV, the idea being to project video on the moon by using large solar farms filled with big moving mirrors to redirect sunlight incident on Earth. Although successful, she agreed that it was culturally unacceptable. In 1998, she co-founded and was chief technical officer at MicroDisplay Corporation in San Pablo, California, holding that position for five years. Her next role was as a technical officer in the display division of Intel Corporation, a position she held until 2004.

Between 2005 and 2007 she was the co-founder (with Nicholas Negroponte) and chief technical officer of One Laptop Per Child and lead architect of the $100 laptop, the lowest-power laptop ever made. For the entirety of 2005 she was the only employee. By 2015 more than three million of these inexpensive computers had been sold to governments worldwide, which then distributed them through the ministries of education to students. The laptops ultimately remained the property of the child, and the operating system and software are specifically adapted to the languages of the participating countries. Over 50 countries were involved that included more than 25 different languages.

In 2008 Mary Lou founded Pixel Qi JOE, Inc., in Hull, Massachusetts. In June the same year she was awarded an Honorary Doctor of Athabasca University by Canada's online university. She also founded and led two moonshots at Google X, reporting to the American business magnate, computer scientist and Internet entrepreneur Sergey Brin who was a co-founder of Google. In this role she oversaw display and consumer electronic programs for Google. Mary Lou was also Executive Director of Engineering at Facebook/Oculus VR where she was at the forefront in advances in Virtual Reality. In 2011 she won the ABIE Award for Innovation from the Anita Borg Institute.

In 2013 Mary Lou was named one of the hundred most influential people in the world by *Time* magazine (Time 100), and in the same year was named as one of CNN's top ten thinkers in science and technology for her work in display innovation. In 2014 she received an honorary Doctor of Science from Brown University. She was appointed to the Board of Directors of Lear Corporation in 2016, a leading global supplier of automotive seating and electrical distribution systems that serves every major automaker in the world.

Also in 2016, Mary Lou founded Openwater, a startup company that explored MRI-type body imaging using holographic and infrared techniques. In 2018 she presented a TED talk on the technology used by Openwater. At the 6th Laser IGNITION 2018 Conference held in Yokohama, Japan, she outlined advances in the resolution progression of Openwater's MRI machines. Mary Lou also demonstrated the potential for technological improvements in telepathy that would permit users to transmit thoughts and feelings electronically. Today Openwater describes itself as 'building a next-generation portable neural imaging system to enable early precision stroke detection and routing for rapid thrombectomy which could save millions of lives'. In 2018 she was included in *Forbes'* America's Top 50 Women in Tech.

Mary Lou is Executive Director of Engineering at Facebook, Inc. and Head of Display Technologies at Oculus where she leads advanced consumer electronics, opto-electronic and display design and manufacturing efforts, as well as being at the forefront in advances in Virtual Reality. She holds more than 200 published or issued patents and has received many honours for her outstanding achievements. These include being elected as a Fellow of the Optical Society (OSA) and receiving the Edwin H. Land Medal from them. The Anita Borg Institute named her as one of the top 50 female computer scientists of all time. She was also awarded two prestigious alumni awards from Brown University, namely the Horace Mann Medal (awarded by the Graduate School) and BEAM award (awarded by the School of Engineering). Mary Lou is married to John Patrick Conor Ryan, formerly a partner at Monitor Group.

Katherine Johnson

Born: 26 August 1918
Died: 24 February 2020 (aged 101)

(Creola) Katherine Coleman was born in White Sulphur Springs, West Virginia. She was the youngest of four children to mother Joylette Roberta (née Lowe), a teacher, and father, Joshua McKinley Coleman, a farmer and handyman who worked at the Greenbrier Hotel. As a child, Katherine displayed outstanding mathematical abilities, but Greenbrier County, where she lived, did not permit African-American pupils to attend school past eighth grade. This necessitated her parents enrolling the 10-year-old Katherine at a high school in Institute, West Virginia, on the grounds of West Virginia State College, where she enrolled in every mathematics subject.

Katherine graduated summa cum laude at age 18 in 1937 with a Bachelor of Science degree in mathematics and French. She then landed a teaching role at a black public school in Marion, Virginia. After marrying her first husband, James Goble, in 1939, she resigned from her teaching role to attend graduate school at West Virginia University in Morgantown, West Virginia, the first African-American woman to do so. At the end of her first year of study she became pregnant and quit her program to concentrate on her home life and family.

At the time, jobs for African-Americans were in short supply, and although she wanted to be a researcher, the only position Katherine could find was as a teacher. This changed in 1952 when she became aware that the National Advisory Committee for Aeronautics (NACA) was hiring both white and African-American mathematicians at the Langley Memorial Aeronautical Laboratory, based in Hampton, Virginia. The roles were in their Guidance and Navigation Department, and in June 1953 she commenced work there. Her initial task was, along with a group of other women, to perform mathematical calculations and read data obtained from an aircraft's black box. Her job changed when she and a colleague were temporarily transferred to an all-male research team, she never returned to her original position. Instead, for the following five years she used her analytical geometry skills to work on various projects, including analysing gust alleviation for aircraft in the West Area Computers section. Due to the workplace segregation laws at the time, Katherine and the other African-American women in the 'coloured computing pool' were required to work, eat, and use restrooms that were separate from those of their white colleagues.

In 1956 her husband James died of an inoperable brain tumour, leaving behind their three daughters Constance, Joylette, and Katherine. In 1959 she married James A. 'Jim' Johnson, an officer in the United States Army.

In 1958 her computing pool was disbanded, at the same time that NACA became NSA and digital computers were emerging. Racial discrimination was still apparent, as Katherine later recalled:

> In the early days of NASA women were not allowed to put their names on the reports – no woman in my division had had her name on a report. I was working with Ted Skopinski and he wanted to leave and go to Houston … but Henry Pearson, our supervisor – he was not a fan of women – kept pushing him to finish the report we were working on. Finally, Ted told him, 'Katherine should finish the report, she's done most of the work anyway.' So Ted left Pearson with no choice; I finished the report and my name went on it, and that was the first time a woman in our division had her name on something.

In the following years Katherine worked as an aerospace technologist before being transferred to the Spacecraft Controls Branch. It was here that she performed invaluable work in the early days of space exploration. In one instance she calculated the trajectory for the first American in space, Alan Shepard, on 5 May 1961. In the same year, Katherine calculated the crucial launch window for Shepard's Mercury mission, the first crewed flight of Project Mercury, the aim to put an astronaut into orbit around the Earth and return him safely. In 1971, at age 47, Shepard became the oldest person to walk on the moon as part of the Apollo XV mission.

The first American to orbit the earth was John Glenn who flew Friendship 7 in 1962. It is reported that he requested that Katherine be assigned to double-check the mathematics involved in the computations. She later related that Glenn had said when he was ready to go, 'Call her. If she says the computer is right, I'll take it.' Katherine had earned a well-deserved reputation for extraordinary accuracy in her calculations, an attribute that enhanced confidence in digital computers.

Katherine assisted in calculating the trajectory for the 1969 Apollo 11 flight to the Moon, and later on the fateful Apollo 13 Moon mission.

Following the decision to abort the mission, it was her calculations on the backup procedures that enabled the crew to return to Earth safely. In 2010, at age 92, she recalled in an interview that 'Everybody was concerned about them getting there. We were concerned about them getting back.' Before her retirement from NASA in 1986, she worked on the Space Shuttle program, the Earth Resources Satellite, along with a planned mission to Mars.

In 2015, President Barak Obama awarded Katherine the Presidential Medal of Freedom, the highest civilian honour in the US, presented to 'individuals who have made especially meritorious contributions to the security or national interests of the United States, to world peace, or to cultural or other significant public or private endeavors'. In the following year she was included on the BBC's list of 100 Women of Influence worldwide.

Two NASA facilities were named in her honour; in May 2016 the Katherine G. Johnson Computational Research Facility in Hampton, Virginia, and in February 2019 the Independent Verification and Validation Facility, in Fairmont, West Virginia, became the Katherine Johnson Independent Verification and Validation Facility.

In March 2019, Katherine's husband Jim passed away at the age of 93. The couple had been married for 60 years. She spent her later years encouraging students to enter the STEM fields of science, technology, engineering, and mathematics. In June 2019, George Mason University named the largest building on their SciTech campus, the Katherine G. Johnson Hall and in 2020 Bethel School District, Washington, named its newest school the Katherine G. Johnson Elementary.

Throughout her life Katherine received many honours: Honorary Doctor of Laws, from SUNY Farmingdale (1998), West Virginia State College Outstanding Alumnus of the Year (1999), Honorary Doctor of Science by the Capitol College, Laurel, Maryland (2006), Honorary Doctorate of Science from Old Dominion University, Norfolk, Virginia (2010), De Pizan Honor from National Women's History Museum (2014), the NCWIT Pioneer in Tech Award (2015), and more.

In 2016 Katherine received three major awards, including the Silver Snoopy award given by NASA to those 'who have made outstanding contributions to flight safety and mission success'; the Astronomical Society of the Pacific's Arthur B.C. Walker II Award, and a Presidential Honorary Doctorate of Humane Letters from West Virginia University, Morgantown, West Virginia, and the Langley West Computing Unit NASA Group Achievement Award at a reception at the Virginia Air and Space Center. In the following year she was awarded the Daughters of the American Revolution (DAR) Medal of Honor, and an Honorary Doctorate from Spelman College.

In the year of her 100th birthday, 2018, she was awarded an Honorary Doctor of Science from the College of William & Mary, Williamsburg, Virginia. On 29 April 2019, the University of Johannesburg and its Faculty of Science conferred on her the degree of Philosophiae Doctor Honoris Causa for her pioneering role at NASA. Later that year, on 8 November, she received the Congressional Gold Medal, this being 'Congress's highest expression of national appreciation for distinguished achievements and contributions by individuals or institutions'.

Katherine passed away age 101 at a retirement home in Newport News on 24 February 2020. On 6 November 2020, a satellite named after her (ÑuSat 15 or Katherine, COSPAR 2020-079G) was launched into space. In February 2021, Northrop Grumman named the Cygnus NG-15 spacecraft, one that supplies the International Space Station, the SS *Katherine Johnson*. In 2021 she was inducted into the National Women's Hall of Fame.

Karen Spärck Jones

Born: 26 August 1935
Died: 4 April 2007 (aged 71)

Karen Ida Boalth Spärck Jones was born in Huddersfield, Yorkshire, England, where she was educated at a grammar school in Huddersfield, which at the time was a textile manufacturing town. Her mother, Ida Spärck, was a Norwegian who worked for the Norwegian government-in-exile in London, while her father, Alfred Owen Jones, was a chemistry lecturer at a technical college. As he taught evening classes, he was unable adequately to care for Karen and so she was sent to live with a family in the country.

After completing high school, in 1953 Karen enrolled at Girton College, Cambridge, where she majored in history with an additional final year in 'Moral Sciences' (philosophy). After graduating in 1956, for a short time she was a schoolteacher, but then changed direction into the field of computer science. She attended the University of Cambridge, earning a Bachelor of Arts degree and a PhD with her thesis 'Synonymy and Semantic Classification' that was considered ahead of its time in the area of Natural Language Processing (NLP).

In the late 1950s Karen worked at the Cambridge Language Research Unit where she collaborated with the British computer scientist Roger Needham. Karen and Roger were married in 1958 when they were both aged about 23. During the 1960s, Karen's research interests were in natural language processing and information retrieval. In 1964, she published 'Synonymy and Semantic Classification', which is now regarded as a foundation paper in the field of natural language processing. One of her most important contributions was the concept of inverse document frequency (IDF) weighting in information retrieval, which she introduced in a 1972 paper 'A Statistical Interpretation Of Term Specificity And Its Application In

Retrieval', published in the *Journal of Documentation* (Vol. 28 No. 1, pp. 11-21). Today, IDF is used in most search engines, often as part of the 'term frequency–inverse document frequency' (tf–idf) weighting scheme.

In 1974 Karen moved to the Cambridge University Computer Laboratory and in 1976 she co-authored a paper with Stephen E. Robertson titled 'Relevance weighting of search terms' that appeared in the *Journal of the American Society for Information Science* (Vol. 27, 129-46). In the 1980s she began working on early speech recognition systems and during 1982 she became involved in the Alvey Programme, a British government sponsored research program in information technology.

In 1986 she co-edited, with Barbara Grosz and Bonnie Webber, *Readings in Natural Language Processing* (published by Morgan Kaufmann). In 1988 she won the Gerard Salton Award that is presented every three years to an individual who has made significant, sustained and continuing contributions to research in information retrieval'. Karen became President of the Association for Computational Linguistics (ACL) in 1994, receiving the ACL Lifetime Achievement Award. In 1997 she co-edited with Peter Willett *Readings in Information Retrieval* (Morgan Kaufman). After being employed on a series of short-term contracts, in 1999 she became a Professor of Computers and Information.

Karen continued to work in the Computer Laboratory, even after her retirement in 2002, receiving an ASIS&T Award of Merit in the same year. In March 2003 her husband Roger passed away of cancer at age 68 at their home in Willingham, Cambridgeshire. The British Computer Society established an annual Roger Needham Award in his honour in 2004. In 2006 Karen won the ACM - AAAI Allen Newell Award and in the following year the ACM Women's Group Athena Award.

Karen passed away from cancer at age 71 on 4 April 2007 after receiving the prestigious BCS Lovelace Medal for 'for contributions to natural language processing'. From 2008 onwards, to recognise her achievements in the fields of information retrieval (IR) and natural language processing (NLP), the Karen Spärck Jones Award is awarded for outstanding research in one or both of her fields. In August 2017, the University of Huddersfield renamed one of its campus buildings in her honour. Formerly known as Canalside West, the Spärck Jones building houses the University's School of Computing and Engineering. In the same year she was one of the women profiled by the Centre for Computing History in the Women in Computing Festival 2017, entitled 'Where Did All the Women Go?'

In 2019, *The New York Times* published Karen's long overdue obituary in its series 'Overlooked', referring to her as 'a pioneer of computer science for work combining statistics and linguistics, and an advocate for women in the field'.

Susan Kare

Born: 5 February 1954

Susan Kare was born in Ithaca, New York, to a father who was a professor at the University of Pennsylvania and a mother who taught her counted-thread embroidery. Her brother, who died in 2017, was the physicist aerospace engineer Jordin Kare who was renowned for his research on laser propulsion. In 1971, Susan graduated from Harriton High School, a public school located in Westchester County. During her time there, for several summers she interned at the Franklin Institute for designer Harry Loucks who introduced her to typography and graphic design. She also undertook photo typesetting with 'strips of type for labels in a dark room on a PhotoTypositor'.

Following high school, Susan attended Mount Holyoke College, graduating summa cum laude with a bachelor degree in Art in 1975. Her undergraduate honours dissertation was on sculpture. She next enrolled at New York University, earning a Master of Arts and a PhD in fine arts in 1978 with her thesis entitled 'The use of caricature in selected sculptures of Honoré Daumier and Claes Oldenburg'.

Susan had by then developed a keen interest in fine art and viewed it as being the cornerstone of her future career. She built up an impressive portfolio with her experience gained by taking many pro-bono graphics jobs, including posters, brochure design, holiday cards, and invitations. After completing her doctorate, she relocated to San Francisco where she was employed as a sculptor and occasionally a curator at the Fine Arts Museums of San Francisco (FAMSF).

In 1982, Susan received an offer via a phone call from a high school friend, the software engineer Andy Jay Hertzfeld. The deal he proposed was that in exchange for an Apple II computer, she would hand-draw several icons and font elements to enhance Apple's Macintosh computer, due for release in January 1984. She later admitted that she 'didn't know the first thing about designing a typeface or pixel art' and also knew nothing about computer graphics. Unfazed, using her background and experience, she designed several 32×32 pixel representations of software commands and applications, including an icon of scissors for the 'cut' command and a finger for the 'paste' command, as well as a paintbrush for MacPaint. Her efforts were so impressive that in January 1983 she was hired as an 'HI Macintosh Artist'.

In the twelve months before the release of the Macintosh, Susan designed the original core visual design language, as well as marketing material, numerous typefaces and icons. Patenting some of these, her designs comprised the first visual language for the identity of the Macintosh, as well as for Apple's pioneering of graphical user interface (GUI) computing. As well as creating new icons, Susan enhanced some of the existing ones such as the trash can, dog-eared paper icon, and I-beam cursor. Other of her classic icons include Clarus the Dogcow seen in the print dialog box, the Happy Mac icon of the smiling computer that welcomes users at system startup, and the Command key symbol on Apple keyboards. Other classics she created were the Lasso, the Grabber, and the Paint Bucket. Her stated aim was 'to bring an artist's sensibility to a world that had been the exclusive domain of engineers and programmers'. She 'hoped to help counter the stereotypical image of computers as cold and intimidating'.

Susan designed the world's first proportionally spaced digital font family that included Chicago and Geneva. She was appointed as a creative director in Apple Creative Services, working for Apple's first creative director, Tom Suiter. Susan later recalled how fortunate she was to be taught directly by engineers how early software was assembled, remarking 'I loved working on that project – always felt so lucky for the opportunity to be a nontechnical person in a software group. I was awed by being able to collaborate with such creative, capable and dedicated engineers. My "work/life balance" has improved since then.'

In 1986, Susan followed one of Apple's founders, Steve Jobs, in leaving Apple Inc.. She became the Creative Director and tenth employee in his next project named NeXT, Inc., a computer and software company founded the previous year. In this role she recreated slideshows to Jobs' precise specifications. However, her main desire was to do bitmaps, and after leaving NeXT she worked independently as a creative designer, building up an impressive client base that included Microsoft, IBM, Sony Pictures, Motorola, General Magic, and Intel. In 1997, Susan and Steve Jobs were listed among *I.D.* magazine's Forty list of influential designers.

One example of Susan's work was designing the card deck for Microsoft Windows 3.0 popular Solitaire game and instructing early computer users to use a mouse to drag and drop objects on a screen. Some of her icons, including those for Notepad and Control Panels, remained basically unchanged by Microsoft until the introduction of Windows XP, released in August 2001. In October 2001, she received the Chrysler Design Award that 'celebrates the achievements of individuals in innovative works of architecture and design'. In 2003 Susan joined the advisory board of Glam Media (now Mode Media), and between 2006 and 2010 produced hundreds of 64×64 pixels icons for the virtual gifts feature of Facebook. In 2007, she designed the identity, icons, and website for the consumer electronics organisation Chumby Industries, Inc.

Susan's designs on various stationery and notebooks have been carried by the Museum of Modern Art (MoMA) store in New York City, and in 2015 they purchased her notebooks of sketches that had led to the early Graphics User Interface (GUI) of the Mac computer. In the same year she was employed by Pinterest, an image sharing and social media service, as a product design lead.

In February 2021, Susan took up a new position as Design Architect for Niantic Labs, a software development company based in San Francisco. She and her husband, Jay Tannenbaum, divorced in January 2012, the couple having three sons.

Mary Kenneth Keller

Born: 17 December 1913
Died: 10 January 1985 (aged 71)

Mary Kenneth Keller was born in Cleveland, Cuyahoga County, Ohio, to father John Adam Keller and mother Catherine Josephine (née Sullivan) Keller. In 1932, at age 18, Mary entered the Sisters of Charity of the Blessed Virgin Mary where she took her vows in 1940. She enrolled at Depaul University in Chicago, graduating with a Bachelor of Science in mathematics in 1943 and a Master of Science in mathematics and physics in 1953.

In 1958 Mary commenced work at the National Science Foundation (NSF) workshop in the computer science center at Dartmouth College which, although a male-only institution at the time, broke its rule so that she could work in the computer science department where she participated in the implementation of the first DTSS BASIC Kernel for the language. Here she also worked, with other students, under John G. Kemeny and Thomas E. Kurtz, two computer scientists and educators who would later become well-known for their development of the BASIC programming language that translated the zeroes and ones of computer code into something more intuitive and straightforward. Mary also worked on the BASIC program that provided many people with their first experience of programming.

Mary enrolled in the PhD program at the University of Wisconsin–Madison, graduating with a doctorate in 1965 for her thesis 'Inductive Inference on Computer Generated Patterns'. It was described as 'constructing algorithms that performed analytic differentiation on algebraic expression, written in CDC FORTRAN 63'. She was the first woman in the US to be awarded a PhD in Computer Science. Her dissertation was supervised by the mathematician, computer scientist and educator Professor Preston Clarence Hammer.

With outstanding foresight, Mary saw the potential for computers to increase access to information and promote education. In the same year as finishing her PhD, she founded the computer science department at Clarke College (now Clarke University), a Catholic women's college founded by Sisters of Charity of the Blessed Virgin Mary, located in Dubuque, Iowa. To begin her venture, in the same year as she received her doctorate she was awarded a grant of $25,000 from the National Science Foundation, payable over two years, for 'instructional equipment for undergraduate education'.

Even though it was at a small college, this was one of the first computer science departments in the US and Mary served as its director for twenty years. She was a tireless advocate for the involvement of women in computing, as well as for the use of computers in education. In 1967 she helped to establish the Association of Small Computer Users in Education (ASCUE), an organisation that still exists today. The first annual technology conference, always held at Myrtle Beach, South Carolina, took place in 1967 and was comprised of attendees/members from mostly small and medium colleges and universities. At the 1975 conference she remarked astutely, 'We have not fully used a computer as the greatest interdisciplinary tool that has been invented to date.' Her vision was that the world would be a better and smarter place, and she lectured adult students, including working mothers who were allowed to bring their small children with them to class.

Clarke College now has the Keller Computer Center and Information Services, which is named after her, and provides computing and telecommunication support to Clarke College students, faculty members, and staff. In addition, the college has also established the Mary Kenneth Keller Computer Science Scholarship in her honour.

Mary was one of the women profiled in the Women in Computing Festival 2017, entitled 'Where Did All the Women Go'?'. She passed away at age 71 on 10 January 1985 in Dubuque, Dubuque County, Iowa. She is buried in the Sisters of Charity Cemetery in the same city.

Maria Margaret Klawe

Born: 5 July 1951

Maria Klawe was born in Toronto, Canada, to Janusz Josef and Kathleen Wreath Klawe. She was raised in such a way as to be primarily interested in things that were supposed to be for boys. The second of four daughters, her father treated her as his son, encouraging Maria to work with him in the garden and workshop. When she was aged four, the family moved to Edinburgh in Scotland, where she attended an excellent girls' school, George Watson's Ladies College, after which she returned to Canada to Edmonton, Alberta, at age twelve.

She developed a love for mathematics, science, art, reading and music, with her father believing she could excel at anything. Maria planned to study engineering followed by architecture as a way to combine her passion love for mathematics, science and art. However, in 1968, while registering as a first-year student at the University of Alberta in Edmonton, she switched her major to honours mathematics upon discovering that engineering students were not allowed to take the honours mathematics courses.

Her all-male mathematics professors often asked why she wanted to study mathematics as there 'were no great women mathematicians'. However, she ignored the not so sage advice as she loved what she was learning, and this triggered her passion in increasing diversity in STEM fields throughout her career. As a student she was also passionate about addressing inequities in society but found it difficult to imagine how she could change the world in significant ways through pure mathematics. She dropped out of university in the middle of her third year to travel the world, returning to earn her Bachelor of Science in 1973. She stayed at Alberta for her graduate studies.

By 1977 she had completed her PhD, solving three twenty-year old problems in functional analysis. Maria then applied for all eighty-three academic positions in North America for pure mathematics, along with about a thousand other mathematicians looking for positions. She was lucky enough to get one of the few tenure track positions that were available and started as an assistant professor at Oakland University, forty kilometres north of Detroit, but stayed there only a year.

Although never studying the subject before, in autumn 1978 Maria then started a second PhD, this time in computer science, at the University of Toronto. By early 1979 she landed a position as a tenure-track assistant professor at the university and did not proceed with her doctorate.

Maria was placed in charge of a research seminar series, the second speaker being Nick Pippenger from IBM Research in Yorktown Heights. Six weeks later she and Nick were engaged to be married. Although Toronto made Nick an offer as a full professor, the couple decided to go to IBM San Jose as Nick was very shy and Martia worried that the combination of getting married, starting a family and teaching might be too much. On 12 May 1980 they were married, and they stayed there for eight years, having a son, Janek, in the second year and a daughter, Sasha, in the fifth. Maria became a manager at the end of the fourth year and a senior manager a year later.

In 1988 the couple moved to the University of British Columbia (UBC) in Vancouver to help build a world-class computer science department there. Maria was the first female faculty member in the computer science department, the first female head of a department in the Faculty of Science, and the eleventh female faculty member in science out of about three hundred. After six and a half years as Head of the department, she successfully applied for the position of Vice President of Student and Academic Services at UBC, becoming the first female to hold that role.

Maria was keen to get the university to invest in IT, network the campus and provide faculty and staff with workstations, as well as making students feel they were valued contributors to the university. She served in that role for three and a half years, and then became the first female Dean of Science. In her four years in that position, Maria put much effort into recruiting more females to the faculty, doubling the number from twenty-four to forty-eight. She was invited to give a talk at the National Academy of Science in the United States about her success in increasing the number of female faculty members in mathematics from two to seven in three years. She decided that if she wanted to increase diversity in STEM more broadly, she needed to move back to the United States.

In January 2003 Maria commenced as the Dean of Engineering at Princeton University. Nick followed her there six months later as a tenured full professor in computer science. Her first six months in her new role proved very challenging, as her best friend, Anita Borg, died of brain cancer in April and her mother passed away in July. Maria had planned to stay at Princeton for several years and then go on to a presidency at a major research university. However, in summer 2006 she was approached by Harvey Mudd College for the presidency there and started as president in July that year.

A big part of the reason for moving to Mudd was that she suspected that attracting and retaining more women and people of colour to fields like computer science and engineering would require changes in both pedagogy and curriculum. When she arrived at Mudd, slightly less than a third of students were female and about seventy per cent were Caucasian. Female computer science majors made up fewer than fifteen per cent, and female engineer majors fewer than twenty-five per cent. Within five years female students were over forty per cent of computer science and engineering majors, as well as the student body. Today, they make up half of computer science, engineering and physics majors as well as the student body. Moreover, only thirty per cent of the students are Caucasian. Over twenty per cent are Hispanic, five per cent are African American, another ten to fifteen per cent are multiracial, and ten per cent are international.

In computer science the introductory course was split into separate sections for students according to prior experience with computer science, so that students with little or no experience would not be discouraged or intimidated. In addition, homework problems helped students see how theoretical concepts could be used to solve real world problems. In engineering the required course on mathematical transforms moved to a flipped classroom approach in which teams collaborated on problem solving and also built an underwater robot that demonstrated every theoretical concept in the course. The modifications to both courses resulted in better learning outcomes for everyone.

Maria has been awarded many honours throughout her career. In 1996 she was inducted as a Fellow of the Association for Computing Machinery, serving as its President between 2002 and 2004 when she won the A. Nico Habermann award. She was a founding fellow of the Canadian Information Processing Society in 2006. and more fellowships followed, including the American Academy of Arts and Sciences in 2009, the American Mathematical Society in 2012, and the Association for Women in Mathematics in 2019. She has also received numerous honorary doctorates, including from Ryerson Polytechnic University (2001), the University of Waterloo (2003), Queen's University (2004), Dalhousie University (2005), Acadia University (2006), the University of Alberta (2007), the University of Ottawa (2008), the University of British Columbia (2010), the University of Toronto (2015)] Concordia University (2016) and McGill University (2018).

On 29 January 2009 Maria became a citizen of the United States and later that year joined the board of directors of the Microsoft Corporation. She won the 2014 Woman of Vision ABIE Award for Leadership from the Anita Borg Institute, and in 2018 was featured among 'America's Top 50 Women in Tech' by *Forbes*.

Maria feels very lucky to have been able to combine a successful career in computer science with a marriage and two children, Janek, and Sasha, who have become significant contributors to society.

Sandra Kurtzig

Born: 21 October 1947

Sandra L. Brody was born in Chicago, Illinois, in 1947, to father Barney Brody, the son of Russian immigrants, and mother Marian (Boruck) Brody, a journalist who came from a wealthy Chicago family. Sandra's parents met on a Greyhound bus when they were seated next to each other and, after Sandra, they later had a son Greg who was six years her junior.

In her early years, Sandra's parents made several trips from Chicago to California, necessitating her mother to home school her as she would miss school for weeks at a time. On their final trip they decided to settle in Los Angeles where Barney built houses which Marian then advertised for sale. Both parents were entrepreneurs who started their business from scratch and this attribute passed on to Sandra.

At high school Sandra was a slow reader, but excelled in, as well as liked, mathematics, chemistry and sciences because 'there was a right or wrong answer'. She was a hard worker and finished with essentially straight A grades. After completing school, Sandra enrolled at the University of California at Los Angeles (UCLA), graduating with a Bachelor of Science degree in mathematics.

Embarking on a PhD program in aeronautical and astronautical engineering at Stanford University, she was one of just two women in a class of 250. In twelve months she had obtained a Master of Science degree, but began to have second thoughts about being an engineer. She spent the summer of 1968 touring Europe and, upon her return, a recent Stanford PhD graduate, Arie Kurtzig, proposed marriage. The wedding took place on 1 December 1968 when Sandra had just turned 21, and she became

Sandra Kurtzig

Sandra Kurtzig. After a brief honeymoon in Acapulco, they resided in a small apartment in Short Hills, New Jersey.

Sandra accepted a position with a start-up company, Virtual Computing, that rented out time on their computers. Although she thought it was a job in sales, her role actually involved writing computer programs. Three months later she was required to sign a nondisclosure and noncompete agreement (forbidding her from taking another job with a competitor). When she refused to sign the document, she was immediately fired. In the early 1970s, they moved to Mountain View, California, where Sandra was employed selling computer time-sharing for General Electric (GE).

In 1972, she left her position at GE to devote time to starting a family, and she had two sons, Ken (b. 1973) and Andy (b. 1976). Using her US$2000 commission from GE, she rented a time-sharing terminal and created a small part-time contract software-programming business out of her second bedroom. The business, named ASK, was never meant to be anything substantial and was only to 'keep her mind occupied'. However, her first client, Halcyon, needed an inventory-tracking program that could efficiently provide manufacturing information. Sandra soon realised that this could also be useful to similar companies in the same field, and she expanded her business by hiring several engineering and computer graduates. She supervised their writing applications, making her one of the first female entrepreneurs in Silicon Valley. Sandra and Arie bought a large five-bedroom house in Los Altos, California, sleeping upstairs and operating the ASK corporate offices downstairs.

As the business expanded, she re-invested the profits back into the company, acquiring access to the Hewlitt-Packard 3000 series of minicomputers after hours. By 1978, ASK released a package of programs called 'Manman' which would become one of the first enterprise resource planning (ERP) software suites. Sandra later arranged with Hewlitt Packard for them to sell it for use on HP-3000 minicomputers. Her company went public on NASDAQ in 1981, making her the first woman to take a Silicon Valley technology company public. At its peak, ASK had 91 offices in 15 countries. In 1983, Sandra's personal stake in ASK was worth more than US$40 million. In the same year she and Arie divorced. It was reported that as part of the divorce settlement, Sandra gave him an estimated $20 million, making it, at the time, one of the largest settlements ever given by a wife to a husband.

By 1985, ASK had sales of US$450 million and Sandra then resigned her role as CEO, only to return four years later to assist in growing the company even further. In November 1990, ASK purchased Ingres Corporation and at its peak the company's annual sales were just under US$1 billion. In 1994 Sandra's autobiography, written with co-author Tom Parker, was published, *CEO: Building a $400 Million Company from the Ground Up* (Harvard Business Review Press). It is described as a book in which 'she shares the business knowledge, resourcefulness, and will to win that made her impressive success possible'. Also in 1994, ASK was purchased by Computer Associates International for $13.25 per share, or $310 million.

In 2010, Sandra founded the enterprise management software company Kenandy that specialises in producing cloud ERP solutions for manufacturing businesses. The operation is named after her two sons Ken and Andy. Sandra served as the CEO of Kenandy until 2015 and is now its Chairman. In June 2013, Kenandy announced a $33 million round of funding led by Lightspeed Venture Partners, the company being valued at $350 million.

Sandra has received many awards, including the Wall Street Transcript's Bronze Award, and was profiled in publications including *The Wall Street Journal*, *The New York Times*, and *The Washington Post*. She certainly has been a remarkably successful woman in computing.

Hedwig Eva Maria Kiesler – 'Hedy Lamarr'

Born: 9 November 1914
Died: 19 January 2000 (aged 85)

Hedwig Eva Maria Kiesler (later known as Hedy Lamarr) was born on 9 November 1914 in Vienna, Austria-Hungary, the only child of mother Gertrud 'Trude' (Lichtwitz) Kiesler, a pianist from Budapest, and father Emil Kiesler who was a prominent bank director. Hedwig was raised a Christian, Trude having come from an upper-class Jewish family that had converted to Catholicism.

In the late 1920s, Hedwig was discovered as an actress and brought to Berlin by producer Max Reinhardt where she trained in the theatre before returning to Vienna to work in the film industry, first as a script girl and then as an actress. In 1933, as a teenager, she married Friedrich ('Fritz') Mandl who was thirteen years her senior and chairman of Hirtenberger Patronen-Fabrik, a leading Austrian armaments firm founded by his father, Alexander Mandl.

In her 1967 autobiography, *Ecstasy and Me*, it was revealed that Hedwig attended a convent school for girls. Her first role was as an extra in the 1930 German film, *Geld auf der Straße* ('Money on the Street'). She performed well enough to be in three more German productions in 1931. However, it would be her fifth film, at age eighteen, that gained her worldwide fame. In 1933, she appeared in a German production called *Ecstasy*, the story of a young girl married to a man much older, but who falls in love with a young soldier. In the movie she is seen swimming and running nude. It made world headlines and was banned by the US government. Her husband is said to have attempted to bring a halt to her acting career in

Germany and to purchase all copies of the film. However, she later described him as extremely controlling, and wrote in her autobiography that she escaped him by disguising herself as a maid and fleeing to Paris, where she obtained a divorce in 1937. The following year she had her first serious acting role in the film *Algiers*, for which she received high praise.

While travelling to London, Hedwig met Metro-Goldwyn-Mayer studio head Louis B. Mayer, who offered her a movie contract in Hollywood, convincing her to change her name to 'Hedy Lamarr', choosing the surname in homage to the silent film star, Barbara La Marr. In 1938, Mayer brought her to Hollywood and promoted her as the 'world's most beautiful woman'. Hedy became a star from the late 1930s to the 1950s, her biggest success being *Samson and Delilah* in 1949. She also went on to play a number of stage roles, including a starring one in *Sissy*, a play about Austrian royalty produced in Vienna, which won accolades from critics.

Being largely self-taught, Hedy worked in her spare time on various hobbies and inventions. Among those who knew of her inventiveness was aviation tycoon Howard Hughes. He actively supported her interests and placed his team of science engineers at her disposal.

Sometime during the Second World War, Hedy learned about the new technology of a radio-controlled guidance system for torpedoes, using spread spectrum and frequency hopping technology to defeat jamming by enemy powers that could send them off course. She came up with the idea of creating a frequency-hopping signal that could not be tracked or jammed and contacted her friend, composer and pianist George Antheil, to help her develop a device for doing just that. They managed to synchronise a miniaturised player-piano mechanism with radio signals. They drafted designs for the system, which was granted a patent on 11 August 1942 (filed using her then married name Hedy Kiesler Markey). It turned out to be technologically difficult to implement, and at that time the US Navy was not receptive to considering inventions coming from outside the military. However, they did adopt it in the 1960s, the principles of their work being arguably incorporated into Bluetooth technology with their findings similar to methods used in legacy versions of CDMA (code-division multiple access) and Wi-Fi. An updated version of this system had been first implemented during the 1962 Cuban Missile Crisis and subsequently emerged in numerous military applications on Navy ships.

It was the 'spread spectrum' technology that Hedy helped to invent that would launch the digital communications era, forming the technical backbone that makes cellular phones, fax machines and other wireless operations possible. She therefore became a pioneer in the field of wireless communications in the US, where she became a naturalised citizen, at age thirty-eight, on 10 April 1953. The great significance of George and Hedy's invention was not realised until decades later when, in 1997, they received the Electronic Frontier Foundation Pioneer Award and the Bulbie Gnass Spirit of Achievement Bronze Award, given to individuals whose creative lifetime achievements in the arts, sciences, business, or invention fields have significantly contributed to society. Hedy was also featured on the Science

Channel, as well as the Discovery Channel and in 2014 she and Antheil were posthumously inducted into the National Inventors Hall of Fame. For her contribution to the motion picture industry, Hedy has a star on the Hollywood Walk of Fame.

In 1981, with her eyesight failing, Hedy retreated from public life and settled in Miami Beach, Florida. In her later years, she became increasingly reclusive. Her only means of communication with the outside world became the telephone, regularly spending up to six or seven hours a day on it. She had also become estranged from her son, James Lamarr Loder, when he was twelve years old, and they did not speak for almost fifty years. She was married and divorced six times, to Friedrich Mandl (1933–1937), Gene Markey (1939–1941), John Loder (1943–1947), Ernest 'Ted' Stauffer (1951–1952), W. Howard Lee (1953–1960) and Lewis J. Boies (1963–1965), who was her own divorce lawyer. Following her sixth and final divorce, Hedy remained unmarried for the final thirty-five years of her life.

Hedy Lamarr died of heart disease in Casselberry, Florida, on 19 January 2000, aged eighty-five. Her son, Anthony Loder, spread her ashes in Austria's Vienna Woods in accordance with her last wishes. In December 2014, an 'honorary grave' was created for her in Vienna's Central Cemetery, Group 33 D No 80. She has certainly earned a place among the twentieth century's most important women inventors, with a vision for computing technology that was well ahead of her time.

Ailsa Land

Born: 14 June 1927
Died: 16 May 2021 (aged 93)

Ailsa H. Dicken was born in West Bromwich, Staffordshire, England, the only child of Harold Horton Dicken and Elizabeth Grieg. She was raised in several semi-rural locations between Birmingham and Litchfield, a village in the Basingstoke and Deane district of Hampshire. Ailsa attended local schools until 1938, when at age eleven she was sent to a small co-ed preparatory boarding school on the clifftops at Hastings.

With war looming in early 1939, Ailsa and her mother visited some relatives in Canada, with an eye to the family possibly emigrating there. Meanwhile, Harold remained in England and served as a Catering Officer in RAF Bomber Command stations until May 1945 when the war in Europe ended. While in Canada, Ailsa attended several more schools before completing high school in 1940 at the Malvern Collegiate Institute in Toronto. At age 16 she enrolled alongside her mother in the Canadian Women's Army Corps in 1943, claiming she was 18. She ended her military service in 1944 in Ottawa at the National Defence Headquarters. She and her mother then returned to the UK to re-join her father.

Ailsa then enrolled at the London School of Economics (LSE), graduating in 1950 with a Bachelor of Science in Economics. This was also the year she met the German-born Frank Land, a fellow graduate whom she married in 1953. As part of her PhD program at LSE, she became interested in the emerging field of Operational Research (OR), especially in mathematical programming (then known as 'activity analysis'). In 1956 she received her doctorate with a thesis on optimal strategies in transporting coking coal, entitled 'An Application of the Techniques of Linear Programming to the Transportation of Coal'. She was supervised by George Morton.

Ailsa Land

Aisla was appointed as a lecturer at LSE in 1953, and several years later, along with her now colleague George Morton, devised a two-year Diploma in Operational Research, in partnership with the British Iron and Steel Research Association whose graduate trainees formed the initial intake. This was one of only two postgraduate degrees in OR in England and in the ensuing seventy years it has produced thousands of graduates.

Progressing through the academic ranks with promotions to senior lecturer, Reader, and then Professor, Ailsa started an active research group in OR, supervising many masters and PhD students. In the late 1950s she began to tackle complex issues in the new field of integer programming (IP), including the well-known travelling salesman problem. These were cases in which the optimal solutions to linear programming problems needed to be all integers, or at least some of them integers, and at the time no satisfactory method had been devised.

Perhaps Ailsa's best-known work came from her collaboration with the Australian statistician Alison Doig (now Harcourt), their pairing leading to the renowned 'branch-and-bound method' for solving optimisation problems that require integer solutions. Their paper, 'An Automatic Method for Solving Discrete Programming Problems', was published in the journal *Econometrica* (Vol. 28, No. 3., July, pp. 497-520) in 1960. Their technique is now the most commonly used to solve such problems. Previously the simple approach to such problems was to enumerate every possible solution and then choose the best one. This was usually an impossible task and their method saved an enormous amount of computation time.

Ailsa also researched a number of other optimisation techniques, including shortest path algorithms, quadratic programming, bi-criteria decision problems, and statistical data fitting. In November 1973, she and co-author Susan Powell published *Fortran Codes for Mathematical Programming: Linear, Quadratic and Discrete* (John Wiley & Sons, Inc., New York) in which they outlined various computer implementations of optimisation techniques, along with providing a mathematical explanation of a number of examples.

In 1987, at age 60 Ailsa retired from LSE after 25 years of service, although she continued her research in a variety of projects, including the quadratic assignment problem, and combinatorial auctions. She declared at the time, 'Now I'm retired I can do some research!' In 1994 she was awarded the Harold Larnder prize by the Canadian Operational Research Society for 'achieving international distinction in operational research'.

Ailsa passed away at age 93 on 16 May 2021. She is survived by her husband Frank, who is an emeritus professor in the Department of Information Systems at LSE, their three children, Frances, Richard and Margi, seven grandchildren and two great-grandchildren.

Ailsa was the first woman professor of Operational Research in the UK and a student award at LSE, the Ailsa Land Prize, is given annually in her honour. In 2019 she was awarded the Operational Research Society's Beale medal, and in 2021, posthumously, the gold medal of the Association of European Operational Research Societies.

Henrietta Swan Leavitt

Born: 4 July 1868
Died: 12 December 1921 (aged 53)

Henrietta Swan Leavitt was born in Lancaster, Massachusetts, the eldest of seven children of George Roswell Leavitt, a Doctor of Divinity and Congregational church minister, and his wife Henrietta Swan Kendrick. Henrietta and her family were quite wealthy, and George's work required them to move several times during her youth. They resided in Cleveland, Ohio, for several years and, in 1885, the 17-year-old Henrietta attended Oberlin College there for a one-year preparatory course. Oberlin is a private liberal arts college, and its Conservatory of Music is the oldest continuously operating conservatory in the US.

At the end of her preparatory year, Henrietta spent a further two years as an undergraduate student, including one year of studying music. Her family then moved back to Cambridge, Massachusetts, where she attended Harvard Annex (now Radcliffe College) as Harvard University at the time was not open to women. The Annex was operated by the Society for the Collegiate Instruction of Women and in 1892, at age 23, Henrietta graduated with the equivalent of a Harvard Bachelor of Arts degree. Throughout her time at Oberlin and Harvard, she studied a wide variety of subjects, including Latin and classical Greek, fine arts, philosophy, analytic geometry, and calculus.

Her chosen subjects not only included mathematics, but in the final year she concentrated on astronomy as it gave her a great deal of enjoyment. So much so, that for the next two years her family supported her to be a volunteer researcher at Harvard's observatory where she accumulated credits for an advanced degree in astronomy. She was hired as one of the 'female computers' by Edward Charles Pickering, director of the Harvard

College Observatory, to measure and catalogue the brightness of stars as they appeared in the observatory's photographic plate collection.

In 1893, Henrietta's work at the observatory had earned her credit towards a postgraduate degree in astronomy, although she did not complete it. In 1898, she joined the staff at Harvard, reportedly as a 'Curator of Astronomical Photographs' and later spent 1896 and 1897 in Europe. On her return to the US, she travelled to Beloit, Wisconsin, where her father was now a pastor. There she got a job as an arts assistant at the liberal arts Beloit College. It was around this time that she experienced eye problems. These eventually healed, but she also contracted an illness that led to a gradual reduction in her hearing.

Henrietta contacted Pickering in May 1902 with a request that he send over to Wisconsin her laboratory notes so that she could continue her report. As the cold weather aggravated her hearing issues, she also asked him if he knew of any positions available somewhere in a warm climate. He replied that he didn't, but instead invited her to return to Harvard Observatory College and she did so, at first without remuneration. Later she was given 30 cents per hour, this being above the then average wage in the US. She was reported as being 'hard-working, serious-minded ... little given to frivolous pursuits and selflessly devoted to her family, her church, and her career'. Throughout her life, Henrietta was devoutly religious and committed to the church.

The tasks undertaken by the 80 or so well-educated women at Pickering's observatory involved data analysis and time-consuming calculations, ones that today would be performed by a computer. While working at the observatory, Henrietta uncovered the relationship between the luminosity and the period of Cepheid variables (stars that experience fluctuations in their brightness). This was a momentous discovery that provided astronomers with the first 'standard candle' that could be used to measure the distance to remote galaxies. Prior to that, the technique to measure these distances were based on parallax and triangulation, these limiting measurable distances to no more than several hundred light years. Using Henrietta's method, distances up to 20 million light years could be determined.

One of the consequences of Henrietta's research was the finding that the Milky Way galaxy has a diameter of between 150,000 and 400,000 light years. She was also assigned by Pickering the task of examining the variable stars of the Small and Large Magellanic Clouds. These were the recordings on photographic plates taken with the Bruce Astrograph of the Boyden Station of the Harvard Observatory in Arequipa, Peru. She subsequently identified 1777 of them, publishing her results in the *Annals of Harvard College Observatory* (Vol. 60, pp.87-108. 3) in 1908. One of her findings was that the brighter variable stars had the longer period.

In another paper published in 1912, this time by Pickering, Henrietta studied the relationship between the periods and the brightness of a sample of 25 of the Cepheids variables in the Small Magellanic Cloud. The paper began with 'prepared by Miss Leavitt' and highlighted her graph that related the period of each star to its maximum and minimum brightness. To be precise, her graph plotted magnitude versus logarithm of period. She wrote that 'A straight line can be readily drawn among each of the two series of points corresponding to maxima and minima, thus showing that there is a simple relation between the brightness of the Cepheid variables and their periods.'

Henrietta later developed and refined the Harvard Standard for photographic measurements, a logarithmic scale that orders stars by brightness over 17 magnitudes. Her analysis of 299 plates from 13 telescopes enabled her to construct her scale, which in 1913 was accepted by the International Committee of Photographic Magnitudes. In the same year she discovered T Pyxidis, a recurrent nova in Pyxis, and one of the most frequent recurrent novae in the sky with eruptions observed in 1890, 1902, 1920, 1944, 1967, and 2011.

The period–luminosity relationship for Cepheids, now known as 'Leavitt's Law', has allowed scientists to calculate the distances to stars too remote for stellar parallax observations to be of use. Henrietta was awarded many honours and was a member of Phi Beta Kappa, the American Association of University Women, the American Astronomical and Astrophysical Society, and the American Association for the Advancement of Science. She was made an honorary member of the American Association of Variable Star Observers and in 1921 was appointed head of stellar photometry.

Unfortunately, she did not serve in that role that long, passing away at age 53 from stomach cancer on 12 December 1921. She was buried in the Leavitt family plot at Cambridge Cemetery in Cambridge, Massachusetts, near to her mother, father, and her two siblings who died in infancy. Henrietta never married and had no children. Her colleague, the American astronomer Solon I. Bailey, wrote of her that 'She had the happy, joyful, faculty of appreciating all that was worthy and lovable in others, and was possessed of a nature so full of sunshine that, to her, all of life became beautiful and full of meaning.'

In her biography *Miss Leavitt's Stars: The Untold Story of the Woman Who Discovered How to Measure the Universe* (2005), written by George Johnson, the author describes her final resting place: 'Sitting at the top of a gentle hill, the spot is marked by a tall hexagonal monument, on top of which sits a globe cradled on a draped marble pedestal.'

Henrietta's work was so fundamental to the development of astronomy and astrophysics that in 1926, the Swedish mathematician Magnus Gösta Mittag-Leffler tried to nominate her for the Nobel Prize in physics, unaware that she had died. Nobel prizes are not awarded posthumously. However, after her death she was honoured with the asteroid 5383 Leavitt. The moon crater Leavitt is named after her as a mark of respect to deaf men and women who have worked as astronomers. One of the ASAS-SN telescopes, located in the McDonald Observatory in Texas, is also named in her honour.

Nicole-Reine Lepaute

Born: 5 January 1723
Died: 6 December 1788 (aged 65)

Nicole-Reine Étable de la Brière was born the sixth of nine children in the Luxembourg Palace in Paris. Her mother, Jean Étable, was a valet in the service of Louise Élisabeth d'Orléans, while her father had worked for the royal family for a number of years. Both were in the service of the duchess de Berry and her sister Louise. Nicole was an intelligent child who was mostly self-taught, staying up all night reading books, including every one of those in the library. The renowned French astronomer and writer, Jérôme Lalande, said that as a child, 'she had too much spirit not to be curious.'

In August 1749, at age 26, Nicole married the 28-year-old Jean-André Lepaute who was a royal clockmaker in the Luxembourg Palace. He would later be celebrated throughout Europe for his outstanding work. The couple lived at the Palais du Luxembourg and during the first few years of their marriage, at her suggestion, the couple constructed a clock with an astronomical function. It was then presented to the French Academy of Science in 1753, where it was inspected and approved by Jérôme Lalande.

Nicole's next project, along with her husband and Lelande, was to write a book entitled *Traite d'horlogerie* (Treatise of Clockmaking) that was published in 1775. Her husband took sole credit for the authorship, leading an unimpressed Lalande to remark 'Madame Lepaute computed for this book a table of numbers of oscillations for pendulums of different lengths, or the lengths for each given number of vibrations, from that of 18 lignes, that does 18000 vibrations per hour, up to that of 3000 leagues.'

So taken was Lalande with her work that he recommended that she, along with the mathematician Alexis Clairaut, compute the predicted return of Halley's Comet, as well as determining the attraction of Jupiter and Saturn of the comet. It took them more than six months to complete their task, hardly stopping to eat as they worked so intensely. In November 1758 they presented their estimation that the comet would arrive in mid-April 1759. They were remarkably close, as the comet reached perihelion on 13 March 1759, within the margin of error given for the prediction.

These were extraordinary calculations as it was the first time scientists had successfully forecast when the comet would cross the perihelion, that is, the point of the comet orbit closest to the Sun. It was shameful that, in announcing their results, Clairault did not recognise her contribution at all, claiming it was all his own work. This infuriated Lalande who viewed Nicole as the 'most distinguished female French astronomer ever'. Lalande refused to work with Clairut again.

Despite the lack of acknowledgement by Clairut of her work, in 1759 she was again a part of Lalande's team and worked with him to compute the ephemeris of the transit of Venus. Once more her contribution was not even documented. However, in 1761 she was recognised by being inducted as an honorary member of the distinguished Scientific Academy of Béziers.

For the next fifteen years, Nicole collaborated with Lalande on the Academy of Science's annual guides for astronomers and navigators by developing ephemerides. These were tables that predicted the location of the stars on each day of the year and were especially useful to mariners.

In 1762, Nicole calculated the exact time of a solar eclipse that occurred on 1 April 1764. She wrote an article, published in *Connaissance des Temps* (Knowledge of the Times), which included a map of the eclipse's extent and timing in 15-minute intervals across Europe. She also created a group of catalogues of the stars which were important for future astronomers, as well as calculating the ephemeris of the Sun, the Moon and the planets for the years 1774–1784.

Although Nicole and her husband did not have any children, she adopted her husband's nephew, Joseph Lepaute Dagelet, training him in astronomy and advanced mathematics. She was so successful in her instruction that at age 26, in 1777, he became a mathematics professor at the French Military School, before being elected deputy astronomer eight years later in 1785 at the French Royal Academy of Sciences.

In 1767, Nicole's husband Jean-André became terminally ill and Nicole cared for him until her death in Saint-Cloud, France, at age 65 in Paris on 6 December 1788. Only a few months earlier she had herself gone blind. Jean-André passed away only a few months later at age 68 on 11 April 1789.

Some 15 years after Nicole's death, Lalande finally acknowledged her role in his work in an 1803 article in *Bibliographie Astronomique*:

During six months we calculated from morning to night, sometimes even at meals... The assistance of Mme Lepaute was such that, without her I should never have been able to undertake the enormous labour, in which it was necessary to calculate the distance of each of the two planets Jupiter and Saturn from the comet, separately for each successive degree for 150 years.

For Nicole's amazing computational and other achievements, the asteroid 7720 Lepaute is named in her honour, as is the lunar crater Lepaute.

Barbara Jane Huberman Liskov

Born: 7 November 1939

Barbara Huberman was born on 7 November 1939 in Los Angeles, California, the eldest of the four children of Jane (Dickhoff) Huberman and Moses Huberman. She attended the University of California, Berkeley, where in 1961 she earned her bachelor's degree in mathematics with a minor in physics. In her classes she was one of only two women. She then applied to graduate programs in mathematics at Berkeley and Princeton, although at the time Princeton was not accepting female mathematics students. Barbara was accepted at Berkeley, but instead chose to move to Boston and began working at Mitre Corporation, a non-profit organisation with a mission of 'solving problems for a safer world'. They operate multiple federally funded research and development centres in the US.

It was at Mitre that Barbara became interested in computers and programming, working there for twelve months as a member of the technical staff. She then accepted a programming position at Harvard University where, in 1962–63, she worked on a language translation project before deciding to return to postgraduate studies, applying for admission to Berkeley, Stanford and Harvard. She settled on Stanford and in 1963 enrolled in a master's degree, which she obtained in 1965. She then entered the doctoral program under the supervision of the eminent computer and cognitive scientist John McCarthy, an expert in artificial intelligence. Her thesis topic was 'A Program to Play Chess End Games' and, in 1968, she became one of the first women to be awarded a PhD from a computer science department in the US. In 1970, she married Nathan ('Nate') Liskov and the couple had a son, Moses, in 1975.

After graduating from Stanford, Barbara returned to her research work at Mitre where she stayed until 1972, when she accepted a role at the Massachusetts Institute of Technology (MIT) as assistant professor in the Department of Electrical Engineering and Computer Science. She led many significant projects, including the 'Venus' operating system, a small, low-cost and interactive timesharing system. Along with her students, between 1974 and 1975 she designed and implemented a programming language 'CLU'. It introduced many features that are still used widely today and is seen as a step in the development of object-oriented programming or 'OOP'. In 1976, she was promoted to associate professor and, in 1980, to full professor. Between 1986–97 she was the NEC Professor of Software Science and Engineering and, since 1997, the Ford Professor of Engineering.

Between 1982 and 1988, Barbara created another programming language, 'Argus', in collaboration with Maurice Herlihy, Paul Johnson, Robert Scheifler and William Weihl. It was an extension of the CLU language and utilised most of the same syntax and semantics. It was the first high-level language to support implementation of distributed programs and to demonstrate the technique of 'promise pipelining'. She also developed 'Thor', describing it as 'an object-oriented database system designed for use in a heterogeneous distributed environment. It provides highly reliable and highly available persistent storage for objects, and supports safe sharing of these objects by applications written in different programming languages.' With Jeannette Wing, Barbara developed what became known as the 'Liskov substitution principle', a particular definition of subtyping.

In 2002, Barbara was recognised as one of the top women faculty members at MIT, and by *Discover* magazine as among the top fifty faculty members in the sciences in the US. In 2004, she won the prestigious John von Neumann Medal, awarded by the Institute of Electrical and Electronics Engineers (IEEE) in honour of the eminent mathematician John von Neumann, for 'fundamental contributions to programming languages, programming methodology, and distributed systems'. On 19 November 2005, Barbara and Donald E. Knuth were awarded Honorary Doctorates from the Eidgenössische Technische Hochschule Zürich (ETH Zürich), the Swiss Federal Institute of Technology, a science, technology, engineering and mathematics university. They were also featured in the ETH Zürich Distinguished Colloquium Series.

In 2007, Barbara was made the Associate Provost for Faculty Equity at MIT, a position she still held in 2019. In March 2009, Barbara received the 2008 A.M. Turing Award from the Association for Computing Machinery (ACM), an international learned society for computing and its most prestigious award and the computer science community's equivalent of the Nobel Prize, for her work in the design of programming languages and software methodology that led to the development of object-oriented programming. The ACM cited her contributions to the practical and theoretical foundations of 'programming language and system design, especially related to data abstraction, fault tolerance, and distributed computing'.

In 2014, Barbara was inducted into the National Inventors Hall of Fame. In 2019, she was leading the Programming Methodology Group at MIT, with a research focus in Byzantine fault tolerance and distributed computing. She is the author of three books and over 100 technical papers. Her legacy lies in her outstanding contributions to building software programs that form the infrastructure of an information-based society.

In 2011, Barbara Liskov was awarded honorary doctorates from both Northwestern University, Chicago and the University of Lugano, Switzerland. The MIT President, Susan Hockfield, said of her,

Barbara is revered in the MIT community for her role as scholar, mentor and leader. Her pioneering research has made her one of the world's leading authorities on computer language and system design. In addition to her seminal scholarly contributions, Barbara has served MIT with great wisdom and judgment in several administrative roles, most recently as Associate Provost for Faculty Equity.

Joyce Currie Little

Born: 20 January 1934

Joyce Currie Little was one of two daughters who were born and raised in Louisiana by her father who worked a farm and was a self-taught engineer, and a mother who had an interest in literature. Joyce attended Pioneer High School and enrolled at Northwest Louisiana University, graduating in 1957 with a Bachelor of Science in Mathematics Education. In 1963 she received a Master of Science in Applied Mathematics from San Diego University, California. While in graduate school she worked in the aerospace industry as a computational test engineer, between 1957 and 1960 developing programs to analyse data from models being tested in a wind tunnel for Convair Aircraft Corporation in San Diego.

After completing her master's degree, Joyce moved to Maryland where she took up a position teaching statistics and managing a computer centre at Goucher College, a private liberal arts institution in Towson. She also enrolled in the PhD program at the University of Maryland, College Park, the state's flagship university and one of the nation's pre-eminent public research universities.

In 1967, Joyce became the chairperson of the Computer and Information Systems Department at the Community College of Baltimore. In January 1971 she published a 438-page book, *RPG: report program generator* (Prentice Hall, USA). In 1975, she chaired the ACM Committee on Curriculum for Community and Junior College Education, its initial meeting being supported by the ACM Special Interest Group on Computer Science Education. This was an important gathering attended by more than a dozen two-year college educators who decided that its highest priority was curriculum work with the aim of improving associated degree career programs in computer programming.

As a result, many workshops ensued, harnessing ideas and developing a report, a draft of which appeared in the June 1977 *SIGCSE Bulletin*. Presentations were given at various computing conferences and a revised draft was sent to hundreds of reviewers for additional comments and feedback. In the fall of 1981, Joyce left the Community College, declaring that 'You don't ever leave the love of the two-year college level of education. It is the most important aspect of the American dream of being able to better oneself and move up in the world ... that major purpose always rang true to my students, and I came to appreciate it more because of them.'

She then immediately accepted a faculty position at Towson University, and in 1984 was named Chairperson of the Department of Computer & Information Sciences. In the same year she received her PhD in Educational Administration for Computing Services from the University of Maryland, College Park.

Joyce has been an active member of the Association for Computing Machinery (ACM) for many years, and in 1992 received their Distinguished Service Award. In 1994 she was inducted as an ACM Fellow with the citation 'Her service to the broad computing community spans some twenty years and includes significant contributions to curriculum development, standards, vocational education professional ethics.' Joyce has many other professional affiliations, including being a Fellow of both the Association for Computing Machinery and American Association for the Advancement of Science. She is also a member of International Society for Technology in Education, the Maryland Association for Educational Uses of Computers, Inc., Institute of Electrical and Electronics Engineers and Association for Information Technology Professionals.

On 6 April 2013 she received the prestigious Distinguished Information Sciences Award (DISA) for 2012, by which time she was Professor Emerita, Towson University. The honour was awarded at the National Collegiate Conference (NCC) in St. Louis Missouri. She also received the SIGCSE Award for Lifetime Service to the Computer Science Education Community for her contributions to computing in two-year colleges, certification, and professional development.

Joyce is a strong advocate for the role of women in computing, with her research interests including metrics and assurance for quality in software engineering, along with the social impact and cyber-ethics for workforce education.

(Augusta) Ada Byron Lovelace

Born: 10 December 1815
Died: 27 November 1852 (aged 36)

Augusta Ada Byron, known as Ada, was born in London, the daughter and only legitimate child of the renowned poet Lord George Gordon Byron, who left the family home when she was just five weeks old and never saw her again. His acrimonious separation from his wife Annabella, a mathematician, meant that Ada's mother was the only significant parent in her life. She did not even see a portrait of her father until her twentieth birthday. Even so, Annabella was not very close to her daughter and, for the most part, Ada was raised by her maternal grandmother Judith, the Honourable Lady Milbanke. At an early age Ada was fascinated by mathematics, music and crafts, especially model building, and these would be her lifelong passion.

Ada suffered from ill-health during her early years, but at age twelve became interested in flight, examining the anatomy of birds to ascertain the correct proportion between wing length and body size. This led to her writing a book, *Flyology*, on the subject. At age fourteen she contracted measles, resulting in paralysis so severe she was bedridden for almost a year, after which she learned to walk again with the aid of crutches.

Ada's technological skills were becoming apparent during her teenage years and her mother arranged a series of private tutors in mathematics and science, including William Frend, William King and the celebrated Mary Somerville (*see entry*). In a letter to Ada's mother in 1832, another of her tutors, the mathematician and logician Augustus De Morgan, wrote that Ada had the capacity to be 'an original mathematical investigator, perhaps of first-rate eminence'. Upon turning eighteen, Ada was presented at court, and it was reported that 'her greatest delight was to go to the Mechanics Institute to hear the first of Dr Dionysius Lardner's lectures on the differential engine.

Miss Byron, young as she was, understood its working and saw the great beauty of the invention.'

At age twenty, Ada married William, 8th Baron King, who in 1838 was made the Earl of Lovelace and Viscount Ockham. Lord Lovelace supported his wife's interests and they spent much of their time in the country where she could research and study. It was the calculating device invented by Charles Babbage, who would become a lifelong friend, that held her interest. Babbage paid her frequent visits.

In 1840, Babbage presented an invited lecture to the Prime Minister of Italy on his proposed 'Analytical Machine' (that had succeeded his 'Difference Engine'). An Italian engineer, Luigi Menabrea, transcribed the presentation into French and it was later published in the *Bibliothèque de Genève* (Library of Geneva) in October 1842. Ada was invited by Charles Wheatstone, a friend of Babbage, to translate it into English, a task that occupied her for some nine months in meticulously explaining the difference between the two devices.

She was very particular about her writing, taking advice from Babbage only when she felt it necessary – 'I cannot endure another person to meddle with my sentences.' In the end, the treatise had been expanded to three times its original size. Her work was much more than a mere translation, with one section including a technique for using the Analytical Engine to calculate a sequence of Bernoulli numbers, although the machine had not yet been built. As a result of her efforts, Ada is now widely regarded as the world's first computer programmer and her method as the first computer program. Her work, 'Sketch of the Analytical Engine with notes by AAL', was published in Taylor's *Scientific Memoirs*. Ada could see that the Analytical Machine had the capacity to be programmed rather than simply performing basic operations:

[The Analytical Engine] might act upon other things besides number, were objects found whose mutual fundamental relations could be expressed by those of the abstract science of operations, and which should be also susceptible of adaptations to the action of the operating notation and mechanism of the engine... Supposing, for instance, that the fundamental relations of pitched sounds in the science of harmony and of musical composition were susceptible of such expression and adaptations, the engine might compose elaborate and scientific pieces of music of any degree of complexity or extent.

In her mid-thirties, in 1850 she developed a fascination with betting on horse racing, but it soon turned to disaster as, after finding herself deeply in debt, she reportedly 'pawned the family jewels and then implored the help of her mother in redeeming them, and in concealing the whole affair from her husband'. In 1852, after several months' illness, Ada passed away from uterine cancer at the age of only thirty-six. At her request, she was buried next to the father she never knew, in the Church of St Mary Magdalene in Bucknall, Buckinghamshire.

(Augusta) Ada Byron Lovelace

Ada was the first person to see the enormous potential of Babbage's device. Her name is honoured in the Lovelace Medal, awarded since 1998 by the British Computer Society, and since 2008 in an annual competition for women students. In 2009, the British journalist, writer and consultant Suw Charman-Anderson launched Ada Lovelace Day as an international celebration of the achievements of women in science, technology, engineering and maths (STEM). Its aim is to increase the profile of women in STEM, thereby creating new role models who will encourage more young women into such careers, as well as supporting women already working in STEM. It is now held every year on the second Tuesday of October, featuring the Ada Lovelace Day Live! 'science cabaret' event in London, in which women in STEM give short talks about their work or about other women who have inspired them. They also perform short comedy or musical interludes with a STEM focus.

Ada Lovelace was a truly remarkable woman who achieved so much in her short life. She holds pride of place in any list of pioneering women in computing.

Marissa Mayer

Born: 30 May 1975

Marissa Mayer was born in Wausau, Wisconsin, the only daughter of two children to Margaret Mayer, an art teacher of Finnish descent, and Michael Mayer, an environmental engineer who worked for water organisations. Marissa was a busy teenager, participating in ballet, ice-skating, piano, swimming, and debating. From an early age she had expressed interest in mathematics and science.

Attending Wausau West High School, she was part of the curling team and the precision dance team, excelling in chemistry, calculus, biology, and physics. Marissa took on many extracurricular activities, including becoming president of her high school's Spanish club, treasurer of the Key Club, captain of the pom-pom squad and captain of the high school debating team that won the Wisconsin state championship. In 1993 she graduated from high school and was selected by the Governor of Wisconsin, Tommy Thompson, as one of the state's two delegates to attend the National Youth Science Camp in West Virginia. She applied to 10 universities — including Harvard, Yale, and Stanford — and got accepted into all of them. She chose Stanford.

Marissa had intended to have a career as a pediatric neurosurgeon, enrolling in pre-med classes at Stanford University. However, she switched her major to symbolic systems, a degree that included the fields of philosophy, cognitive psychology, linguistics, and computer science. During her junior year, supervised by the computer science educator Eric S. Roberts, she taught a class in symbolic systems that went so well that he asked her to teach another class over the summer.

In 1997 Marissa graduated with honours with a Bachelor of Science in symbolic systems and in 1999 a Master of Science in computer science. Her specialisation for both degrees was artificial intelligence, while the basis of her undergraduate thesis was devising travel-recommendation software that advised users in natural-sounding human language.

After graduating from Stanford, Marissa received 14 job offers, ultimately selecting Google where she became employee number 20. Her initial tasks involved writing code and leading small teams of engineers, along with developing and designing Google's search engines. She was later promoted to the position of product manager and then director of consumer web products. In this role she oversaw the layout of Google's prominent search homepage and was part of the three-person team responsible for Google AdWords, an advertising platform that allows businesses to show their product to relevant potential customers based on their search terms.

In 2002, Marissa devised the Google Associate Product Manager (APM) program, an initiative to recruit new talents and cultivate them for leadership roles. Each year she selected several junior employees for the two-year program, where they took on extracurricular assignments and intensive evening classes. In 2005, Marissa became Vice President of Search Products and User Experience and subsequently held other important positions in Google Search, Google Images, Google News, Google Maps, Google Books, Google Product Search, Google Toolbar, iGoogle, and Gmail.

In 2010, she headed the Local, Maps, and Location Services, and in the following year she secured Google's acquisition of survey site Zagat at a cost of $125 million. While still at Google, Marissa lectured on introductory computer programming at Stanford and mentored students at the East Palo Alto Charter School. For this, Stanford awarded her both the Centennial Teaching Award and the Forsythe Award.

In July 2012, Melissa was appointed president and CEO of Yahoo! and made a member of the company's board of directors. To revive the company's failing fortunes, she replaced some senior executives with new people whom she perceived to be more growth-oriented, as well as improving the culture of the workplace. She decided to go back to the basics and the company's core products including search, mail, and advertisements, as well as focusing more aggressively on mobile internet in the future.

To make the culture 'the best version of itself', Marissa launched a new online program called PB & J that collected employee complaints, as well as their votes on problems in the office; if a problem generates at least 50 votes, online management automatically investigates the matter. In February 2013, she introduced a major personnel policy change at Yahoo! that required all remote-working employees to convert to in-office roles. Two months later she changed Yahoo!'s maternity leave policy, lengthening its time allowance and providing a cash bonus to parents.

In May 2013, Marissa led Yahoo! to acquire Tumblr in a US$1.1 billion acquisition, although by February 2016, Yahoo! acknowledged that the value of Tumblr had fallen by US$230 million since it was acquired. In 2014, Marissa was ranked sixth on *Fortune*'s 40 under 40 list, and the 16th most-powerful businesswoman in the world in the same year. She announced her resignation from Yahoo! on 13 June 2017.

After leaving Yahoo!, Marissa started Lumi Labs, which was rebranded as Sunshine in November 2020, with former colleague Enrique Munoz Torres. The company is based in Palo Alto and is focused on artificial intelligence and consumer media. Their first product, Sunshine Contacts, aimed to improve the users iPhone contacts and Google contacts via, among other things, intelligent algorithms, contact data, public sources.

Marissa sits on the boards of directors of Walmart, Maisonette, and Jawbone, along with a place on the non-profit boards of such as Cooper–Hewitt, National Design Museum, New York City Ballet, San Francisco Ballet, and San Francisco Museum of Modern Art. She was named in *Fortune* magazine's annual list of America's 50 Most Powerful Women in Business in 2008, 2009, 2010, 2011, 2012, 2013, and 2014. At age 33, in 2008 she was the youngest woman ever listed.

In 2009 she was named one of *Glamour* magazine's Women of the Year and was listed in *Forbes*' List of The World's 100 Most Powerful Women in 2012, 2013 and 2014. In September 2013, Marissa became the first CEO of a Fortune 500 company to be featured in a *Vogue* magazine spread. On 24 December 2015, she was listed by UK-based company Richtopia at number 14 in the list of 500 Most Influential CEOs.

In 2009, the Illinois Institute of Technology granted Marissa an honoris causa doctorate. On 12 December 2009 she married lawyer and investor Zachary Bogue and on 30 September 2012 gave birth to a boy, Macallister. She also gave birth to identical twin daughters, Marielle and Sylvana, in December 2015.

In 2013, Marissa was named in the Time 100, becoming the first woman listed as number one on *Fortune* magazine's annual list of the top 40 business stars under 40 years old. In the same year she made history by being the only person to feature in all three of *Fortune*'s annual lists during the same year: Businessperson of the Year (No. 10), Most Powerful Women (at No. 8), and 40 Under 40 (No. 1).

Marlyn Meltzer

Born: 4 December 1922
Died: 7 December 2008 (aged 86)

Marlyn Wescoff was born in Philadelphia, Philadelphia County, Pennsylvania, USA and graduated from Temple University in 1942 with a major in mathematics and a minor in business machines. Later that year, because of her minor, she was hired by the Moore School of Engineering to perform weather calculations, as she knew how to operate an adding machine. In the following year her duties included performing calculations for newly arrived ballistic missile trajectories, as by now she was skilled in using manual desktop mechanical calculators. The Moore School at the University of Pennsylvania (UPenn) was funded by the U.S. Army during the Second World War and Marlyn was one of a group of about 80 women who worked manually on the complex differential calculations. These women physically hand-wired the machine, an arduous task using switches, cables, and digit trays to route data and program pulses.

In 1945, Marlyn was selected as one of six women to become the first group of ENIAC (Electronic Numerical Integrator and Computer) programmers. The ENIAC was the first all-electronic digital computer, an enormous machine comprising forty black eight-foot panels. In all, it was eight feet high and eighty feet long, containing 17,468 vacuum tubes, 7200 crystal diodes, 1500 relays, 70,000 resistors, 10,000 capacitors and around 5,000,000 hand-soldered joints. It weighed around 30 tons, occupied 167 square metres of space and consumed 150 kW of electricity. It was rumoured that its power requirement led to the lights across Philadelphia dimming every time it was switched on.

The project presented a huge challenge for the programmers as they had none of the programming tools available today. They had to physically conduct the ballistic program using 3000 switches and dozens of digital trays to route the data and program pulses through the machine.

Marlyn was in a special team with Ruth Teitelbaum within the ENIAC project who used analogue technology to calculate ballistic trajectory equations. The women chosen for the job were sent to Aberdeen Proving Grounds in Maryland to learn the punch card system for the machine. Six months after the end of the Second World War, on 14 February 1946, the ENIAC computer was finally unveiled before the public and the media, capturing the attention of the nation.

The programmers were not even introduced at the event and, although some of them appeared in photographs, they were reportedly assumed to be just models. The six women were the only generation of programmers to program it. At the time she and the others did not receive the recognition they deserved.

In 1947 Marlyn resigned from the team to get married to Dr. Philip Meltzer, before ENIAC was relocated to the Ballistics Research laboratory at Aberdeen, Maryland. In 1997, she was inducted into the Women in Technology International Hall of Fame with the five other original programmers of the ENIAC, Kathleen McNulty Mauchly Antonelli, Jean Jennings Bartik, Frances Elizabeth Holberton, Frances Spence and Ruth Teitelbaum. This award was established in 1996 by WITI to 'recognize, honour, and promote the outstanding contributions women make to the scientific and technological communities that improve and evolve our society'.

For the remainder of her life, Marlyn enjoyed volunteering at Shir Ami Library and Sunday school story hour, while her charity work included delivering Meals on Wheels for more than 10 years for the Greenwood House in Ewing, New Jersey. She was the treasurer of the Trenton/Lawrenceville chapter of Hadassah and an active member of Women for Greenwood House. During her last four years, she had knitted more than 500 chemotherapy hats for the Susan B. Komen Foundation in Philadelphia.

Marlyn passed away on age 86 on 7 December 2008, surrounded by her family at Yardley, Bucks County, Pennsylvania. She was survived by her son, Hugh Meltzer, and a daughter, Joy.

Ann Katharine Mitchell

Born: 19 November 1922
Died: 11 May 2020 (aged 97)

Ann Williamson was born in Oxford on 19 November 1922 to father Herbert Stansfield Williamson and mother Winifred Lilian Williamson (née Kenyon). Herbert had been based in Simla, the summer capital of British India, as a commissioner in the Indian civil service. Winifred was a former nurse who, as assistant secretary to the Oxford Family Welfare Association, helped conduct one of Britain's earliest family planning clinics.

In 1930, when aged seven, Ann won a scholarship to Headington School in Oxford. She stayed there until 1939 before gaining a place to study mathematics at Lady Margaret Hall in the University of Oxford. She remained there until 1943 when she graduated with a degree in mathematics. In those days relatively few women went to Oxford, but it was even rarer for them to study mathematics – there were only five women in her year. It had been suggested to her by the headmistress of her school that studying mathematics was 'unladylike'. In fact, her parents had to overrule her school to allow her to take up her place at Oxford.

After graduation, Ann was recruited to work at Bletchley Park in September 1943 and remained there until May 1945. Here she was a temporary worker in Hut 6 on German Army and Air Force Enigma decryptions with the Foreign and Commonwealth Office, on an annual salary of £150, increased to £200 after her 21st birthday in November 1943. She was initially among 6000 women and 2000 men involved in every aspect of organising, decrypting and analysing German messages.

The Enigma machine was a cipher device developed and used in the early-to mid-twentieth century to protect commercial, diplomatic, and military communication. It was used extensively by Nazi Germany during the Second World War. Ann's role mainly involved converting 'cribs' into 'menus', the operating instructions for the Bombe decryption devices, to identify the settings of the Enigma machine that day. The Germans changed their code every night at midnight, so Ann and her colleagues had to restart trying to crack the new codes for each 24-hour period.

The Head of Hut 6, Stuart Milner-Barry, found it difficult to recruit men during wartime, and to make matters worse the British civil service rules prevented men and women from working together on the essential night shifts. As a result, Hut 6 consisted solely of female workers, one of whom was Ann.

At the conclusion of the war, the women at Bletchley were instructed to forget about their work there and never discuss it with anyone. However, once their activities at Bletchley became public and the ban was lifted, Ann gave many illustrated talks and interviews about her role during that period. Her story is included in the 2015 *The Bletchley Girls: War, Secrecy, Love and Loss: The Women of Bletchley Park Tell Their Story* (Hodder Paperbacks) by historian Tessa Dunlop.

On 13 December 1948, Ann married John Angus Macbeth Mitchell. The couple had four children, Jonathan, Charlotte, Catherine and Andy, and lived in Edinburgh. John died in 2018 after retiring as a senior civil servant. During his life in the army, civil service and in the voluntary sector, he was awarded Companion of the Bath, Commander of the Royal Victorian Order and the Military Cross.

During the 1950s Ann worked as a marriage guidance counsellor with the Scottish Marriage Guidance Council (now known as Relate Scotland), but in the 1970s returned to education and in 1980 she graduated with a Master of Philosophy in social policy from the University of Edinburgh. This led to the position of research associate in the Department of Social Administration at the University of Edinburgh, publishing research articles on the subject of marriage breakup and divorce. Her particular interest was the effect of marriage breakups on children.

Ann authored several books, including *Someone to Turn To: Experiences of Help before Divorce* (1981), *When Parents Split Up* (1982), *Children in the Middle* (1985), *Coping with Separation and Divorce* (1986), and *Families* (1987), a number of which have been translated into several languages. Her work is referred to in several works on divorce and was used as supporting evidence in two reports by the Scottish Law Commission, 'Family Law: Report on Aliment and Financial Provision' in 1981 and 'Report on Reform of the Ground for Divorce' in 1989.

In a 2014 article in the *Scots Law Times*, the family law barrister Janys Scott QC reviewed Ann's output on the workings of the Scottish divorce court. She remarked that 'Mitchell has had a profound influence on family law in Scotland' and that her 1985 book *Children in the Middle* was 'a seminal work'.

In 1993, age 70, her book *The People of Calton Hill* (Mercat Press) was published, described as 'a brief history of the lives of inhabitants of overcrowded tenements, of Carlton Jail and of the gracious houses in Regent, Royal and Carlton Terraces'; and in 1998 *No More Corncraiks: Lord Moray's Feuars in Edinburgh's New Town* (Scottish Cultural Press).

Ann passed away age 97 on 11 May 2020 in Edinburgh, and was survived by four children and six grandchildren. Shortly before her death she had tested positive for COVID-19 during the pandemic in Scotland.

Maria Mitchell

Born: 1 August 1818
Died: 28 June 1889 (aged 70)

Maria Mitchell was born on in Nantucket, Massachusetts, the third of ten children, to a large Quaker family. Her mother was Lydia (Coleman) Mitchell and her father, William Mitchell, was a cooper as a young man, then conducted his own school and was the principal officer in a bank from 1836 to 1861. As was the case with other Quakers, Maria's parents were very supportive of education for all their offspring, including the girls. They insisted that the girls receive an equal education to the boys.

By all accounts Maria was a quiet child who enjoyed reading and was diligent in her schoolwork, attending Elizabeth Gardener's small school when quite young, then moving to the North Grammar School in 1827, where her father was principal. When she reached the age of eleven, Maria's father established his own school on Howard Street, and she became his teaching assistant. William had a passion for astronomy and the family owned a small telescope which he used to teach Maria the finer points of astronomy to the extent that, when was aged just twelve, she aided him in calculating the exact moment of an annular eclipse. When her father's school closed, the now fifteen-year-old attended Unitarian Minister Cyrus Peirce's 'school for young ladies' for the next two years.

After completing her schooling, Maria worked at Peirce's school as a teaching assistant before opening her own school in 1835, a controversial move as she allowed non-white children to attend in a time when there was segregation at the local public school. Twelve months later she accepted a position as a librarian at the Nantucket Atheneum, meanwhile continuing her astronomical observations.

Her father's connections meant that Maria was able to meet some of the country's most eminent scientists and she took every chance to go to the roof of the house to survey the heavens. Although some comets had been discovered by others, it was still viewed as a significant event and King Frederick VI of Denmark offered a gold medal prize for the discovery of each new 'telescopic comet', one too faint to be seen with the naked eye.

Two months after her twenty-ninth birthday, at 10.30 p.m. on the evening of 1 October 1847, Maria went to the roof of the Pacific National Bank to sweep the sky with the family's telescope. She noticed a small blurry streak that, although invisible to the naked eye, was clear in the telescope. Suspecting immediately that it may well be a comet, she ran to tell her father, who was inclined to announce her discovery right away. But Maria asked him to wait until she could be certain and continued to observe it and record its position. Determined that his daughter's discovery be recognised, on 3 October William wrote to his friend and colleague William C. Bond, who was the director of the Observatory at Harvard College (now University) in Cambridge, Massachusetts, announcing the discovery. The President of Harvard, Edward Everett, then wrote to William Mitchell, asking whether he was aware that Maria could claim a medal from the King of Denmark for her new comet.

As it happened, several others, including Father de Vico in Rome, had also independently observed the comet on 3 October and reported it to European authorities, but Maria received priority and she was recognised for the feat with the medal from the new King Christian VIII of Denmark. This brought her immediate fame and honours, the following year being the first woman elected to the membership in the American Academy of Arts and Sciences and becoming a Fellow of the American Association for the Advancement of Science. The only women to have previously discovered a comet were the renowned astronomers Caroline Herschel and Maria Margarethe Kirch. Maria Mitchell's comet was originally designated as Comet 1847 VI but was later referred to as C/1847 T1.

Maria was frequently mystified by all the attention she received, an entry in her diary after one scientific meeting reading, 'It is really amusing to find oneself lionised in a city where one has visited quietly for years; to see the doors of fashionable mansions open wide to receive you, which never opened before. One does enjoy acting the part of greatness for a while! I was tired after three days of it, and glad to take the cars and run away.'

She was not only struck by the knowledge she gained from her observations, but also the beauty of the sky. She recorded this observation in her journal:

Feb. 12, 1855. I swept around for comets about an hour, and then I amused myself with noticing the varieties of colour. I wonder that I have so long been insensible to this charm in the skies, the tints of the different stars are so delicate in their variety... What a pity that some of our manufacturers shouldn't be able to steal the secret of dyestuffs from the stars.

In 1865, Maria was appointed a professor of astronomy at Vassar College, making her the first such female professor in the US and was also appointed director of the College Observatory. She began recording sunspots in 1868 but from 1873 she and her students made daily photographic records, thereby obtaining more accuracy. These were the first photographs of the sun and a total solar eclipse. In July 1878 she travelled 3500 kilometres with five assistants to Denver where they used a 10 cm telescope to make their observations.

Maria never married and remained close to her family throughout her life. After retiring from Vassar College on Christmas day in 1888, she returned to live in Lynn, Massachusetts, where she had previously lived with her father after the death of her mother in 1861. On 28 June 1889, Maria passed away at age seventy and was buried in Lot 411 in Prospect Hill Cemetery, Nantucket. The Maria Mitchell Observatory in Nantucket is named in her honour and is part of the Maria Mitchell Association (formed after her death) located there. She is the namesake of the SS *Maria Mitchell,* a cargo ship built in the Second World War. A crater on the moon is named after her and her name appears on the front of the Boston Public Library. She was awarded two honorary doctorates, one from Hanover College in Indiana in 1853 and the other from Columbia University in 1887. She also received an honorary PhD from Rutgers Female College in 1870.

As the first American woman astronomer, Maria Mitchell paved the way for others. In addition to her scientific work, she was also active in opposing slavery and in advocating women's rights.

Vera Molnár

Born: 5 January 1924

Vera Molnár was born in Budapest, Hungary, where she enrolled for a diploma in art history and aesthetics at the Budapest College of Fine Arts, graduating in 1947. In 1946 Vera had created her first non-representational images in the form of abstract geometrical and systematically determined paintings. After graduation, she received an artists' fellowship to study in Rome at the Villa Giulia, and shortly after moved to France.

In 1959 Vera iterated combinatorial images, and in 1960 she co-founded several artist research groups, including GRAV (Groupe de Recherche d'Art Visuel) who investigated collaborative approaches to mechanical and kinetic art, and Art et Informatique, with a focus on art and computing. They were instrumental in the Op-art and Kinetic Art movements of that decade. In 1963 GRAV produced a labyrinth for the third Bienniale de Paris that invited viewers to walk through twenty environmental experiences, and in 1966 the group created the 'Day in the Street' itinerary (*Une Journée dans la rue*) in Paris where they invited the public to involve themselves in various kinetic activities.

GRAV was dissolved in November 1968, the same year that Vera began working with computers, creating algorithmic paintings based on simple shapes and geometrical themes. Her initial work involved transformations of geometric objects, such as a square, by rotating, deforming, erasing all or parts of them, or replacing portions with basic elements of other geometric shapes. Then she would repeat the process while fracturing or breaking them as she transformed them, finally sending them to a plotter for the output.

Vera learned the early programming languages of Fortran and BASIC, gaining access to a computer at a research laboratory in Paris. She did much of this early work at the Centre Pompidou, ARTA (Atelier du Recherche des Techniques Avancées). Between 1974 and 1976, Vera and her husband, François, developed the MolnArt computer program and in 1979 she took part in the Ars Electronica art festival. In 1985 she was appointed as a lecturer in the fine arts and art studies department at the Sorbonne University in Paris.

Vera's art works are represented in the permanent collections of the Museum of Modern Art (MoMA), the Centre Pompidou, the Morgan Library, the National Gallery of Art, and the Victoria and Albert Museum among others. In her MoMA exhibit, she has displayed 'On Line: Drawing Through the Twentieth Century'.

In 2001 she co-authored with Laurence Barbier the book *Musée de Grenoble; [à l'occasion de l'exposition présentée ... du 7 octobre 2001 au 6 janvier 2002* (Réunion des musées nationaux). Vera received the Digital Art Museum's Digital Arts Award in 2005 for her life's work, which included a €20,000 prize and a catalogued exhibition. Her exhibit (Un)Ordnung. (Dés) Ordre, displayed at the Museum Haus Konstruktiv, shows her early freehand drawings that were never previously exhibited, including her works from the late-1960s.

Another book, edited by Wulf Herzogenrath and Barbara Nierhoff-Wielk and illustrated by Vera, was published in 2006. It was titled *Vera Molnar – monotonie, symétrie, surprise: Preisträgerin des d.velop digital art award (ddaa)* 2005. Also in 2006, Vera co-founded the Open Structures Art Society (OSAS) in Budapest and in the following year she was appointed Chevalier of Arts and Letters. Several of her early works were included in a 2015 retrospective exhibition in New York City called 'Regarding the Infinite | Drawings 1950-1987'.

In 2018, at age 94, Vera won the outstanding merit award AWARE (Archives of Women Artists Research and Exhibition), supported by the French Ministry of Culture. She is still active in her work and is regarded as a pioneer of computer and generative art.

Sudha Murthy

Born: 19 August 1950

Sudha Murty was born into a Deshastha Madhwa Brahmin family in Shiggaon, Haveri in Karnataka, India, the daughter of surgeon Dr. R.H. Kulkarni and his wife Vimala Kulkarni. She was raised both by her parents and maternal grandparents, with her experiences as a child forming the basis for her first book entitled *How I Taught my Grandmother to Read, and other Stories*.

After completing high school, Sudha enrolled at the B.V.B. College of Engineering & Technology (now known as KLE Technological University) where she completed a Bachelor of Engineering, specialising in Electrical and Electronics Engineering. She was the top student and received a gold medal from the Indian Institute of Engineers.

Sudha became the first female engineer hired at India's largest auto manufacturer TATA Engineering and Locomotive Company (TELCO), at first joining the company as a Development Engineer in Pune. While there, in 2009 she married N.R. Narayana Murthy and the couple have two children, Akshata and Rohan. Her daughter Akshata married Rishi Sunak, her classmate from Stanford, a British Indian who became Prime Minister of the UK in October 2022.

Later she worked at Walchand Group of Industries at Pune as Senior Systems Analyst and in 1996 started Infosys Foundation and became its Trustee. Two institutions of higher learning, the H.R. Kadim Diwan Building housing the Computer Science & Engineering (CSE) department at IIT Kanpur and the Narayan Rao Melgiri Memorial National Law Library at NLSIU were both endowed and inaugurated by her foundation.

Sudha has won many awards for her work. Among these are the Karnataka Rajyotsava State Award for the year 2000, for achievement in the field of literature and social work, the 2001 Ojaswini award for excellent social work for the year 2000; the 2004 Raja-Lakshmi Award from the Sri Raja-Lakshmi Foundation in Chennai in 2004; the R.K. Narayana's Award for Literature in 2006; the Daana Chintamani Attimabbe Award from the Karnataka Government in 2010; an honorary LL.D (Doctor of Laws) degree for contributions to the promotion of formal legal education and scholarship in India in 2011; Basava Shree-2013 Award to Narayan Murthy & Sudha Murthy for 'their contributions to society'; the Life Time Achievement Award at the Crossword-Raymond Book Awards in 2018; and the Hemmeya-Kannadiga award from television in 2019. She has also won India's fourth highest civilian award, Padma Shri. In 2023 she was awarded the Padma Bhushan by the government of India for her contributions to the field of social work. In 2021 she retired as the chairperson of the Infosys Foundation.

Sudha is a prolific author with many books to her name. She has published over 30 books, including two travelogues, two technical books, six novels and three educative books, among others. She also lectures at Bangalore University.

As well as her computing prowess, Sudha is famous for many of philanthropist works and the empowerment of women. She spreads the awareness of rural education, public hygiene, poverty alleviation and is passionate in helping people in flood-affected areas. Through the Infosys Foundation, she has built 2,300 houses in the flood-affected areas. She is also a member of the Bill and Melinda Gates Foundation that is committed to tackling the greatest inequities in our world.

Susan Hubbell Nycum

Susan Hubbell Nycum was raised in Pittsburgh, Pennsylvania, USA. Her grandmother on her father's side was college-educated as a chemical engineer, something that was quite unusual for that era. On her grandfather's side, her great uncle was the eminent Edwin Hubble who has the famous telescope named after him, while her father, Dean Hubble, had hundreds of patents and was instrumental in her education. She later described her mother as 'the practical brain in the household' and she encouraged Susan to stay at home and undertake a course to be a secretary, which consisted of typing and shorthand. Susan, along with a friend, completed the course in a quarter of the allocated time.

She then found a position at a German engineering company in Pittsburgh. Susan met her husband, a PhD in psychology, while he was teaching locally at Duquesne University. He and Susan and married after their first year in law school and continued to study there, having a daughter after the second year. After she was born, Susan did not work again until her daughter was six years old and in grade school.

Susan graduated from Duquesne University School of Law and later also earned a law degree from Stanford Law School, specialising in computer security and intellectual property issues. Her research into information security led her to co-author, with Donn B. Parker, a 1973 study *Computer Abuse* (Stanford Research Institute), this being one of the first attempts to define and document computer-related crime. She has since produced studies on the law surrounding software patents, serving an adviser to the United States.

Susan has also been an adviser to the governments of Australia, Brazil, Canada, Finland, Germany, India, Israel, Singapore, Thailand and the USA for IT and IP policy. In her role as an advisory board member for the National Science Foundation (NSF) in the US, Susan approved funding for the Internet. In 1975 she co-authored, with Robert Pratt Bigelow, *Your Computer and the Law* (Prentice-Hall). In the early 1980s she was Chairwoman of the National Information Systems Advisory Panel.

Susan worked at the law firm of Chickering and Gregory in San Francisco and later as an international partner of Baker & McKenzie. She was Chair of the organisation's North America Intellectual Property (IP) and Information Technology (IT) practice group, a coordinator of their global IT practice group and a member of their governing bodies for North America and for Asia Pacific.

At the time of writing, Susan is a full-time neutral domestic and international arbitrator, serving as an officer of the College of Commercial Arbitrators. She was a founding Executive Committee member of the Silicon Valley Arbitration & Mediation Center (SVAMC) that 'works with leading technology companies, law firms, ADR institutions and universities in Silicon Valley and around the globe to provide educational programming and related resources regarding the effective and efficient resolution of technology-related disputes'. She is on their Board of Directors.

In 1988 Susan was a co-author, along with Nancy W. Collins and Susan Gilbert, of *Women Leading: Making Tough Choices on the Fast Track* (published by Stephen Greene). She is a former Chair of the American Bar Association (ABA) section of Science and Technology and twice the ABA appointee to the National Conference of Lawyers and Scientists. She is a past president of the ITECH Law Association, a Fellow of the American Bar Foundation, a Fellow of the Association for Computing Machinery (ACM) and member of its Council, a member of the National Academy of Distinguished Neutrals, a former board member of the Mediation Society and several other international mediation organisations. She is listed in the Best Lawyers of America and the Northern California Super Lawyers

Susan was an early member of the Special Interest Group on University and College Computing Services (SIGUCCS), an association of professionals who support and manage the diverse aspects of information technology services at higher education institutions by providing professional development opportunities for SIGUCCS members and other individuals in the field. In 2004 Susan was inducted into its Hall of Fame.

Susan is a pioneer in the development of the legal aspects of electronic storage of information, computer security and the international legal protection of software, semiconductor chips and databases. Her work has led to the passage of laws in every state in the US, as well as for the federal government. The U.S. Supreme Court cited her work in the 1981 landmark case of *Diamond v. Diehr* in which the Court held that 'controlling the execution of a physical process, by running a computer program did not preclude patentability of the invention as a whole.'

Cases that are within Susan's expertise include software and telecom disputes, biotech patent matters, electronic data storage and privacy, cyber security and numerous high-tech commercial disputes concerning outsourcing and development and distribution projects.

Ellen Lauri Ochoa

Born: 10 May 1958

Ellen Lauri Ochoa was born in Los Angeles, one of five children to Joseph and Rosanne (née Deardorff) Ochoa and was raised in in La Mesa, California. Her paternal grandparents immigrated from Sonora, Mexico, to Arizona and later to California where her father was born. In 1975 Ellen graduated from Grossmont High School in El Cajon. While she was in high school her parents divorced and she then lived with her mother and her brothers.

She enrolled in a Bachelor of Science degree in physics at San Diego State University, graduating Phi Beta Kappa in 1980. She then attended Stanford Department of Electrical Engineering, earning a Master of Science degree in 1981 and a PhD in 1985. During her doctoral studies, Ellen investigated optical systems for performing information processing. After graduation, she applied to the National Aeronautics and Space Administration (NASA) to enter its highly competitive astronaut program, being admitted in 1990.

As a doctoral student at Stanford, and later as a researcher at Sandia National Laboratories at the NASA Ames Research Centre, she led a research group that mainly worked on optical systems for automated space exploration. Ellen patented an optical system to detect defects in a repeating pattern and was a co-inventor on three separate patents for an optical inspection system, an optical object recognition method, and a method for noise removal in images. As Head of the Intelligent Systems Technology Branch at Ames, she supervised 35 engineers and scientists in the research and development of computational systems for aerospace missions.

In January 1991 Ellen was selected by NASA and became an astronaut in July that year. She was delegated several important technical assignments in the Astronaut Office, including serving as the crew representative for flight software, computer hardware and robotics, Assistant for Space Station to the Chief of the Astronaut Office and as acting as Deputy Chief, and lead spacecraft communicator (CAPCOM) in Mission Control.

In April 1993 Ellen became the first Hispanic woman to go into space when she served as a mission specialist on a nine-day mission aboard the Space Shuttle *Discovery* STS-56, whose directive was to study the Earth's ozone layer along with other experiments. As part of the study, she released a research satellite using the shuttle's robotic arm. In November 1994, Ellen was payload commander on the Space Shuttle *Discovery* mission STS-66, then a mission specialist and flight engineer on STS-96 in May 1999 and STS-110 in April 2002.

On 1 February 2003, the Space Shuttle *Columbia* disaster occurred when it disintegrated as it re-entered the atmosphere, killing all seven crew members. Ellen was in Mission Control at the time and was one of the first personnel informed of television coverage showing *Columbia's* disintegration.

Ellen retired from spacecraft operations in 2007 after logging nearly 1000 hours in space on four space flights. She then took up the position of Deputy Director of the NASA Johnson Space Center in Houston, Texas, where her role included managing and directing the Astronaut Office and Aircraft Operations. On 1 January 2013, she became the first Hispanic and second female director of the centre.

Between 2018-2020 Ellen served as Vice Chair of the National Science Board and currently chairs the committee evaluating nominations for the National Medal of Technology and Innovation. She has received many awards, including an Outstanding Leadership Medal (1995); an Exceptional Service Medal (1997); Space Flight Medals (1993, 1994, 1999, 2002); NASA's Distinguished Service Medal (2015) – NASA's highest award; International Air and Space Hall of Fame class (2018). In 2017 Ellen was recognised in Hispanic Executive's 2017 'Best of the Boardroom' issue for her work as a board director for Johnson Space Center.

There are a number of institutions that honour Ellen's achievements. These include the Ochoa Middle School located in Pasco, Washington; the Ellen Ochoa Elementary School in Cudahy, California; and the Ánimo Ellen Ochoa Charter Middle School in East Los Angeles. There is also, in Grand Prairie, Texas, the Ellen Ochoa STEM Academy at Ben Milam Elementary School; in Pico Rivera, California there is the Ellen Ochoa Prep Academy; and in Tulsa the Union Public Schools in Tulsa named a new elementary school after her.

On 27 May 1990 Ellen married Coe Fulmer Miles, a Houston-based intellectual property attorney in emerging technologies. The couple have two sons. She is a classical flautist and played with the Stanford Symphony Orchestra, at one time receiving the Student Soloist Award. While an undergraduate at San Diego State University, she played the flute for two years as part of the university marching band and for five years as a member of the university wind ensemble. She brought a flute with her on her first mission to space.

Ellen Lauri Ochoa

Ellen is a Fellow of the American Institute of Aeronautics and Astronautics (AAAS), and the National Academy of Inventors. In 2019 an animated version of her was featured in the episode 'Astronaut Ellen Ochoa' of the children's television program, *Ready Jet Go!* She serves on several boards and chairs the Nomination Evaluation Committee for the National Medal of Technology and Innovation.

She is also a private pilot and regularly travels to schools to address students on her experiences in space. Ellen encourages them to set big goals, with the advice, 'Don't be afraid to reach for the stars. I believe a good education can take you anywhere on Earth and beyond.'

Cathy Helen O'Neil

Born: 1972

Catherine ('Cathy') Helen O'Neil, born in the USA, studied as an undergraduate at the University of California, Berkeley, and is an American mathematician, data scientist, and author. In 1993 she won the Alice T. Schafer Prize from the Association for Women in Mathematics, awarded annually to an undergraduate woman for excellence in mathematics. Cathy obtained a master's degree in mathematics from the Courant Institute and another in operations research from Stanford University. From there she enrolled in the PhD program at Harvard, graduating with her doctorate in 1999. Her thesis was 'Jacobians of Curves of Genus One', supervised by the mathematician Barry Charles Mazur. Her statistical research interests include modelling, epidemiology, Bayesian statistics and analysing social networks.

Cathy then found positions in the mathematics departments of both MIT, first as a post-doctoral student, and Barnard College where she engaged in research in arithmetic algebraic geometry while publishing several papers. In 2007 she left the world of academia, taking roles in business, including two years at D.E. Shaw, a hedge fund company founded in 1988 that was once described by *Fortune* magazine as 'the most intriguing and mysterious force on Wall Street'.

Her next role was at RiskMetrics, a risk software company launched in 1994 that provided investors with better information on managing market risks. After working for four years in finance, in 2011 Cathy assumed the role of a data scientist in a New York start-up, creating models designed to predict people's purchases.

Cathy then became involved with the Occupy Wall Street movement, protesting against economic inequality. It commenced in September 2011 in Zuccotti Park, part of New York City's Wall Street financial district. She also participating in its Alternative Banking Group.

In 2013, along with co-author and data science consultant Rachel Schutt, Cathy published *Doing Data Science: Straight Talk from the Frontline* (O'Reilly Media). In the following year she launched the Lede Program in Data Journalism at Columbia, described as 'An intensive, remote-friendly summer program from Columbia's Graduate School of Journalism and Department of Computer Science designed to equip journalists and storytellers of all kinds with the computational skills needed to turn data into narrative, break out of Excel, perform in-depth investigations, harness APIs, explain complex subjects, write data-driven stories, process document dumps, and find insights'.

In 2016 Cathy published her outstanding book *Weapons of Math Destruction: How Big Data Increases Inequality and Threatens Democracy* (Penguin), sounding 'an alarm on the mathematical models that pervade modern life and threaten to rip apart our social fabric'. It was longlisted for the National Book Award, was a *New York Times* Bestseller 2019 and was awarded the MAA's Euler Book Prize. In 2017 it was translated into Italian (Bompiani), in 2018 into French (ARENES), and in 2021 into Portuguese (Editora Rua do Sabão). In a lecture she made this point:

> Algorithms are opinions embedded in code. It's really different from what you think most people think of algorithms. They think algorithms are objective and true and scientific. That's a marketing trick. It's also a marketing trick to intimidate you with algorithms, to make you trust and fear algorithms because you trust and fear mathematics. A lot can go wrong when we put blind faith in big data.

Cathy is the founder of O'Neil Risk Consulting & Algorithmic Auditing (ORCAA), an algorithmic auditing company. Its website states: 'We work with an organisation to audit the use of a particular algorithm in context, identifying issues of fairness, bias, and discrimination and recommending steps for remediation.'

Bloomberg View publishes Cathy's opinion columns and she now works as a data scientist for start-ups in the New York area, also serving on the advisory board of the *Harvard Data Science Review*. Her blog can be found at 'mathbabe.org', described as a platform for 'exploring and venting about quantitative issues'.

Cathy married Johan de Jong, a Belgian-born Dutchman who is a professor of mathematics at Columbia University. The couple reside in New York City, along with their three sons.

Christine Paulin-Mohring

Born: 31 May 1962

Christine Paulin-Mohring attended a number of education institutions in her early life. The first was Maternelle Guy Moquet (Guy Môquet Kindergarten) in Montreal between 1965 and 1968, followed by Ecole Estienne D'orves 1968-1972 and Collège Jean Jaurès 1972-76. In 1976 she attended high school at Lycée Jean Jaurès in Montreal before transferring to Lycée Turgot in Paris from 1978 to 1980. Her next school was Lycée Saint-louis until 1982, after which she attended Université Pierre Et Marie Curie (Paris 6), between 1980 and 1982.

In 1989 she graduated with a PhD in Computer Science from Université Paris Diderot (Paris 7) while working at INRIA Rocquencourt and Ecole Normale Supérieure. Her thesis, *Extraction de programmes dans le Calcul des Constructions*, was supervised by the French computer scientist Gérard Pierre Huet. In 1991 Christine was one of the primary developers of a language and tool based on the Calculus of Inductive Constructions and it was named Coq, in honour of Thierry Coquand.

In addition to specifying formal proofs of mathematical theorems, the Coq Proof Assistant System, as it known, is also used for software certification. The other developers of Coq were Thierry Coquand, Gérard Huet, Bruno Barras, Jean-Christophe Filliâtre, Hugo Herbelin, Chetan Murthy, Yves Bertot and Pierre Castéran. An initial version of it was Coquand's Calculus of Constructions, known as CoC.

Coq is a key enabling technology for certified software. The system is open source, is supported by a substantial and useful library as well as full documentation and has attracted a large and active user community. Some of the significant results that were accomplished using Coq include proofs for the four colour theorem, the development of CompCert (a fully verified compiler for C), the development at Harvard of a verified version of Google's software fault isolation, and the fully specified and verified hypervisor OS kernel CertiKOS.

In 1997, Christine was appointed a professor at Paris-Saclay University, leading the research group ProVal (INRIA Saclay – Île-de-France, Université Paris-Sud and CNRS) where she worked on the use of proof technologies for developing correct programs until 2011, the same year she was awarded Doctor Honoris Causa, University of Gothenburg (Göteborgs universitet), Sweden.

Between 2012 and 2015 she assumed the role of the Scientific Coordinator of the Labex DigiCosme, a laboratory of excellence in the field of computer science and communication, involving research teams in 14 different laboratories which are part of the Université Paris-Saclay. Christine was also the director of the doctoral School of informatics at Université Paris-Sud from 2005 to 2012 and since then she has led the Collège des Ecoles Doctorales of Université Paris-Sud. In 2014 she was elected to the Academia Europaea.

Christine is a member of the editorial board of the *Journal of Formalized Reasoning,* as well as a professor at Paris-Sud 11 University. She has also co-edited two books, the first (with Jean-Christophe Filliatre and Benjamin Werner) being *Types for Proofs and Programs: International Workshop, TYPES 2004, Jouy-en-Josas, France, December 15-18, 2004, Revised Selected Papers: 3839 (Lecture Notes in Computer Science, 3839),* published by Springer Berlin Heidelberg, 2006. The second (co-edited with Sandrine Blazy and David Pichardie) was *Interactive Theorem Proving: 4th International Conference, ITP 2013, Rennes, France, July 22-26, 2013, Proceedings: 7998 (Lecture Notes in Computer Science),* published by Springer, 2013.

Radia Perlman

Born: 18 December 1951

Radia Joy Perlman was raised near Asbury Park, New Jersey, in a Jewish family. Both of her parents were employed as engineers for the US government, her father Julius Perlman working on radar and her mother Hope Rae Sonne, a mathematician, as a computer programmer. At school, Radia found mathematics and science to be 'effortless and fascinating', also achieving high grades in the other subjects. Her hobbies included playing the piano and French horn, and she often discussed literature and music with her mother.

An outstanding science and mathematics student in her high school, Radia's interests lay in a career in computing. She enrolled as the only female student in a programming class. She later remarked 'I was not a hands-on type person. It never occurred to me to take anything apart. I assumed I'd either get electrocuted, or I'd break something.' It was while a student at MIT that she took a class in physics that involved learning how to program. In 1971 she secured her first paid job as a part-time programmer for the LOGO Lab at the (then) MIT Artificial Intelligence Laboratory. It was there that she programmed system software, including debuggers.

Supervised by the late South African-born American mathematician and computer scientist, Seymour Papert, Radia developed a child-friendly version of the educational robotics language LOGO that she named TORTIS (Toddler's Own Recursive Turtle Interpreter System). Between 1974 and 1976, children as young as three could program a LOGO educational robot called a 'Turtle'. For this, among other achievements, Radia has been described as a pioneer of teaching young children computer programming.

When enrolled at MIT in the late 60s and early 1970s, she was one of around 50 women in a class of about 1,000 students. At the beginning of her degree studies there, MIT only had one women's dormitory, limiting the number of women students that could study. When the male dormitories became co-ed, Radia moved out of the women's dorm into a mixed dorm, where she became the 'resident female'.

Radia graduated from MIT with a B.S. in 1973 and a M.S. degree in 1976, both times majoring in mathematics. She joined the MIT group at BBN Technologies where she became involved with designing network protocols, before enrolling in the PhD program in Computer Science there, completing her doctorate in 1988. Under the supervision of the computer scientist and Internet pioneer David D. Clark, her thesis was titled 'Network layer protocols with Byzantine robustness' that examined the issue of routing in the presence of malicious network failures.

In 1984, while working as a consulting engineer at Digital Equipment Corporation (DEC), Radia was allocated the task of developing a simple protocol which would enable network bridges to locate loops in a local area network (LAN). A necessary requirement was that the protocol should use a constant amount of memory when implemented on the network devices, independent of the size of the network. The building and expanding bridged networks were made more difficult because loops, where more than one path leads to the same destination, could result in a network collapse. Redundant paths in the network meant that a bridge could forward a frame in multiple directions, resulting in loops causing Ethernet frames to fail to reach their destination, in turn flooding the network.

Radia devised a network protocol so that bridges within the LAN communicated with one another, the algorithm allowing the bridges to designate one root bridge in the network. Each bridge then mapped the network and determined the shortest path to the root bridge, deactivating other redundant paths.

The protocol was standardised as 802.1d by the Institute of Electrical and Electronics Engineers (IEEE). Radia remarked that the benefits of the protocol amount to the fact that 'you don't have to worry about topology' when changing the way in which a LAN is interconnected. The invention of her Spanning Tree Protocol (STP), which is fundamental to the operation of network bridges, is for what Radia is best known. She holds more than 100 issued patents and is the author of several books, including *Interconnections: Bridges, Routers, Switches, and Internetworking Protocols* (1999, Addison Wesley Professional), *Internet Security* (2002, Prentice Hall) with co-authors Charlie Kaufman, Mike Speciner and *Network Security: Private Communication in a Public World* (Prentice Hall PTR, 2002) with co-authors Charlie Kaufman and Mike Speciner.

Radia, who was a fellow at Sun Microsystems, has lectured at several universities, including Washington, Harvard University and MIT, as well presenting keynote addresses across the globe. She has won many awards, including the Silicon Valley Intellectual Property Law Association Inventor of the Year in 2003, the Anita Borg Institute Women of Vision Award for

Innovation in 2005 and the USENIX Lifetime Achievement Award in 2006. She was inducted into the Internet Hall of Fame in 2014 and the National Inventors Hall of Fame in 2016. She also has Lifetime Achievement awards from USENIX and the Association for Computing Machinery's Special Interest Group on Data Communication (SIGCOMM), and an honorary doctorate from the KTH Royal Institute of Technology in Sweden in 2000. Radia has been twice named as one of the 20 most influential people in the industry by Data Communications magazine: in the 20th anniversary issue (January 15, 1992) and the 25th anniversary issue (January 15, 1997). She is the only person to be named in both issues.

From 2010 to 2014, Radia worked as a fellow for Intel Labs, and since then has worked as fellow at Dell EMC. In recent years, Radia has invented the TRILL (transparent interconnection of lots of links) protocol to correct some of the shortcomings of spanning-trees.

Modest in describing her achievements, Radia declares 'I did indeed make some fundamental contributions to the underlying infrastructure, but no single technology really caused the Internet to succeed. And sometimes, things get invented multiple times until the time just happens to be right. The thing that happened to be there at the right time isn't necessarily better than the other ones.'

Radia and the computing engineer Michael Speciner have two children, Dawn Perlner and Ray Perlner. Her hobbies include reading literature, writing poetry, and playing the piano.

Rózsa Péter

Born: 17 February 1905
Died: 16 February 1977 (aged 71)

Rózsa Politzer was born in Budapest, Hungary, on 17 February 1905 and was raised in a country torn by war and civil unrest. She attended the Maria Terezia Girls' School until 1922 before enrolling at Pázmány Péter University (in 1950 renamed Eötvös Loránd University). She intended to major in chemistry, but her interest soon turned to mathematics and she studied with world-famous mathematicians, including Lipót Fejér and Jósef Kürschák.

After graduating in 1927, Rózsa was unable to find a permanent teaching position, although she had passed the qualifying exams to be a mathematics teacher. Due to the effects of the Great Depression, many university graduates could not find work and so she began private tutoring, along with some high school teaching as a substitute teacher. At this time, Rózsa also began her graduate studies, initially concentrating her research on number theory. Before long she found that her results had already been independently proven by the work of Robert Carmichael and L.E. Dickson, and so she abandoned mathematics to focus on poetry. However, she was convinced to return to mathematics by her friend and longtime collaborator, the Hungarian mathematician László Kalmár, who suggested she research the work of Kurt Gödel on the theory of incompleteness. Rózsa prepared her own, different proofs from Gödel's work on the recursive functions. These involved a branch of mathematical logic, of computer science, and of the theory of computation that later included the study of computable functions and Turing degrees.

In 1932 she presented a paper, '*Rekursive Funktionen*' (Recursive Functions) at the International Congress of Mathematicians in Zürich, Switzerland, proposing for the first time that such functions be studied as a separate subfield of mathematics. to More papers followed, and she received her PhD *summa cum laude* (with the highest distinction) in 1935. The following year, Rózsa presented her paper '*Über rekursive Funktionen der zweite Stufe*' (About recursive functions of the second stage) to the International Congress of Mathematicians in Oslo and her papers formed the foundation of the modern field of recursive function theory as a separate area of mathematical research as she suggested. The German mathematician Walter Felscher spoke of his admiration of Rózsa's work, that 'it may well be said that she forged, with her bare hands, the theory of primitive recursive functions into existence.' In 1937, Rózsa became a contributing editor of the *Journal of Symbolic Logic*.

As a result of the fascist laws passed in 1939, Rózsa was forbidden to teach and was briefly confined to the Jewish ghetto in Budapest. In the 1930s, Rózsa had changed her German-style name of 'Politzer' to a Hungarian one, 'Péter'. She continued working during the war years and, in 1943, wrote and printed a book, *Playing with Infinity: Mathematical Explorations and Excursions*, a discussion of ideas in number theory and logic for the lay person. A review of the book described it as 'a perfect compromise between rigour and clarity'. Unfortunately, many of the copies were destroyed by bombing and the book was not distributed until the war had ended. Originally published in Hungarian, her book has since been translated into English and at least fourteen other languages. Rózsa lost her brother, a number of friends and fellow mathematicians to fascism, something she outlined in the foreword of later editions of the book.

After the end of the Second World War, she obtained her first regular teaching position at the Budapest Teachers Training College. In 1951 she published a book, *Recursive Functions*, which went through many editions. In 1952, Rózsa was the first Hungarian woman to be made an Academic Doctor of Mathematics and continued to apply recursive function theory to computers from the mid-1950s.

She was committed to improving mathematical education in Hungary, writing school textbooks and working on improving the curriculum. In 1951, she was awarded the Kossuth Prize by the Hungarian Government and, in 1953 she received the Manó Beke Prize from the János Bolyai Mathematical Society, awarded since 1950 to people prominent in furthering mathematical education.

When the Teachers Training College was closed in 1955, Rózsa became a professor at Eötvös Loránd University and in 1959 she presented a major paper, '*Über die Verallgemeinerung der Theorie der rekursiven Funktionen für abstrakte Mengen geeigneter Struktur als Definitionsbereiche*' (On the generalisation of the theory of recursive functions for abstract sets of suitable structure as domains of definition), to the International Symposium in Warsaw (later published in two parts in 1961 and 1962). In 1970, Rózsa won the Silver State Prize and, in 1973, the Gold State Prize, both high national civilian honours. In the same year, she became the first woman to be elected to the Hungarian Academy of Sciences.

In 1975, Rózsa retired from Eötvös Loránd University. Her popularity among students led her to being known as 'Aunt Rózsa', and she was an avid supporter of increased opportunities in mathematics for girls and young women. The following year she published her final book, *Recursive Functions in Computer Theory*, originally published in Hungarian. This was only the second Hungarian mathematical book to be published in the Soviet Union because its subject matter was considered indispensable to the theory of computers. In 1981 it was translated into English.

In her lectures to general audiences, which were often given under the general title 'Mathematics is Beautiful', Rózsa declared that 'no other field can offer, to such an extent as mathematics, the joy of discovery, which is perhaps the greatest human joy.'

Rózsa Péter passed away from cancer on 16 February 1977, the day before her seventy-second birthday. In her eulogy, her student Ferenc Genzwein recalled that she taught that 'facts are only good for bursting open the wrappings of the mind and spirit [in the] endless search for truth.' Her legacy is such that she is now referred to as the 'founding mother of recursion theory'.

Maria Petrou

Born: 17 May 1953
Died: 15 October 2012 (aged 59)

Maria Petrou was born in Thessaloniki, Greece, and her scientific abilities were evident as a child. At age 15 she began tutoring children in mathematics and science after school. In 1975 she graduated with a degree in physics at the Aristotle University of Thessaloniki, her performance so outstanding that she was awarded a studentship that provided an opportunity to study abroad. Maria selected the United Kingdom where she enrolled in Mathematics Part III at Churchill College, Cambridge. She then joined their PhD program in Astronomy, graduating with her doctorate in 1981. In the same year she married a fellow PhD researcher and British astronomer, Phil L. Palmer, with whom she later had one son, Costas. At the time of the marriage, Maria was 28 and Phil aged 27.

Following her PhD, Maria returned to Greece to assume the role as a lecturer in the Department of Astronomy at the University of Athens. However, in 1983 she returned to the UK to take up a Research Fellowship at St Hilda's College, Department of Theoretical Physics, Oxford, in 1983.

In 1986 Maria changed her research field from astronomy to engineering, accepting a postdoctoral research position in image processing, first at Reading University, and later at the Rutherford Appleton Laboratory, located on the Harwell Campus in Oxfordshire, UK. Her research now began to focus more on machine vision and other aspects of robotic intelligence, joining the University of Surrey as a lecturer in Image Analysis in 1988. It was here that she played a vital role in the development of the Centre for Vision, Speech and Signal Processing, expanding and developing the areas of Remote Sensing and Medical Imaging. As a result of her achievements, she was soon promoted through the academic ranks to Professor of Image Analysis in 1998.

In September 2005 she moved to Imperial College London where she took up the Chair of Signal Processing, serving as the Head of the Communications and Signal Processing Group at the Department of Electrical and Electronic Engineering until 2009. In that year she returned to Greece to become Director of the Informatics and Telematics Institute of CERTH, Thessaloniki, a position she held until her death. She was also a Visiting Professor of Image Analysis at Surrey University between 2005 and 2011, and at Jiatong University, Shanghai, between 2006 and 2009.

During her career Maria developed a number of important image recognition techniques, including methods for robotic texture analysis, image comparison and 3D measurement. Among her more notable projects, along with Dr Alexander Kadyrov, she co-invented the trace transform, a method of image processing that allows for more efficient facial recognition systems. Her work in this technology has resulted in many applications in commerce, medicine and environmental imaging. She was considered a leading authority in the field. Her work assisted doctors to identify incipient tumours and produced evidence of environmental degradation.

Maria also developed sophisticated 'segmentation' procedures for sharply identifying edges and delineating simple shapes within a fuzzy image. Apart from mapping the contour of a tumour, there were also military uses, including in surveillance, where shapes of objects must be extracted from images to distinguish between, for example, an enemy tank or a dummy.

She was elected as a Fellow of the Royal Academy of Engineering, 2004, a Distinguished Fellow of the British Machine Vision Association, 2006, a Fellow of the Institute of Physics, 2008, and a Fellow of the City and Guilds Institute, 2009. Also in 2009, she was awarded a Doctor of Science (DSc) in Engineering by the University of Cambridge.

As well as a prolific publisher of research papers herself, she served on the Editorial board of the journals *Electronic Letters on Computer Vision and Image Analysis* (ELCVIA), the *Journal Pattern Analysis and Applications* (PAA), *Pattern Recognition and Image Analysis*, (PRIA), and the *Journal of Applied Intelligence* (AI). In November 1999 her *Image Processing: The Fundamentals* was published (John Wiley & Sons) and a second edition appeared in 2010 co-authored by her son Costas Petrou.

Maria passed away on 15 October 2012 at age 59 from a cancer that she had bravely fought for six months. She was survived by her son Costas. A Special Edition of the journal *Pattern Recognition Letters* celebrating her life and work was published in January 2014. The International Association for Pattern Recognition created The Maria Petrou Prize, 'to be awarded biennially to a living female scientist/engineer who has made substantial contributions to the field of Pattern Recognition, and whose past contributions, current research activity and future potential may be regarded as a model to both aspiring and established researchers.'

Maria had been a fierce campaigner for human rights and helped to publicise abuses, including the ill-treatment of servants by wealthy employers.

Rosalind Wright Picard

Born: 17 May 1962

Rosalind Wright Picard was born in Massachusetts, USA, and holds a bachelor's degree with honours in electrical engineering and a certificate in computer engineering from the Georgia Institute of Technology in 1984. During her degree she worked in several positions, including as a Scientific Atlanta Technical Assistant, Satellite Communications (June 1981–September 1981), sales assistant at Hewlett Packard, Technical Computers (June 1982–September 1982) and an IBM Junior Design Engineer (June 1983–September 1983).

After her undergraduate studies she enrolled at MIT, from which she graduated with a master's degree in 1986 and a PhD in 1991, both in electrical engineering and computer science. Her PhD thesis was titled 'Texture Modeling: Temperature Effects on Markov/Gibbs Random Fields', supervised by Alex Pentland, Jae Soo Lim and Sanjoy K. Mitter.

Prior to completing her PhD, Rosalind was a technical staff member at AT&T Bell Laboratories in New Jersey where she designed VLSI chips for digital signal processing and developed new methods of image compression and analysis. In 1991 she joined the MIT Media Lab faculty. Her international reputation was established when she constructed mathematical texture models for content-based retrieval of images, for creating new tools including the Photobook system, and for pioneering methods of automated search and annotation in digital video.

In September 1997, Rosalind MIT Press published her book *Affective Computing*, which began a new field by that name. Her focus lies in human–computer interaction, and her goal for affective computing is to 'give computers the ability to recognise, express, and in some cases, have emotions'. This is achieved by sensing the emotional state of a user (via sensors, microphone, cameras and/or software logic) and responding by performing specific, predefined product/service features. An example of this would be to recommend a set of videos to fit the mood of the learner.

Rosalind outlined her views on the importance of monitoring emotional cues:

> Whatever his strategy, the good teacher detects important affective cues from the student and responds differently because of them. For example, the teacher might leave subtle hints or clues for the student to discover, thereby preserving the learner's sense of self-propelled discovery. Whether the subject matter involves deliberate emotional expression as is the case with music, or is a 'non-emotional' topic such as science, the teacher that attends to a student's interest, pleasure, and distress is perceived as more effective than the teacher that proceeds callously. The best teachers know that frustration usually precedes quitting and know how to redirect or motivate the pupil at such times. They get to know their student, including how much distress that student can withstand before learning breaks down.

Rosalind holds many patents, including a variety of new sensors, algorithms, and systems for sensing, recognising, and responding in a respectful manner to human affective information. Some of their applications can be found in autism, epilepsy, autonomic nervous system disorders, sleep, stress, human and machine learning, health behaviour change, market research, customer service, and human-computer interaction. She is the author of over two hundred scientific articles and chapters in multidimensional signal modelling, computer vision, pattern recognition, machine learning, human-computer interaction, and affective computing.

The many advisory boards she sits on include the National Science Foundation's (NSF's) division of Computers in Science and Engineering (CISE) and the advisory board for the Georgia Tech College of Computing. She has also served on dozens of international and national science and engineering program committees, editorial boards, and review panels.

Rosalind's awards constitute a long list that includes AT&T Bell Laboratories One Year On Campus Fellow (1984); Georgia Institute of Technology Department of Electrical Engineering Faculty Award (1984); AAUW The Outstanding Georgia Institute of Technology Woman Graduate (1984); IAPR Pattern Recognition Society Best Paper Prize (with Tom Minka) (1991); GA Tech College of Engineering Outstanding Young Engineering Alumni Award 1995; NEC Career Development Chair in Computers and Communications (1992, 1996); ICALT 2001 Best Theory Paper Prize (with Rob Reilly and Barry Kort) 2001; Creapole's Committee of Honour (Paris) (2002); Chamblee High School Hall of Fame (2005); Groden Network Distinguished Honorees, Research Award (2008); *New York Times* Best Ideas of the Year (w/el Kaliouby) (2006); *Popular Science* Top Ten Inventions of 2011: A mirror that reads vital signs 2011 (with Ming-Zher Poh and

Dan McDuff); Best Paper of the Decade, 2000-2009 IEEE Transactions on Intelligent Transportation Systems (with Jennifer Healey) (2013); Sigma Xi 2014 Walston Chubb Award for Innovation (2014); Epilepsy Foundation Innovation Seal of Excellence (with Empatica) (2015); CNN's 7 tech Superheroes to Watch (2015); 30 Most Innovative Women Professors (2016); Red Dot Award, Product Design, Life Science and Medicine (with Empatica) (2016).

Since 1991 Rosalind has been a member of the faculty at the MIT Media Laboratory, gaining tenure in 1998 and a full professorship in 2005, the same year she was honoured as a Fellow of the IEEE for contributions to image and video analysis and affective computing. Between July 2005 and June 2006, she was also a Visiting Scholar in the Department of Psychology at Boston College.

In April 2014, Rosalind co-founded Empatica, a business that designs and develops AI systems to monitor human health through wearable sensors. Their claim is 'Our technology empowers thousands of patients, clinicians and researchers with real-time human insight, driven by physiological and behavioural biomarkers.'

In 2019 Rosalind was elected to the National Academy of Engineering for her contributions on affective computing and wearable computing. This is one of the highest professional honours accorded an engineer. She is the Faculty Chair of the MIT MindHandHeart Initiative, described as 'a coalition of students, faculty, and staff with fresh insights, new ideas, and diverse perspectives working collaboratively and strategically to strengthen the fabric of our MIT community'. She also works with Sherry Turkle and Cynthia Breazeal in the field of social robots and has published significant work in the areas of digital image processing, pattern recognition, and wearable computers.

Johanna Camilla ('Hansi') Piesch

Born: 6 June 1898
Died: 28 September 1992 (aged 94)

Johanna Camilla ('Hansi') Piesch was raised in Vienna, the daughter of a cavalry officer, Oswald Piesch. After completing elementary school she attended secondary school at the Reform Realgymnasium Dr. Wesely, matriculating on 5 July 1916. She enrolled at the University of Vienna, graduating with a PhD in physics in 1921. Hansi then passed the Theoretical State Examination for Insurance and in 1928 the Teacher's Examination in Mathematics and Physics.

She joined the Austrian Post and Telegraph Service (Post- und Telegraphenverwaltung) in 1928 but was forced to leave under the National Socialist regime in 1938. She was then sent to Berlin, where she wrote her publications on switching algebra and was one of the first authors to study the technical application of Boolean algebra. Her publications on Boolean algebra in the following year made her the first to address applications. In doing so she paved the way for Austrian mathematicians Adalbert Duschek and Otto Plech, who later took over the modification of the algebra.

In July 1945, Hansi returned to work, becoming a member of the board of the laboratory of the Postal and Telegraph Administration (PTT) in Vienna. Until her retirement in 1962, she worked as a board member in the library of the Vienna University of Technology and Economics from 1956.

Hansi published a number of important papers. These included 'Concept of general circuit technology' in *Archive of Electrical Engineering*, 33, 1939, 672-686; 'About the simplification of general circuits' in *Archive of Electrical Engineering*, 33, 1939, 733-746; 'Systematics of automatic circuitry', *OFT*, 5, 1951, 2-43; 'The matrix in the circuit algebra for planning relay-controlled networks' in *Archive for Electrical Transmission*, 9, 1955, 460-468;

'Contributions to modern switching algebra', *Conference in Como*, 1956, 16-25; and, with Heinrich Sequenz, 'The Austrian pioneers of the theory of electrical circuits' in *Electrical Engineering & Mechanical Engineering*, 75, 1958, 241-245.

Hansi passed away at age 94 on 28 September 1992 in a Vienna Hospital. She was a quiet lady who did not trumpet her achievements and did not write her autobiography. A brief outline of her life was published by Heinz Zemanek in an article that appeared in *Annals of the History of Computing*, Vol. 15, No. 1, 1993, page 73. Her work on switching algebra is considered to be important and pioneering work in the development of computer science.

Hu Qiheng

Born: 15 June 1934

Hu Qiheng was born and raised in Beijing, China, and attended Experimental High School attached to Beijing Normal University. She travelled to Moscow where she was educated as an engineer, receiving a PhD in Technical Science in 1963. Between 1980 and 1982 she was a visiting professor at Case Western Reserve University in the USA. Returning to China, she worked for the Institute of Automation at the Chinese Academy of Sciences as a research associate, then as an associate research professor before being promoted to research professor. Her next role was as director of the institute, a position she held for 26 years.

Qiheng also served as deputy general secretary and vice president of the Chinese Academy of Sciences in Beijing. Serving in this role in 1994, at age 60, she visited the National Science Foundation and assisted in arranging a consensus on establishing the first direct TCP/IP connection in China. In 1997 she facilitated China's access to the Internet using several proposals, including the establishment of the China Internet Network Information Center.

In 2001 Qiheng co-founded the Internet Society of China (ISC) and became its inaugural president and chair. During her tenure she initiated charity programs that promoted internet access for disadvantaged students in China. She has held many other important roles, including Vice President of China Science and Technology Association, is a Member of China Academy of Engineering and Chair of the Steering Committee for China Internet Network Information Center (CNNIC). She is also a member of the Advisory Board for State Informatization.

Qiheng was President of the China Automation Society, President of the China Computer Society, and Chair of the National Committee for an International Computer Center in China. Among her other impressive achievements, since the 1990s she has developed and researched a World Bank loan project while playing an important role in promoting China's internet connection with the USA. In 2004, age 70, she was appointed by the UN as a member of the Working Group on Internet Governance and was a member of the Internet Corporation for Assigned Names and Numbers (ICANN) Internationalized Domain Name Committee. ICANN, formed in 1998, is a not-for-profit partnership of people from all over the world, dedicated to keeping the Internet secure, stable and interoperable. It promotes competition and develops policy on the Internet's unique identifiers.

In 2013 Qiheng was inducted into the Internet Hall of Fame (released by the Internet Society ISOC) for her contribution to global Internet development and is now a Research Professor of the Chinese Academy of Sciences and a member of the Chinese Academy of Engineering. She is married and has two children.

Qiheng's legacy is that she essentially connected China to the Internet and is still dedicated to encouraging the wholesome development of the Internet in China. She also facilitating the vocation communication platform, advocating cyberspace public welfare, and promoting the straightway communicating for the disabled.

Virginia Marie 'Ginni' Rometty

Born: 29 July 1957

Virginia Marie 'Ginni' Nicosia was born the eldest of four children in Chicago, Illinois, to an Italian-American family who lived in a property owned by her grandparents until she was in the third grade. At that time the family was finally able to purchase their own house. When Ginni was aged 15, her parents divorced and her father left the home. The family then had to get by on food stamps and financial aid until her mother could find employment. She did so, working at a number of odd jobs during the day to support the family and went to a night school to earn a college degree. Ginni looked after her siblings in the evenings.

In 1975, Ginni enrolled in the Robert R. McCormick School of Engineering and Applied Science at Northwestern University in Illinois, courtesy of a scholarship from General Motors, where she interned between her junior and senior years. During her undergraduate years she was a member of the Kappa Kappa Gamma sorority, eventually serving as its president. She was the only woman in most of her classes and supplemented her scholarship money by working at the post office, sorting mail on the night shift.

In 1979 Ginni graduated with a Bachelor of Science degree in computer science and electrical engineering, receiving high honours. She then worked for General Electric in Flint for two years, her position entailing systems development and applications. It was during this time she met and married, in 1981, a private-equity investor, Mark Anthony Rometty.

Ginni joined IBM as a systems analyst and systems engineer in Detroit in 1981 beginning by working with clients in the insurance industry. For the next ten years she was in technical positions, before moving up to management roles. During the early 1990s she worked in sales, joining IBM's

Consulting Group in 1991. Later in the decade she was assisting important clients such as Prudential Financial, Inc. with their internet features.

Her next role was as general manager of IBM's global services division, and in 2002 she helped negotiate the purchase of Monday, the consulting arm of professional services firm PricewaterhouseCoopers for US$3.5 billion. This was reportedly the largest acquisition in professional services history and helped launch IBM into the services business. In 2002 *Time* placed her its 2002 Global Business Influential list.

In 2005 Ginni was promoted to senior vice president of IBM Global Business and was given the task of integrating PricewaterhouseCoopers and its consultants with IBM. She became senior vice president of Enterprise Business Services-IBM Global Services in July that year. Ginni also held other senior positions within the company, including as general manager of IBM Global Services, Americas, general manager of IBM's Global Insurance and Financial Services Sector, managing partner at IBM Business Consulting Services, Inc. and general manager of Insurance Industry Group. She received the Carl Sloane Award in 2006 from the Association of Management Consulting Firms. This is awarded to 'an individual who has contributed substantially to the development of the consulting profession, either through leadership, the development of intellectual capital, innovation in consulting processes, value added to clients served, or a combination of the above'.

Along with other IBM executives, Ginni was instrumental in devising a five-year growth plan for IBM, concentrating on revenue growth and capital allocation. Their '2015 Roadmap' strategy saw the company move away from the hardware industry to focus on businesses such as software and services. In 2009 she became senior vice president and group executive for sales, marketing, and strategy and focused on IBM's emerging analytics unit.

In January 2009, Ginni had responsibility for IBM's sales force, serving as senior vice president of global sales and distribution until 2010. During her tenure in this role she encouraged the development of IBM's growth-markets unit to focus on emerging markets such as Brazil and Vietnam. Between 2010 and 2012 she was an IBM senior vice president, as well as IBM's Group Executive of Sales, Marketing & Strategy. As from 1 January 2012, she would be IBM's president and CEO, becoming the ninth, and first female, chief executive in its history. She also took on the additional role of IBM chairman on 1 October 2012. That year, Bloomberg named her among the 50 Most Influential People in the World.

Sensing that the next big growth areas for IBM were big data and analytics, Ginni brokered a partnership for Apple to design applications for IBM's enterprise customers. To this end, she announced that IBM would partner with SAP on cloud computing and with Twitter on data analytics. Between 2012 and 2015, Ginni oversaw IBM spending $8.5 billion acquiring around 30 companies, and by 2016 she had overseen the divestment of about $7 billion in commoditised assets, including chip manufacturing.

On 28 June 2017, Ginni was awarded the KPMG Inspire Greatness Award and in January the following year she announced IBM's first quarter of year-over-year revenue increase since 2012. By 2018, she declared that around half of IBM's 9,043 patents were in artificial intelligence, cloud computing, cybersecurity, blockchain and quantum computing. In March 2019 she was part of a White House panel on workforce development.

On 30 January 2020, it was announced that Ginni would be stepping down as IBM's CEO although she remained executive chairman until the end of that year. She had held many senior roles, including as a member of the Women in Technology Council, Women's Executive Council, and Women's Leadership Council. Ginni also served as a former director at APQC (American Productivity & Quality Center), as well as on the board of directors of AIG (American International Group) from 2006 until 2009.

Ginni still sits on the board of overseers and board of managers for the Memorial Sloan Kettering Cancer Center and since 2013 has been a council member at the Latin America Conservation Council. She also serves on the Council on Foreign Relations and is also on the board of trustees of her alma mater, Northwestern University.

She is co-chair of the Aspen Institute's Cyber Group, a member of the advisory board of Tsinghua University School of Economics and Management, and a member of the Singapore Economic Development Board International Advisory Council. In May 2019, Ginni received the Edison Achievement Award for her commitment to innovation throughout her career.

Ginni has received honorary doctoral degrees from Rensselaer Polytechnic Institute (2014), Northwestern University (2015) and an honorary degree from North Carolina State University (2019).

In May 2020, Ginni was elected to the board of JPMorgan Chase. She and husband Mark enjoy Broadway plays and scuba diving, as well as spending time in Bonita Springs and New York.

Jean E. Sammet

Born: 23 March 1928
Died: 20 May 2017 (aged 89)

Jean E. Sammet was born in New York City, New York, five years before her younger sister Helen. Their parents, Harry and Ruth Sammet, were both lawyers. The sisters attended public elementary schools in Manhattan where Jean exhibited a strong interest and ability in mathematics but was unable to attend the Bronx High School of Science as it was only for boys. Instead, she attended Julia Richman High School located on the Upper East Side neighbourhood of Manhattan.

For her tertiary education, Jean selected Mount Holyoke College as it had a strong reputation in mathematics, her chosen major. She also took education courses, allowing her to be certified to teach high school mathematics in New York. In 1948 she graduated with a Bachelor of Arts degree with a major in mathematics and a minor in political science.

After Mount Holyoke, Jean enrolled at the University of Illinois, where she received her Master of Arts in 1949. She then embarked on a PhD program at the same university at Urbana-Champaign, working as a teaching assistant. In 1949 she encountered a computer for the first time and was not all impressed, considering it 'an obscene piece of hardware'. She did not complete her PhD there.

In 1951, as New York City was not hiring new teachers, Jean began looking for a teaching position in New Jersey. However, she was told by the authorities in New Jersey that she was missing two subjects from her degrees: a course in education and one in the history of New Jersey. Although she objected to the ruling, she had no choice but to consider other occupations.

As a result, in 1951 Jean took a position at the Metropolitan Life Insurance Company as a trainee actuary, agreeing to participate in an in-house training program to learn about punched card accounting machines, which she mastered. However, she left her position at the insurance office and enrolled at Columbia University to again pursue a PhD in mathematics. She worked as a teaching assistant at Barnard College during the 1952-1953 school year but decided that she did not want the life of an academic and left the program.

Between 1953 and 1958 Jean worked as a mathematician for Sperry Gyroscope in New York, spending her time solving mathematical analysis problems for clients and operating an analog computer. During her time there she also worked on the Department of the Navy's submarine program. In early January 1955 she commenced her career as a programmer on a digital computer, the Sperry Electronic Digital Automatic Computer (SPEEDAC). Jean's first task was to write the basic loader for the SPEEDAC, this being a 20-line program that took three days to toggle into the computer by hand in binary.

Before long Jean became the group leader of an 'open shop' comprised of programmers acting as consultants to the engineers, as well as scientists who assisted them in writing and testing their routines. More programmers were hired, and the group produced other system software while focussing on scientific and engineering computations. In 1955, Sperry Gyroscope and Remington Rand merged and became Sperry Rand. This merger gave Jean access to the UNIVAC I computer and the remarkable Grace Hopper.

In the fall quarter 1956 she lectured one of the earliest graduate-level courses in computer programming in the Applied Mathematics department of Adelphi College (now Adelphi University) on Long Island. Even though Adelphi did not then have a computer, Jean lectured two programming courses for two years, largely without textbooks as very few existed at the time.

With her ability increasing and interest now aroused in the field of computing, Jean left Sperry to take up an engineering position at Sylvania Electric Products in Needham, Massachusetts. Her role was to oversee software development for the MobIle DIgital Computer project (MOBIDIC) project led by Carl Hammer who was responsible for the company's software development. In 1959, Jean and five other programmers established much of the design of the influential COBOL programming language. Their proposal was written in just two weeks and was accepted by Sylvania's US government clients. By 1960 the Pentagon had announced it would not buy computers unless they ran COBOL, thereby creating an industry standard.

In the mid-1960s Jean was appointed as Chairperson of the Special Interest Committee on Symbolic and Algebraic Manipulation (SICASM). In June 1966, she was elected the Northeast Regional Representative of the Association for Computing Machinery (ACM), serving until 1968. She was also a member of the ACM Council and ACM lecturer (1967, 1968, and 1972). In August 1968 she became Chairperson of the ACM Committee on the special interest groups SIG and SIC.

Her book *Programming Languages: History and Fundamentals* (Prentice Hall) was published in 1969, its contents providing an overview of

120 programming languages being used in the United States as of the late 1960s. In 1971 Jean was elected chair of the ACM Special Interest Group on Programming Languages (SIGPLAN). She served one year of a two-year term before resigning, as in June 1972 she was elected vice president of ACM, serving until June 1974.

Between 1977 and 1979 she organised and was appointed as first chairman of the American Federation of Information Processing Societies (AFIPS) History of Computing Committee. In this role she oversaw many projects, including the archiving of important material. In 1978, aged 50, Jean received an honorary Doctor of Science from Mount Holyoke College. Also in 1978, she helped to establish the AFIPS journal, *Annals of the History of Computing*, serving on its editorial board for many years. She initiated and produced the Self-Study Department in the journal until 1991.

From 1983 to 1993 Jean was on the board of directors of the Computer Museum, as well as being a member of its collections committee. In 1991 she was appointed to the original executive committee of the Software Patent Institute (and served as its education committee chairman in 1992 and 1993.

In 2001 Jean was made a Fellow of the Computer History Museum and in 2009 she received the IEEE Computer Society Computer Pioneer Award 'for pioneering work and lifetime achievement as one of the first developers and researchers in programing languages'. In 2013, the National Center for Women & Information Technology (NCWIT) awarded her its Pioneer Award.

After a brief illness, Jean passed away at age 89 on 20 May 2017 in Silver Spring, Maryland. She never married and did not have children.

Lucy Sanders

Born: 1954

Lucinda 'Lucy' Sanders was born in Indianapolis but grew up mainly in Louisiana. Her mother was politically active with the League of Women Voters as well as being an elected official, while her father ran a corporate computing data centre that included large mainframe computers at AT&T Inc. Both of her parents encouraged their two daughters to excel academically, so Lucy took the most advanced college-prep science courses available in school.

Her elder sister graduated with a Bachelor of Science majoring in computing, the first woman at her university to do so, and there were always family discussions about the emerging field. At high school, Lucy was fortunate to have a teacher who taught her pupils how to program in BASIC and FORTRAN languages, as well as obtaining a small desktop Olivetti computer. Lucy's curiosity was very much awoken by such an excellent instructor.

Lucy attended Louisiana State University, where she obtained her own degree in computer science. Then she and her future husband, Bruce Sanders, went to graduate school at the University of Colorado where she received a master's degree in computer science. During her program, in 1977 she was hired by Bell Labs for its part-time student program. At the time, there were very few female engineers and none of those were in management. Her first supervisor there, Ken Fong, remarked 'She was usually a pleasure to work with. Sometimes, however, she would push an issue to the point of annoying people; usually, though, she turned out to be right.'

In her early career, Lucy worked as a Research and Development (R&D) Manager at Bell Labs, and until 1999 was an executive vice president, assuming the role of CTO of Lucent Customer Care Solution. She moved on from Bell Labs to work at Inc CRM Solutions at Avaya Labs for two years, until 2004 when she co-founded the National Center for Women and Information Technology (NCWIT), courtesy of a grant from the National Science Foundation. Lucy, along with Telle Whitney and Robert Schnabel, aimed to use NCWIT to increase the number of women in computer fields. She declared that 'from all of them, I learned about computing ... and I learned about community give-back from my mother and her wide range of interests, from civic to environmental.'

Before accepting this role, Lucy had previously held a number of other positions, including on the Board of the Alliance for Technology, Learning, and Society (Atlas), the Denver Public Schools Computer Magnet Advisory Board, and the MSRI, the Engineering Advisory Council at the University of Colorado at Boulder. She is also a Trustee for the Center for American Entrepreneurship and the International Computer Science Institute.

Lucy has won many awards and honours for her achievements, including the Bell Labs Fellow Award in 1996, the highest accolade bestowed by the company. She holds six patents in the communications technology area. Other awards include the Silicon Valley Tribute to Women in Industry Award for business excellence and community outreach (2000); CU Boulder Distinguished Engineering Alumni Award for Industry and Commerce (2004); Soroptimist International of Los Angeles Women of Vision Award (2006); George Norlin Distinguished Service Award (2011); A. Nico Habermann Award (2012), and Bob Newman Lifetime Achievement Award, Colorado Technology Association (2016) for her ongoing commitment to further innovative technology.

In 2007 Lucy was inducted into the Women in Technology Hall of Fame and in 2013 into the US News STEM Leadership Hall of Fame. She currently works as CEO of NCWIT and serves as Executive-in-Residence for the ATLAS Institute at the University of Colorado at Boulder. She is also a Trustee for the Colorado School of Mines, the Center for American Entrepreneurship in Washington D.C. and the International Computer Science Institute at the University of California, Berkeley.

Patricia Selinger

Born: 15 October 1949

Patricia Griffiths Selinger attended Saint Ann School West Palm Beach, Florida, between 1957 and 1961, later graduating from Harvard University with three degrees, all in applied mathematics. These comprised a Bachelor of Science in 1971, a Master of Science in 1972 and a PhD in 1975. She then joined IBM and was selected to lead the IBM Almaden Research Computer Science department. In 1986 Patricia established and managed the Database Technology Institute (DBTI) with the aim of accelerating technology into IBM's database products.

The Institute invented and partnered with IBM development to deliver a number of fundamental technologies in DB2 for OS/390, IMS, and DB2 for Linux, Unix and Windows. DBTI was very successful in providing a fast technology pipeline from research to development with technical contributions in the areas of database optimisation, data parallelism, distributed data, and unstructured data management.

Patricia was instrumental in the development of System R, a pioneering relational database implementation and wrote the official paper on relational query optimisation. The dynamic programming algorithm for determining join order proposed in that paper still forms the basis for most of the query optimisers used in modern relational systems. It was the first implementation of SQL, which has since become the standard relational data query language.

In 1994 Patricia was appointed an IBM Fellow, the company's highest technical recognition, and in 1997 was made a member of the National Academy of Engineering. She received the SIGMOD Edgar F. Codd Award in 2002, as well as the ACM Innovation Award in the same year, the highest Association for Computing Machinery (ACM) award given in the area of data management. SIGMOID is the ACM Special Interest Group on Management of Data. In 2009 she became an ACM Fellow.

Patricia was elected as a Fellow of the American Academy of Arts and Sciences as well as receiving an ACM Systems Software Award for her work on System R. A prolific researcher with over 40 scientific publications to her credit, she is a co-holder of three patents. In 2012 the book *Patricia Selinger*, authored by Ronald Cohn and Jesse Russell, was published by VSD.

Between 2014 and 2016, Patricia was the Chief Technology Officer at Paradata where she worked on problems involving data harmonisation, curation, provenance, and entity resolution to provide transparency to the supply chain. Paradata technology aims to transform real-time data into confirmed perceptions and executable actions.

Patricia rose to the rank of Vice President of Data Management Architecture and Technology at IBM in 2017, serving in that role until 2018 when she retired. She is currently a project consultant for IBM.

Priti Shankar

Born: 20 September 1947
Died: 17 October 2011 (aged 64)

Margarida Priti Shankar was born in Vanxem, Loutolim, Goa, India, to Agostinho Gracias (Innocencio) Monteiro, a Brigadier in the Indian Army, and Maria Especiosa Sofia Monteiro, a mathematics and French teacher. Her siblings notably included Dr Vivek Monteiro, a theoretical physicist turned trade-union leader and low-cost science educator; Professor Anjali Monteiro, the documentary film-maker and professor of media studies at the Tata Institute of Social Sciences; and Dr. Nandita de Souza, the Goa-based developmental and behavioural paediatrician.

In 1958 her parents moved from Khadakwasla, Pune, to Jammu where her father served along the India-Pakistan border in Surankote. The move resulted in Priti missing six months of school, during which time she was home schooled by her mother. Several years later, Priti returned to Pune, attending Fergusson College and later enrolling at the Indian Institute of Technology (IIT) in Delhi. In 1968 she became the first female to graduate with a Bachelor of Technology degree in electrical engineering. This was a time when very few women in India studied science, and those that did were largely in the biological sciences.

Priti then travelled overseas to the USA. The next step in her academic endeavours was to enrol in the PhD program at the University of Maryland, College Park, obtaining her doctorate in 1972. The following year she returned to India where she was appointed as an assistant professor at the Centre for Automation at the Indian Institute of Science (IISc) in Bangalore. She played a vital role in steering it to a pre-eminent position in the country.

In 1974 she married P.N. Shankar, a theoretical fluid dynamicist at the National Aerospace Laboratories of Bangalore. Two years later the couple had a son, Nachiket, and in 1983 a daughter, Mridula. In 1979 Priti pioneered the science field by developing a Bose–Chaudhuri–Hocquenghem (BCH) code, which were defined over finite fields and therefore became operational over finite rings. In 2002 she was a co-editor, with Y.N. Srikant, of CRC Press, which in 2003 became part of Taylor & Francis and in the following year formed part of the UK publisher Informa. Priti also served on leadership board of *Resonance*, a peer reviewed science education journal in India.

Priti's research focused on the areas of compiler design, formal language theory and algorithmic coding theory. She made many contributions to the development of a theory for tree parsing, her research enabling the automatic generation of code generators from formal machine specifications in the form of regular tree grammars. This was an important outcome, with her results being published in the journal *ACM TOPLAS* in 2000. She also co-edited (with Y.N. Srikant) in 2002 the first handbook of compilers, *The Compiler Design Handbook: Optimizations and Machine Code Generation* (published by the CRC). The second edition appeared in 2018.

In 2007 Priti received the Jaya Jayant award for teaching excellence, and between 2006 and 2009 she was named a Distinguished Lecturer by the Institute of Electrical and Electronics Engineers. The *Priti Shankar Library of Popular Math and Science* is located in the UMED building of the Navnirmiti Learning Foundation. In 2012 Priti co-edited (with Deepak D'Souza) the book *Modern Applications of Automata Theory (Iisc Research Monographs)* published by World Scientific Publishing Company.

Priti passed away from cancer at age 64 on 17 October 2011. Her last written words were that the Lord had given her an opportunity to live her life on her terms, and left it with no regrets. 'I've pretty much done what I wanted to, most of my life. I consider myself very lucky to have been born into an enlightened family where independent thinking was encouraged, and to be associated with an institution where complete academic freedom is given to faculty members.'

Stephanie 'Steve' Shirley

Born: 16 September 1933

(Vera) Stephanie Buchthal was born in Dortmund, Germany. Her father was Arnold Buchthal, a Jewish judge sacked by the Nazi regime. Her mother, a non-Jewish Viennese, was a tailor's assistant. In July 1939 the 5-year-old Stephanie, along with her 9-year-old sister Renate, arrived in Britain as Kindertransport refugees.

Placed in the care of foster parents who lived in the town of Sutton Coldfield, Birmingham, Stephanie was later reunited with her biological parents, but said she never really bonded with them. She attended a convent school before the family moved to Oswestry, near the Welsh border, where she attended the Oswestry Girls' High School. As mathematics was not taught at the school, Stephanie received permission to take lessons at the local boys' school. She later recalled that, following her wartime experiences, she had 'six wonderful years of peace' there.

After completing high school, Stephanie chose not to attend university but rather look for a position in a mathematical or technical field. At age 18 she became a British citizen and changed her name to Stephanie Brook. During the 1950s, Stephanie worked at the Post Office Research Station at Dollis Hill in northwest London, building computers from scratch and writing code in machine language. For the next six years she attended evening classes, graduating with a Bachelor of Science honours degree in mathematics.

In 1959 Stephanie changed employers, moving to CDL Ltd, the designers of the ICT 1301 computer. In 1962 she married a physicist, Derek Shirley. She also founded – with capital of £6 – the software company Freelance Programmers that was later known as F International and then Xansa. It was later acquired by Steria and is now part of the Sopra Steria Group.

As she had experienced sexism in the workplace, Stephanie was determined to create job opportunities for women with dependants As a result, her workplace was essentially all female with only three male programmers among the first 300 staff. 'It was really a female-friendly organisation. It was set up as a crusade rather than to make money, and indeed it took a long time before it did make any money, and I was very proud eventually when it succeeded that I'd set up this special women's company. Again, another first, I thought, because I have to justify my existence.'

Stephanie discovered that when she wrote company letters signed with her real name, many of them did not receive a response. Considering that it was simply because she was a woman, Stephanie adopted the name 'Steve' so they would take more notice of her. Stephanie's team projects included programming Concorde's black box flight recorder, and it was also instrumental in helping develop software standards, management control protocols, and other standards that were eventually adopted by NATO.

Stephanie was appointed Officer of the Order of the British Empire (OBE) in the 1980 Birthday Honours for services to industry. In 1985, she was awarded a Recognition of Information Technology Award. The UK-based Shirley Foundation was set up by her in 1986 with a substantial gift to establish a charitable trust fund. Its current mission is facilitation and support of pioneering projects with strategic impact in the field of autism spectrum disorders with particular emphasis on medical research. The fund has supported many projects through grants and loans.

In 1987, Stephanie was granted the Freedom of the City of London, and between 1989 and 1990 was the first female President of the chartered British Computer Society. In 1991 she was awarded an honorary doctorate from the University of Buckingham and made Master of the IT livery company 1992–93. In 1993, Stephanie retired at the age of 60.

In 1999 she received the Mountbatten Medal which is awarded annually for an outstanding contribution, or contributions over a period, to the promotion of electronics or information technology and their application. In the 2000 New Year Honours, Stephanie was made Dame Commander of the Order of the British Empire (DBE) and in the following year was appointed a Fellow of the Royal Academy of Engineering and of Birkbeck College.

From May 2009 until May 2010, Stephanie served as the UK's Ambassador for Philanthropy, a government appointment aimed at giving philanthropists a voice. In 2012, she donated her entire art collection, including works by Elizabeth Frink, Maggi Hambling, Thomas Heatherwick, Josef Herman and John Piper, to Prior's Court School and the charity Paintings in Hospitals. In an appearance on BBC Radio 2's *Good Morning Sunday*, Stephanie revealed that she had given away more than £67 million of her personal wealth to different projects.

In February 2013, Stephanie was assessed as one of the 100 most powerful women in the United Kingdom by Woman's Hour on BBC Radio 4, and in January 2014 the Science Council named her as one of the Top 100 practising scientists in the UK. In 2018 she was made Fellow of the Computer History Museum and became the first woman to win the lifetime achievement award of the Chartered Management Institute 'for her stellar contribution to British engineering and technology'.

Through the Shirley Foundation, she has donated most of her wealth (from the internal sale to the company staff and later the flotation of FI Group) to charity, with beneficiaries including the Worshipful Company of Information Technologists and the Oxford Internet Institute (part of Oxford University). She was an early member of the National Autistic Society and has pioneered and funded research in this field, for example through the Autism Research Centre led by Professor Simon Baron-Cohen and via Autistica. She has also served as an independent non-executive director for Tandem Computers Inc., the Atomic Energy Authority (later AEA Technology) and the John Lewis Partnership.

Stephanie's company has been valued at $3 billion, making millionaires of 70 of her team members. Since her retirement with her husband Derek of over 50 years, she focusses on her philanthropy.

Megan Smith

Born: 21 October 1964

Megan Smith was raised in Buffalo, New York, and Fort Erie, Ontario, spending many summers at the Chautauqua Institution in Chautauqua, New York. Her mother, Joan Aspell Smith, was director of the Chautauqua Children's School. In 1982 Megan graduated from City Honors School and then enrolled at the Massachusetts Institute of Technology (MIT). She earned a Bachelor of Science degree in 1986 and an S.M. (Master of Science) degree in 1988, both in mechanical engineering. Her master's degree was completed in the MIT Media Lab. She was a member of the MIT student team that designed, built and raced a solar car 3200 kilometres miles across the Australian outback in the first cross-continental solar car race.

Following her graduation from MIT, Megan worked at a variety of organisations, including Apple in Tokyo and General Magic located in Mountain View, California, as product design lead on emerging smartphone technologies. She then joined Planet Out in 1995, becoming its Chief Operating Officer in 1996 and the Chief Executive Officer in 1998, presiding over their merger with Gay.com. In 1999 Megan married the American journalist Kara Anne Swisher and the couple had two sons, Louis and Alexander. In the same year she won the GLAAD Interactive Media Award for Internet Leadership. In 2000 she was named as one of the Top 25 Women on the Web.

In 2003, Megan joined Google, eventually rising to the role of vice president of new business development. Here she led early-stage partnerships, pilot explorations and technology licensing across Google's global engineering and product teams. The early acquisitions she led included Keyhole (Google Earth), Where2Tech (Google Maps), and Google Picasa, a now discontinued cross-platform image organiser and image viewer. Later she also became general manager of Google's philanthropic arm, Google.org. During 2003–4 she was a Reuters Digital Vision Program Fellow at Stanford University.

Megan co-hosted, along with Google executives Astro Teller and Eric Schmidt, Google's Solve for X solution acceleration programs that ran between 2012 and 2014. The program commenced on 1 February 2012 at a three-day convention at CordeValle Resort in San Martin, California. A third co-creator of the project was another executive, Eric 'Astro' Teller. At the same time, in 2012 Megan founded Google's 'Women Techmakers' diversity initiative to expand visibility, community and resources for technical women around the world. In both 2012 and 2013 she was listed by *Out* magazine as one of the 50 most powerful LGBT people in the US.

In 2014, Megan left Google to assume the role of 3rd U.S. Chief Technology Officer (CTO) under the administration of President Barack Obama, the first woman to do so. The role involved recruiting top tech talent to serve across government to collaborate on important issues, including artificial intelligence, data science and open source, economic growth, entrepreneurship, structural inequalities, government tech innovation capacity, STEM/STEAM engagement, workforce development, and criminal justice reform. Her role lasted three years, after which she helped launch the Tech Jobs Tour, which brought together diverse and non-traditional talent with companies who needed their skills. In 2015 she was entered into the prestigious Matrix Hall of Fame, an award for outstanding women in communications.

Megan serves on the board of MIT, Vital Voices, LA2028 (Los Angeles Olympics in 2028), and Think of Us (a firm that focusses on 'transforming child welfare by leveraging lived experience and system proximity to drive systems change'). She is also on the advisory boards for the MIT Media Lab and the Algorithmic Justice League, as well as being a member of the Award Selection Committee for the distinguished Carroll L. Wilson Award at MIT.

Megan is an active supporter of STEM education and innovation. In 2018 she was the CEO and Founder of shift7 which works on tech-forward, inclusive innovation for faster impact on systemic economic, social, and environmental challenges. In that year she and Kara divorced. In 2019 she was named by *Business Insider* as among the 23 Most Powerful LGBTQ+ People in Tech and in early 2021 opened the first-ever Horasis Extraordinary Meeting on the United States of America today, during a plenary discussion on 'Rebuilding Trust'.

Cynthia Jane Solomon

Born: 7 September 1938

Cynthia Jane Solomon was born in Somerville, Massachusetts, USA. In 1959 she graduated with a Bachelor of Arts in history from Radcliffe College, after which she lectured for seven years at Milton Academy in Milton, Massachusetts. She was Technology Integration Coordinator at Monsignor Haddad Middle School in Needham, Massachusetts. Cynthia continued her studies at Boston University where she received her Master of Science in computer science in 1976. She later received her Doctor of Philosophy (PhD) in education at Harvard University in 1985, her work being largely focused on research on human-computer interaction using children as designers. Her thesis led to the publication of her 1986 book, *Computer Environments for Children: A Reflection on Theories of Learning and Education* (The MIT Press). She also worked full-time as a computer teacher in elementary and secondary schools.

During her studies, Cynthia worked for several years as a researcher with artificial intelligence pioneers Marvin Minsky and Seymour Papert at MIT, later finding a position at the research and development company Bolt, Beranek and Newman (now Raytheon BBN). It was here that she, along with other researchers, set about creating a programming language for children based on words and sentences instead of number and symbols. It was named 'Logo', and improvements were made by teaching it to 7th grade pupils in the late 1960s. Cynthia had begun her journey in computer science by teaching herself 'Lisp', a practical mathematical notation for computer programs that was the then preferred programming language for artificial intelligence (AI) research.

Among the many types of robots created for children, one of the most popular was the Turtle robot that could carry out commands including drawing simple geometric shapes using a pen. In the 1980s Cynthia was hired by the Machine Intelligence Research Artificial Intelligence Laboratory where in time she took charge of the creation of Apple's Logo implementation at a time when she was the vice president of R&D for Logo Computer Systems, Inc. Logo was the forerunner of later educational programming languages, such as Smalltalk, the first graphical language tool to support live programming and advanced debugging techniques in a user-friendly format, and Scratch, a free programming language and online community where one can create one's own interactive stories, games, and animations.

Cynthia is a prolific author of articles on child education and technology in the classroom, along with leading workshops on academic research and writing. In 1988 her *Computer Environments for Children* (Cambridge: MIT Press) was published and in 1996 *Designing Multimedia Environments for Children* (Wiley) co-authored with Allison Druin.

Cynthia served as the Director of the Atari Cambridge Research Laboratory and has won several awards for her life's work, including in 2016 the National Center for Women & Information Technology (NCWIT) Pioneer Award. She was on the program committee of Constructing Modern Knowledge and the Marvin Minsky Institute on Artificial Intelligence.

Today, Cynthia continues to make her mark by speaking at conferences and working with the One Laptop per Child Foundation, described as 'a non-profit initiative established with the goal of transforming education for children around the world'. She consults, teaches and publishes, as well as working with a number of notable foundations.

Frances Spence

Born: 2 March 1922
Died: 18 July 2012 (aged 90)

Frances Veronika Bilas was born in in Philadelphia in 1922, the second of five sisters. Her parents both worked in education with her father, Joseph Francis Bilas, an engineer for the Philadelphia Public School System and her mother, Anna Elizabeth (Hughes) Bilas, a schoolteacher.

Frances attended the South Philadelphia High School for Girls where she completed her studies in 1938. After initially enrolling at Temple University, she was awarded a scholarship and switched to Chestnut Hill College where she graduated in 1942 with a major in mathematics and a minor in physics. During her time there she met Kathleen Antonelli, who later also became an ENIAC programmer.

In 1947, Frances married Homer Weldon Spence, an Army electrical engineer from the Aberdeen Proving Grounds. He had been assigned to the ENIAC (Electronic Numerical Integrator and Computer) project and later became head of the Computer Research Branch. Frances worked as a programmer on the ENIAC for several years following the Second World War, but not long after her marriage she resigned to raise a family. She and Homer would have three boys, Joseph, Richard, and William.

The ENIAC project conducted by the U.S. Army had a mission to construct the first all-electronic digital computer. Although it was men who built the hardware, the complex computations were carried out by a team of six female programmers called 'computers'. Unfortunately, the role that she and the other female programmers took on was largely ignored as it was felt that women were not interested in technology. Any photos that appeared did not mention them by name, and when the ENIAC was unveiled to the public on 15 February 1946, the U.S. Army failed to mention any of their names.

Frances Spence and the other women were originally hired by the University of Pennsylvania's Moore School of Engineering to create the ENIAC. Its purpose was in ballistics, to track trajectories of missiles. As many men were fighting in the war, the US Army funded Moore School to hire a team of eighty women. Frances and Kathleen Antonelli were part of a smaller group within the larger team that was assigned to the operation of an analog computing machine known as a 'Differential Analyzer'. After the war, Frances continued working with the ENIAC and collaborated with other eminent mathematicians.

Along with the other original ENIAC programmers, in 1997, Frances was inducted into the Women in Technology International Hall of Fame, their pioneer work paving the way for the advancement of electronic computing. In 2010, a documentary *Top Secret Rosies: The Female 'Computers' of WWII* was released, based on in-depth interviews with three of the six women programmers. The ENIAC team also inspired the award-winning 2013 documentary *The Computers* that included footage of the team in interviews.

Frances passed away at age 90 on 18 July 2012 in Nassau County, New York. Her husband Homer had died at age 78 on 27 February 1995.

Janese Swanson

Born: 21 November 1958

Janese Swanson was born the second oldest of six children in an era when girls were generally not considered to have any interest or ability in technology or inventing. After her father was killed in Vietnam, Janese was raised by her mother and as a teenager held odd jobs as a teenager to help support her family. She took care of her younger siblings and learned to repair broken toys and appliances. Through this work she developed an interest in science education, especially the perception of gender roles. Her grandfather encouraged her to become a fashion model and even became a cover girl. Through this Janese gained valuable experience with styling and layouts. She also worked in retail sales at Sears. Although she was the youngest and only female salesperson in the television and sound system department at Sears, she won several sales awards helped by her technical knowledge.

Janese attended Orange Glen High School, one of the five public high schools in the Escondido Union School District in Escondido, California. In 1976–1980 she attended San Diego State University where she graduated with a bachelor's degree in liberal studies in 1981. She then became a schoolteacher before being laid off, along with nearly 40 of her colleagues, when the school system ran short of funds. Unable to find another teaching position, she briefly returned to modelling and finally gained employment as a flight attendant. During this employment she convinced a large computer company to donate laptop computers. During her spare time, she taught several of her co-workers how to use them, usually among small groups in private homes.

In the late 1980s, Janese was employed by Broderbund Software as a product manager where she led teams that produced educational toy and game products, including such as 'Playroom' and 'Treehouse' and 'Where in the World is Carmen San Diego?, The latter stemmed from her own experience as a flight attendant. In 1988 she enrolled at the University of San Francisco, graduating with an MA in Education in 1990. In 1992 she started her own company, Kid One For Fun, where she developed and licensed toys including the Yak Bak, a handheld voice recorder for kids. She stayed there until 1995.

All the while she continued with her tertiary studies, earning six degrees, including from the University of San Francisco a Doctor of Education in organisation and leadership, with her thesis examining gender issues in product design. Following her doctorate, in 1995 she founded the company Girl Tech and two years later launched the website girltech.com, as well as publishing the *Tech Girl's Internet Adventures* (John Wiley & Sons Inc.) that introduced girls to the Internet and explained how to use it. The website had content aimed at girls aged 8 to 14, including articles profiling worthy role models, a 'Chick Chat' discussion board, advice columns and referrals to other recommended sites.

Janese was inspired to start Girl Tech when her 8-year-old daughter, Jackie, was watching commercials. Janese remarked: 'I was tired of seeing that "pink" aisle in the toy store. I was looking at the research that showed that both boys and girls said that boys are more "highly valued" in our society. I couldn't let that happen to my own daughter. (She) was a driving factor in this.' At first the toy manufacturers told her that 'If you build it for boys, the boys and girls will buy it, but if you build it for girls, the boys won't buy it.'

Girl Tech was then born, including products such as the Friend Frame, a talking picture frame, and the Beam-It Projector, which allows the user to write messages and beam them across the room using a torch. Another was The Door Pass, a device that monitors intruders to a child's room by using voice recognition and motion sensors. The products sold were usually priced between $10 and $20 and often coloured bright purple or green, although rarely pink. Other toys included the Snoop Stopper Keepsake Box, Me-Mail Message Center, Zap N' Lock Journal and Swap-It Locket. There were also several magazines especially for girls: *Tech Girl's Internet Adventures*, *Tech Girl's Activity Book*, and *Girlzine: A Magazine for the Global Girl*.

Girl Tech was acquired for US$6 million by Radica Games (Mattel), a company listed on NASDAQ and that Janese said was founded by men who are 'the fathers of daughters' and who vowed not to interfere. In 2006 Radica Girl Tech introduced, for example, the 'Radica Girl Tech Voice Recognition Password Journal' that automatically opens with voice recognition and a password, as well as recognising voice commands for reading light, calendar, alarm and more. Janese felt that privacy was 'a huge issue among girls 8 to 12'.

Janese has won many awards for her efforts to assist young girls with technology. These include the Annual Leading Change Award from Women in Communications, Webgirls, Top 25 Women on the Web, Advancement of Girls and Technology, and Women Entrepreneur of the Year Nominee from the National Association of Women Business Owners. She was also featured in the 1997 issue of *Ms.* magazine's Women of the Year.

Janese has worked as the Education Coordinator at the United States Mint and was a founder of 'The Art Apprentice' – 'Learn to paint alongside other amateur artists on their journey to creating a masterpiece.' For sixteen years she was an art teacher in the Del Mar Union School District where she used computer technology to encourage students' creativity. Her students received an Innovative Video In Education (iVIE) award in 2008 from the San Diego County Office of Education. In 2007, Janese was the education chair of SIGGRAPH (Special Interest Group on Computer Graphics and Interactive Techniques). Since August 2020 she has been a Curriculum Coordinator and STEM Resource Teacher at Hawaii State Department of Education.

Janet Taylor

Born: 13 May 1804
Died: 26 January 1870 (aged 65)

Jane Ann Ionn was born on 13 May 1804 in Wolsingham, Durham, England, the 6th child of the Reverend Peter Ionn and Jane Deighton, the daughter of a country gentleman. Peter Ionn was the curate and schoolmaster at the Free Grammar School in Wolsingham where he taught, among many other things, the subject of navigation. When Jane Ann's' mother died in May 1811, two months after giving birth to her sixth child Frederick, Jane Ann was still only six years old. When she was nine, a scholarship became available for girls aged fourteen and over to attend The Royal School for Embroidering Females that had been established at Ampthill in Bedfordshire, under the patronage of Queen Charlotte.

With the backing of the Member of Parliament for Durham City, Michael Angelo Taylor, and notwithstanding her young age, Jane Ann was accepted as a pupil, and stayed there until the death of the Queen on 17 November 1818, when the school was then closed. Then aged seventeen, Jane Ann obtained a position as governess to the family of the Vicar of Kimbolton, the Reverend John Huntley. Kimbolton was a small town of only 1,500 people about 25 miles (40 km) north of Ampthill.

On 2 May 1821, her father Peter died suddenly when Jane Ann was sixteen years old. She then went to live with her brother Mathew Ionn who had opened a linen draper's shop at 44 Oxford Street in London. On 30 January 1830, now aged twenty-nine, Jane Ann married George Taylor Jane, aged forty-one, at the British Embassy in The Hague, The Netherlands. George was a widower with three children, a former naval man during the Napoleonic wars and now a publican. He was also a 'Dissenter', brought up outside the Church of England. On their marriage, George changed his name to 'George Taylor' and she became Mrs Janet Taylor for the rest of her life. The couple set up residence at 6 East Street, Red Lion Square, near Oxford Street in London.

Janet became a prodigious author of nautical treatises and textbooks, born of a particular fascination about the measurement of longitude by the lunar distance method. She conducted her own Nautical Academy in Minories in the east end of the City, not far from the Tower of London. She was a sub-agent for Admiralty charts, ran a manufacturing business for nautical instruments, many of which she designed herself, and embarked on the business of compass adjusting at the height of the controversies generated by magnetic deviation and distortions on iron ships.

Her singular contribution to the maritime community and to the welfare of mariners was recognised in her being awarded gold medals (the highest award possible) by the King of Prussia, the King of The Netherlands and even by the Pope, culminating in the eventual award of a Civil List pension in her country, with the support of the Bishop of Durham. That her role was significant is also evident in that she was the only woman included among 2,200 entries in the encyclopaedic work, *The Mathematical Practitioners of Hanoverian England 1714–1840*, by Professor Eva G.R. Taylor, notwithstanding that Janet's contribution continued well after the 1840s, beyond the period considered by Professor Taylor.

Janet's entry into publishing began in 1833, at the age of twenty-nine, and she went on to produce a number of major works of importance to the maritime community, most of which went into many editions. There were seven editions of her first book, *Luni-Solar and Horary Tables* (or *Lunar Tables*) alone, appearing between 1833 and 1854. Her *Principles of Navigation Simplified: with Luni-Solar and Horary Tables*, first published in 1834 had three editions, while *An Epitome of Navigation and Nautical Astronomy* went to twelve editions between 1842 and 1859. Her *Planisphere of the Fixed Stars with Book of Directions*, with its beautiful plates of star charts, was first published in 1846 and reached its sixth edition in 1863. And then there were the *Diurnal Register for Barometer, Sympiesometer, Thermometer and Hygrometer* (seven editions); *A Guide Book to Lt Maury's Wind and Current Charts* (seven editions); and the *Handbook to the Local Marine Board Examinations for Officers of the British Mercantile Marine Board* (twenty-seven editions). Each was dedicated to a member of the royal family – King William IV, whose mother had sponsored Janet's scholarship as a child; Queen Adelaide; and the Duchess of Kent (then Princess Victoria's mother). This was a remarkable volume of work and, almost without exception, her work was highly praised and well received.

Her nautical tables – a vital tool in the determination of longitude at sea – were widely recognised as an invaluable aid to merchant seamen. She also discussed the use of the marine chronometer developed by John Harrison. In September 1834, Janet obtained a British patent for 'A Mariner's Calculator', claiming 'improvements in instruments for measuring angles and distances, applicable to nautical and other purposes'. Between 1617 and 1852 only seventy-nine patents were awarded in the category 'Compasses and Nautical

Instruments', the patents were awarded to renowned leaders in the field, but during this 235-year period Janet was the only woman.

Her Mariner's Calculator, an early type of computer, was an ingeniously clever concept, combining several nautical instruments in one. Janet delivered a prototype of her new device to the Admiralty for assessment, and it was given to their own Hydrographer, Captain Francis Beaufort. Captain Beaufort's report in May 1834 was not favourable. It was not that he thought it would not work but, in the 'clumsy fingers of seamen', he thought not. He also thought it would encourage slovenliness (perhaps because it would do too much of the hard work).

By 1845, the Taylors had opened business premises at 104 Minories where she sold a wide range of nautical and mathematical instruments, illustrated by an advertisement in the Mercantile Marine Magazine, October 1854, declaring that the firm manufactured 'every description of nautical and mathematical instruments'. It was in Minories that Janet also ran her 'Nautical Academy', which would continue for over thirty years.

Perhaps the most distinctive of Janet's instruments was the exquisite Prince of Wales quintant, entered for the Great Exhibition of 1851. It was much more than a working nautical instrument. Magnificent and flamboyantly ornate, it combined the principal aspirations of the exhibition in one, arts and manufacturing, and of the Royal Society that had championed the Exhibition. At the centre of the instrument was the Prince of Wales crest, '*Ich Dien*' (I serve), which was also on the box. The elegance of Janet's creation, however, was lost on the jury. In the section relating to 'Instruments made in the United Kingdom', it was simply reported that Janet had exhibited a sextant 'intended for show rather than use' and there was no mention of any award. The Prince himself was only eleven years old, but in time the instrument came to be presented to the Royal Family, and, in turn, it came to the National Maritime Museum in May 1936.

Janet's contributions in the maritime world also extended to compass adjusting. She ran a large compass adjusting business, based on the application of techniques for correcting magnets to counteract the effects of iron on ships' compasses advocated by the Astronomer Royal, Professor George Airy.

Janet Taylor passed away on 26 January 1870, at the Vicarage, St Helen Auckland, the home of her sister and brother-in-law, Canon Matthew Chester, the incumbent of the parish. Her death certificate recorded her occupation simply as 'Teacher of Navigation'. But she was far more than this. Her story is a remarkable one, especially for a woman in the nineteenth century.

Ruth Teitelbaum

Born: 1 January 1924
Died: 8 August 1986 (aged 62)

Ruth Lichterman was born in New York City, New York, on 1 January 1924, to Sarah and Simon Lichterman. She attended Hunter College and graduated with a bachelor's degree, majoring in mathematics. Soon after, she was hired by the Moore School of Electrical Engineering at the University of Pennsylvania, a school being funded by the U.S. Army during the Second World War. It was here that a group of about eighty women, known as 'computers', worked doing manual calculations of ballistic trajectories through complex differential calculations with the aid of desktop calculators, an analogue technology of the period. In 1945, the Army decided to fund an experimental project involving the first all-electronic digital computer. Six of the women 'computers' were selected to be its first programmers, including Ruth.

The computer on which the group worked was called ENIAC (Electronic Numerical Integrator and Computer), a machine with about 18,000 vacuum tubes and forty black 8ft (243 cm) panels. It was 8 ft (243 cm) tall and 80 ft (2.4 m) long. The total cost was about $487,000, equivalent to $8,000,000 in 2023. The construction contract was signed on 5 June 1943 and work on the computer began in secret at the University of Pennsylvania's Moore School of Electrical Engineering the following month, under the code name Project PX.

As the ENIAC project was classified, the programmers were denied access to the machine until they received their security clearances. As the first programmers, there were no programming manuals or courses, only the logical diagrams to help them determine how to make ENIAC work. This involved them physically programming the ballistics program by using the 3,000 switches and dozens of cables and digit trays to route the data and program pulses through the machine.

After the war, Ruth relocated with ENIAC to Aberdeen, Maryland, where she taught the next generation of ENIAC programmers. She worked closely with another programmer, Marlyn Meltzer and the pair performed a vital function for the 15 February 1946 demonstration to the world's public and press. This was to carry out a manual calculation to prove the machine was working properly. Their work helped debug the machine as the engineers and programmers prepared for the public unveiling. On the day, ENIAC ran the ballistics trajectory programmed by the six women with perfect results, captivating the world's imagination. The following year, ENIAC was turned into the world's first stored program computer and these six programmers were the only generation of programmers to program it at the machine level.

The women all left the program and most of them, including Ruth, did so to marry. Ruth remained for two more years to train future ENIAC programmers. She was the last of the original six to remain employed at Aberdeen, retiring on 10 September 1948 when she married Adolph Teitelbaum. Although the male engineers that built the machine soon became famous, little is known of the women programmers. To remedy this, the ENIAC Programmer Project was founded by lawyer and historian Kathy Kleiman, who devoted years to researching the University of Pennsylvania Archives and Library of Congress, as well as recording extensive broadcast-quality oral histories with four of the original six ENIAC programmers in the late 1990s with senior PBS Producer, David Roland. As she undertook the research, Kathy said that people kept coming forward 'with stories of grandmothers, their great aunts, their mothers – there were so many women involved in early technology that we don't know about.'

Kathy says that the women not only programmed the first computer, but 'dedicated years after the war to making programming easier and more accessible for all of us who followed'. In 2013, she teamed up with award-winning documentary producers Jon Palfreman and Kate McMahon of the Palfreman Film Group to tell this incredible story in *The Computers*.

On 9 August 1986, Ruth Teitelbaum passed away in Dallas, Texas, aged sixty-two, having received little credit for what she had achieved during her lifetime. In 1997, more than a decade after her death, Ruth was inducted into the Women in Technology International Hall of Fame, along with the other original ENIAC programmers. Ruth's husband, Adolph, accepted the award.

Janie Tsao

Born: 1953

Janie Tsao (née Wu Chien) was born in Wu Jian, Taiwan, and graduated with a Bachelor of Arts degree in English literature from the Tamkang University in Taiwan. It was at the university that she met her future husband and business associate, Victor Tsao. In 1975 the couple moved to the USA where they were married. They moved to Chicago in 1977, where they both attended graduate school.

The pair later relocated to California where Janie taught Information Technology at Sears Roebuck for eight years. She also worked as a systems manager at TRW and Carter Hawley Hale where she was responsible for the programming computer systems at seven retail outlet divisions, as well as mainframe systems among the division. At age 35, in April 1988, Janie quit this role to follow her idea for a product that would allow multiple computers to share a single printer. She and Victor started their company, that they named Linksys, out of their garage in Irvine, California.

By 1991 the business had done so well that Victor also quit his job to work full-time alongside Janie. Taking control of the company's sales, Janie persuaded the major retailers Fry's Electronics and Best Buy to sell Linksys products, in 1995 and 1996, respectively. These were very important deals for Linksys, enabling it to quadruple its revenue to US$21.5 million in 1996. Two years later it tripled this figure to US$65.6 million.

Janie developed Linksys' retail channel and oversaw the development of the company's distribution, e-commerce and international channel market strategies and programs. She also developed Linksys's broadband strategy, partnering with cable and telecom companies to 'provide high-speed Internet sharing access via wired or wireless solutions to PC users across the country'.

She partnered with leading cable and telecom companies including AT&T Broadband, Verizon, Charter, AOL, Time Warner, Sprint, Telus and British Telecom. These partnerships provided high-speed Internet sharing access via wired or wireless solutions to PC users across the US.

In 2000, Janie was named Entrepreneur of the Year by the Orange County Business Association and in 2002 she was awarded a BridgeGate 20 award which honoured the top 20 leaders that year. In a deal valued at over US$500 million, Janie and Victor sold their Linksys company to Cisco Systems where they continued to serve as senior vice presidents until 2007, when they retired. In 2004, the couple were jointly named Entrepreneur of the Year by *Inc.* magazine.

Janie served as the vice president of Worldwide Sales, Marketing and Business Development for the Linksys division of Cisco Systems, Inc., in the same way she had since she co-founded Linksys in April 1988. Between 1988 and 2004, Linksys grew to be the number one provider of networking hardware through consumer retail in North America, owning more than 40 per cent of the market. Linksys was then the leading vendor of wireless, broadband routers, USB and networking hardware in both the retail and e-commerce sales.

In 2005 Janie was the winner of the ABIE Award for Technical Leadership from the Anita Borg Institute. In the same year, Janie and Victor founded an investment firm Miven Venture Partners, the name derived from a combination of their sons' names, Michael and Steven. It invests in private equity, VC, hedge funds, real estate, and public securities.

In 2013 Linksys was sold to Belkin, which in turn in 2018 was acquired by Foxconn, the largest provider of electronics manufacturing services. Linksys products are sold direct-to-consumer from its website, through online retailers and marketplaces, as well as off-the-shelf in consumer electronics and big-box retail stores. As of 2021, Linksys products were sold in retail locations and value-added resellers in 64 countries and was the first router company to ship 100 million products.

Today, through the Tsao Family Foundation, Janie works with the Center for Asian American Media to produce documentaries 'promoting understanding and communication'.

Dana Lynn Ulery

Born: 2 January 1938

Dana Lynn Mueller was born in East Saint Louis, Illinois, USA, to her father Harry H. Tanzer Mueller, who died when she was two years old, and mother Meriam (Corn) Mueller. She attended Grinnell College, a small private liberal arts college in Grinnell, Iowa, and in 1959 graduated with a Bachelor of Arts, including a double major in mathematics and English literature. On 15 January the same year she married Harris Elsworth Ulery.

In 1961 Dana became the first female engineer at the NASA Jet Propulsion Laboratory in Pasadena, California, where she designed and developed algorithms to model NASA's Deep Space Network capabilities. She also became involved in automating real-time tracking systems for the Ranger and Mariner space missions using a North American Aviation Recomp II, 40-bit word size computer. During 1963 and 1964 she was a programmer for Getty Oil Company.

Dana then enrolled at the University of Delaware in Newark, graduating with a Master of Science in 1972 and a PhD in computer science in 1975. Following this she became a postdoctoral research associate at the university. Her thesis was titled 'Computer science's reincarnation of finite differences'. In 1976 Dana relocated to Egypt where she accepted visiting faculty appointments at Cairo University and the American University in Cairo. She then returned to the United States where she joined the Engineering Services Division of the DuPont Company, where she worked as a computer scientist and technical manager. In January 1979 she and Harris divorced, and on 29 February 1980 she married William Henry Fellner, an engineer at Dupont.

In the early 1980s, Dana's work at DuPont saw her leading initiatives to develop and deploy enterprise application systems to evaluate and control product quality. Her work was so outstanding that she was awarded the DuPont Engineering Award for Leadership of Corporate Quality Computer Systems.

Dana had an active involvement in the establishment of Electronic Data Interchange (EDI) standards that were set for electronically exchanging technical information used by business and government. She initiated and led multidisciplinary programs at the United States Army Research Laboratory (ARL) in Adelphi, Maryland, to commence research into multi-source information fusion and situational understanding applied to non-traditional battle environments and homeland defence.

During the 1990s, Dana served as the Pan American Delegate to the United Nations Electronic Data Interchange for Administration, Commerce, and Trade (UN/EDIFACT), a position she held for many years. She was Chair of both the UN/EDIFACT Multimedia Objects Working Group and the UN/EDIFACT Product Data Working Group, leading early international development of standards for electronic commerce. In 1999 she published two books: *BuyIt Software Development Plan: A C-BASS Component* and *ARL Intranet Analysis and Development Study*.

In 2007, Dana retired from her position as Chief Scientist of the Computational and Information Sciences Directorate at the United States Army Research Laboratory (ARL). She has two children with her former husband Harris, a daughter Terrie L. Ulery and son Bradford T. Ulery. A short biography of her life was published in 2017 in an article by Irina Nikivincze in 'Dana Ulery: Pioneer of Statistical Computing and Architect of Large, Complex Systems' in the *IEEE Annals of the History of Computing* (Volume 39, Issue: 2, 91 - 95).

Manuela Maria Veloso

Born: 12 August 1957

Manuela Maria Veloso was born and raised in Lisbon, Portugal, attending Lisbon's Instituto Superior Técnico from which she graduated with her Licenciatura (Bachelor of Science degree) in electrical engineering in 1980 and a Master of Science degree in electrical engineering in 1984. She then relocated to the USA where she received a Master of Arts in Computer Science from Boston University in 1986. From there she enrolled in the PhD program at Carnegie Mellon University located in Pittsburg, Pennsylvania, graduating with her doctorate in computer science in 1992. Her thesis, 'Learning by Analogical Reasoning in General Purpose Problem Solving', was supervised by the eminent computer scientist Jaime Carbonell.

Soon after receiving her PhD, Manuela was appointed as an assistant professor at the Carnegie Mellon School of Computer Science. Five years later she was promoted to associate professor and made a full professor in 2002. In the academic year 1999–2000 she was a visiting professor at the Massachusetts Institute of Technology (MIT) and was program co-chair of AAAI-05, held on 9–13 July 2005, in Pittsburgh. During 2006–2007 she was a Radcliffe Fellow of the Radcliffe Institute for Advanced Study at Harvard University. In 2009 she won the ACM/SIGART Autonomous Agents Research Award, and in 2013–2014 she held the post of visiting professor at the Center for Urban Science and Progress (CUSP) at New York University (NYU).

Manuela is one of only a handful of women whose research entails robotics and artificial intelligence at the highest levels. She has been President of the Association for the Advancement of Artificial Intelligence (AAAI) and co-founding trustee of the RoboCup Federation. 'We propose that the ultimate goal of the RoboCup Initiative be stated as follows: By the middle of the twenty-first century, a team of fully autonomous humanoid robot soccer players shall win a soccer game, complying with the official rules of FIFA, against the winner of the most recent World Cup.' Manuela's robot soccer teams have been RoboCup world champions on several occasions, while her CoBot mobile robots have autonomously navigated over than 1,000 kilometres throughout university buildings.

Manuela has been a member of the Editorial Board of both CACM and the AAAI Magazine. In 2015 she edited the book *Planning by Analogical Reasoning* (Springer-Verlag), described as 'the integration of analogical and case-based reasoning into general problem solving and planning as a method of speedup learning'. In 2016 she was appointed as the head of Carnegie Mellon's Machine Learning Department.

Manuela's research activities lie in the area of Artificial Intelligence, her long-term goal being 'the effective construction of autonomous agents where cognition, perception, and action are combined to address planning, execution, and learning tasks'. She also has a keen interest in the continuous integration of reactive, deliberative planning and control learning for teams of multiple agents acting in dynamic and uncertain environments. This includes adversarial modelling, reuse, and abstraction in control learning for multiple agents.

Her investigations include effective planning, execution, and learning algorithms for deterministic and nondeterministic multiagent domains within the research projects CORAL (Collaborate, Observe, Reason, Act, and Learn), MAPEL (Multi-Agent Planning, Execution, and Learning), and the MultiRobot Lab. To this end, she has used robot soccer to test her research, developing teams of robot soccer agents in three different leagues. She also researches the integration of planning and information retrieval, and the application of evolutionary computation and machine learning to the performance prediction of signal processing algorithms.

Manuela has been the recipient of many awards for her research, including the National Science Foundation CAREER Award (1995), the Allen Newell Medal for Excellence in Research (1997), being elected as an AAAI Fellow (2003) and a Fellow of the Institute of Electrical and Electronics Engineers (IEEE) (2010) and American Association for the Advancement of Science (AAAS) (2010). In 2009 she won the ACM/SIGART Autonomous Agents Research Award and in 2012 was appointed as the Einstein Chair Professor at the Chinese Academy of Sciences. She was made a Fellow of the ACM in 2016 for 'contributions to the field of artificial intelligence, in particular in planning, learning, multi-agent systems, and robotics'. In 2018 she took a leave of absence to join J.P. Morgan.

Manuela is featured in the Notable Women in Computing cards and in 2021 was named among the most influential women in engineering, according to a new list compiled by Academic Influence. She is married to José Manuel Fonseca and they have two children, André Veloso and Pedro Veloso.

Mary Allen Wilkes

Born: 25 September 1937

Mary Allen Wilkes was born in Chicago, Illinois, and graduated from Wellesley College in 1959 where she majored in philosophy and theology. At first she had ambitions to be a lawyer, but was discouraged by friends from entering the legal profession as women faced significant challenges and a lack of opportunities. Instead, she took the advice of her eighth-grade geography teacher who told her: 'Mary Allen, when you grow up, you ought to be a computer programmer.'

Mary then looked for employment in a field other than law and after she graduated from high school her parents drove her to the Massachusetts Institute of Technology (MIT), where she inquired about programming jobs. She was hired in 1959 to work under the direction of Oliver Selfridge and Benjamin Gold on the Speech Recognition Project at their Lincoln Laboratory in Lexington, Massachusetts. During 1959 and 1960, she programmed the IBM 704 and the IBM 709 computers, joining the laboratory's Digital Computer Group. In June 1961, work commenced on the LINC (Laboratory INstrument Computer) design under American physicist Wesley A. Clark who had earlier designed Lincoln's TX-0 and TX-2 computers.

In the summer of 1964, a small group from the LINC development team, including Mary, left MIT to form the Computer Systems Laboratory at Washington University in St. Louis. Mary had spent 1964 travelling around the world, rejoining the group later in the year, although she lived and worked from her parents' home in Baltimore until late 1965. During that time the team had doubled the size of the LINC memory to 2048 12-bit words. This enabled Mary to develop the more sophisticated operating system LAP6, which incorporated a scroll editing technique that utilised an algorithm proposed by her colleagues, Mishell J. Stucki and Severo M. Ornstein.

Mary made a number of important contributions to the LINC development, including simulating the operation of the LINC during its design phase on the TX-2, designing the console for the prototype LINC and authoring the operation manual for the final console design.

It is speculated that the LINC may well have been the first 'personal computer' as it had its own monitor, keyboard, and storage. In addition, it was intended for use by individuals, unlike a giant timesharing computer that required punch cards. One of Mary's more notable quotes is 'We had the quaint notion at the time that software should be completely, absolutely free of bugs. Unfortunately, it's a notion that never really quite caught on.'

In 1972 Mary left the field of computing to enrol in the Harvard Law School from which she graduated with a law degree. She practised as a trial lawyer for many years, both privately and as head of the Economic Crime and Consumer Protection Division of the Middlesex County District Attorney's Office in Massachusetts. Between 1983 and 2011 she also lectured in the Trial Advocacy Program at the Harvard Law School, as well sitting as a judge for the school's first- and second-year Ames (moot court) competition for 18 years.

Mary became an arbitrator for the American Arbitration Association in 2001, primarily being involved in cases involving computer science and information technology. Between 2005 and 2012, she served as a judge of the Annual Willem C. VIS International Commercial Arbitration Moot competition in Vienna, Austria, organised by Pace University Law School located in White Plains, New York.

Mary's achievements have been honoured in several ways, including the 2013 Great Britain's National Museum of Computing's exhibition 'Heroines of Computing' at Bletchley Park. In its 2015–16 exhibition, she was recognised by the Heinz Nixdorf MuseumsForum in Paderborn, Germany, in *Am Anfang war Ada: Frauen in der Computergeschichte* (In the beginning was Ada: Women in Computer History).

Sophie Wilson

Born: 1957

Born Roger Wilson, Sophie Wilson was born and raised in Leeds, Yorkshire, England. Her parents were both schoolteachers, her father in English and her mother in physics. An outstanding mathematics student, in 1975 at age 18 Sophie studied computer science and the Mathematical Tripos at Selwyn College, Cambridge University. She was also a member of their Microprocessor society and designed a microcomputer with a MOS Technology 6502 microprocessor during her Easter break there.

Sophie created a device that prevented cigarette lighter sparks triggering payouts on poker machines and in 1978 joined Acorn Computers Ltd where her computer designs were used to construct the first of many computers sold by the company. In 1981 Sophie enhanced the Acorn Atom's BASIC programming language into an improved version for the Acorn Proton microcomputer. Over a three-day period, she designed the system including the circuit board and components that required fast new DRAM integrated circuits to be sourced directly from Hitachi. By the evening she had constructed a prototype, spending the following 24 hours debugging the software.

As a result of her work, Acorn was awarded a contract with the British Broadcasting Corporation (BBC) for their national Computer Literacy Project. She was present backstage when the Proton computer made its first appearance on television, being on hand in case any issues arose. She later described the experience as 'a unique moment in time when the public wanted to know how this stuff works and could be shown and taught how to program.'

The Proton computer became the 'BBC Micro' and its BASIC language evolved into 'BBC BASIC', and for the following 15 years she oversaw its development, including producing instruction manuals and technical specifications. In 1983 she began designing the instruction set for one of the first reduced instruction set computer (RISC) processors, the Acorn RISC Machine ARM. The ARM1 computer worked the first time in April 1985. The processor later became one of the most successful IP cores, a licensed CPU core, and 95% of smartphones were using it by 2012. The video architecture Sophie designed was known as Acorn Replay and included operating system extensions for video access, as well as the codecs, optimised to run high frame rate video on ARM CPUs from the ARM 2 onwards.

Sophie was a board member of the technology and games company Eidos plc, which bought and created Eidos Interactive, for the years following its flotation in 1990. She was a consultant to ARM Ltd when, in 1990, it separated from Acorn. In January 1999, Acorn Computers Limited was renamed Element 14 Limited and was later purchased by Broadcom, going on to win most of the Central Office DSL business. Sophie was the driving force behind Broadcom's Firepath processor. Acorn remained active in various forms until it was dissolved in December 2015.

In 1994 Sophie underwent gender reassignment surgery. She has received many honours for her outstanding achievements, including in 2012 the Fellow Award by the Computer History Museum in California for 'her work, with Steve Furber, on the BBC Micro computer and the ARM processor architecture.' In the following year she was elected as a Fellow of the prestigious Royal Society and in 2014 received the Lovie Lifetime Achievement Award in acknowledgement for her invention of the ARM processor. Cambridge University awarded her an honorary Doctor of Science.

Sophie became an honorary fellow of her alma mater, Selwyn College, Cambridge, in 2016, and was one of the women profiled in the Women in Computing Festival 2017. In the June 2019 Birthday Honours she was appointed Commander of the Order of the British Empire (CBE) for services to computing. In 2020, she was honoured as a Distinguished Fellow of the British Computer Society and now serves as the Director of IC Design in Broadcom's Cambridge, UK, office. In her private life she enjoys photography and is involved in a local theatre group, where she oversees costumes and set pieces. She has also acted in several productions. Of her philosophy in life:

'You can have anything you want if you want it badly enough. You can be anything you want to be, do anything you set out to accomplish if you hold to that desire with singleness of purpose.' Not my own words, Abraham Lincoln says it better than I could. Your life is defined by what you do – actions speak louder than words and just knowing is not enough. Be a doer, be creative, be persistent, believe in yourself.

Anna Winlock

Born: 15 September 1857
Died: 4 January 1904 (aged 46)

Anna Winlock was born in Cambridge, Massachusetts, the eldest of five children of astronomer Joseph Winlock, the third director of the Harvard College Observatory, and Isabella Lane Winlock. She had a distinguished ancestry. On both sides of the family her lineage could be traced back to old families in Virginia that helped to win America's independence, as well as founding the states of Kentucky and Missouri. Anna attended the Cambridge Schools as a child and developed an interest in both mathematics and Greek.

Joseph encouraged her interest in astronomy, taking her at age twelve to attend a solar eclipse in his home state of Kentucky. Not long after Anna graduated from high school, in June 1875 her father passed away and she now became the one to provide financial support for her mother and four siblings. She approached the Harvard College Observatory seeking a job in calculations as they had decades worth of data in a condition that rendered them useless.

Anna demonstrated that she could reduce these observations that her father had left unfinished. He had introduced her to the principles of mathematical astronomy and so she was an attractive proposition to the observatory, especially as she could be paid less than half the then prevailing rate for performing calculations. She was offered a pay rate of twenty-five cents an hour to do the computations and she accepted the position. In doing so, she became one of the first female paid staff members of the Harvard College Observatory.

Following the death of Anna's father Joseph, Edward Charles Pickering became the next director of the Harvard Observatory in 1877 and realised that the volume of data coming in was exceeding his staff's ability to analyse it. In less than a year, Anna was joined at the observatory by three other women who also served as 'computers', becoming known as Pickering's Harem. They gained fame by producing high quality output despite the low wages and arduousness of the work.

Anna was a great believer that women were quite capable of carrying out important work in astronomy. She demonstrated her outstanding abilities as a scientist and left a lasting legacy in the work carried out by the observatory. In particular, she made the most complete catalogue of stars near the north and south poles of her era. She also performed complex calculations and studies of asteroids, including a determination of the path of the asteroid Eros, one of the largest inner asteroids. Anna found the circular orbit for the asteroid Ocllo, later assisting in determining its elliptical elements. She contributed to many other projects, one of which involved the continuous and arduous task of reducing and computing meridian circle observations.

Five years before she commenced work at the observatory, her father oversaw a project that involved collaboration with multiple countries to prepare a comprehensive catalogue of stars. This mission was divided into sections or zones by circles parallel to the celestial equator, and one of Anna's first tasks was to commence work on the section called the 'Cambridge Zone'. She worked on this mission for over twenty years.

The work done by her team on the Cambridge Zone contributed significantly to the Astronomische Gesellschaft Katalog (AGK), a catalogue that contains information on more than one hundred thousand stars and is still used worldwide by many observatories and their researchers. In addition, Anna supervised the creation of the Observatory Annals (a collection of tables that provide the positions of variable stars in clusters) into 38 volumes.

Anna's career at the Harvard College Observatory spanned thirty years. Throughout his tenure from 1877 to his death in 1919, Pickering employed more than 80 women as his 'human computers'.

Anna passed away unexpectedly at age 46 on 4 January 1904 during a visit to the Harvard College Observatory. She had worked through the holiday season and her last notebook entry was on New Year's Day. Her funeral service was held at St John's Chapel in Cambridge. She was a talented observer, mathematician, calculator, and analyst of astronomical data with the ability to take large amounts of raw information and assimilate it into a more accessible form.

Beatrice Worsley

Born: 18 October 1921
Died: 8 May 1972 (aged 50)

Beatrice ('Trixie') Helen Worsley was born in Querétaro, Mexico. While her father, Joel Worsley was born in Manchester, England, he moved with his wife Beatrice Marie (née Trinker) to Xia in Mexico where he worked at her family's textile mill. It was destroyed in 1917 by Mexican rebels, after which the family relocated to El Salto, also in Mexico. It was here that their son Charles Robert was born in 1920, and daughter Beatrice Helen in the following year. The family kept to themselves and had little to do with their neighbours, reportedly for security reasons. As a result, both Beatrice and Charles were home schooled, but their parents were determined to find a better educational arrangement for them. This meant leaving Mexico.

In 1929 the family moved to Toronto, Ontario, where 8-year-old Beatrice enrolled at Brown Public School. In 1935 she switched to Bishop Strachan School, an Anglican day and boarding school for girls. She elected to enrol in the more challenging of the two options on offer, this being the one involving courses for university preparation. Her results were outstanding, the principal declaring that she was one of the best students ever to attend the school. In 1939 she graduated with awards in mathematics, science, and Divinity English, as well as winning the Governor General's Award for having the highest overall grade.

As a result of her high school performance, Beatrice was awarded the Burnside Scholarship in Science from Trinity College, part of the University of Toronto, and in September 1939 at age 17, commenced her undergraduate studies there. Her exceptional performance in the first year of study won her the first Alexander T. Fulton Scholarship in Science. The following year she transferred to the more applied division of

Mathematics and Physics and was awarded the James Scott Scholarship in Mathematics and Physics at the end of her third year. In 1942 she took a summer vacation job in the actuarial department of the Manufacturers Life Insurance Company in Toronto, and it was here that she first encountered mechanical calculators. By the time she had graduated with a Bachelor of Science in 1944, Beatrice had an astonishing record of earning the highest mark in every class, every year.

Following graduation, Beatrice enlisted in the Women's Royal Canadian Naval Service ('Wrens') and, after completing winter basic training at HMCS *Conestoga* in Galt (now Cambridge, Ontario), she was assigned to the Naval Research Establishment (NRE) in Halifax. Here she researched, among other things, torpedo guidance systems. The next five months were spent at sea, mainly on defences and degaussing (the process of decreasing or eliminating a remnant magnetic field). Her time was largely spent on the NRE's Bangor-class minesweeper, HMCS *Quinte*. After the conclusion of the Second World War, Beatrice was the only Wren to remain in service, and in September 1945 was assigned to a new project examining hull corrosion. She was also promoted to the rank of lieutenant.

Beatrice left the service in August 1946 and enrolled in a one-year master's program in mathematics and physics at MIT, her subjects including solid-state physics. Under the supervision of Henry Wallman, a member of the renowned MIT Radiation Laboratory, she completed her thesis 'A Mathematical Survey of Computing Devices with an Appendix on Error Analysis of Differential Analyzers'. It examined essentially every computer that existed at the time. She then returned to Canada and explained to her family that she wanted to work with computers, despite there then being no computing industry in the country. She accepted a position in the aerodynamics department with the National Research Council of Canada (NRC).

Meanwhile, the University of Toronto was developing its own interest in computers, and in September 1947 the NRC provided funds for it to purchase two IBM punch card mechanical calculators and two assistants to operate them. In January 1948 Beatrice successfully applied for one of these positions (the other going to J. Perham Stanley), with one of her first tasks involving a contract to provide computational support to the Atomic Energy of Canada (AECL). This involved Beatrice and Stanley constructing a differential analyser from Meccano parts in the summer of 1948. Following that, the pair were sent to Cambridge University's Mathematical Laboratory which was building an Electronic Delay Storage Automatic Calculator (EDSAC). Their involvement was mainly to help bring it online for its first test run on 6 May 1949.

Beatrice assisted in writing the first program to successfully calculate the squares of numbers as well as tables of primes. Her programming code made her recognised in the field. She then enrolled in the PhD program at Newnham College at Cambridge University while still working in the laboratory. Her initial supervisor was the numerical analyst Douglas Hartree, but she returned to Canada to continue her research under Byron Griffith at the University of Toronto. In 1951 she was rehired by the Computation Centre there and obtained her PhD, with the approval of Hartee, from the University of Cambridge in 1952. Her thesis, 'Serial Programming for Real and Idealized Digital Calculating Machines', is reportedly the first PhD dissertation written about modern computers. Apart from Hartee, her co-supervisor was the eminent mathematician and computer scientist Alan Turing.

In the summer of 1952, a computer designated 'FERUT' (Ferranti Electronic computer at the University of Toronto) was in operation and was at the time one of the most powerful computers in the world. In autumn 1953, Beatrice and Patterson Hume designed a new computer language, Transcode, to perform its operations. This was an improvement on previous languages as it enabled programmers to enter numbers in decimal form and they could be converted to binary and back again.

Despite her outstanding work, Beatrice had great difficulty in gaining promotion at the University of Toronto, and it was not until 1960 that she was promoted from a staff member to an academic position as assistant professor. It took four more years for her promotion to associate professor of physics and computer science, in the same year the university began its graduate studies in computer science.

In 1965, Beatrice was offered a position at Queen's University in Kinston, Ontario, where she assisted in the launch of their new Computer Centre based on an IBM 1620, an inexpensive computer used mainly in education and research. However, Beatrice spent most of her time teaching in the classroom, and in 1971 she earned a sabbatical at the Department of Applied Analysis and Computer Science at the University of Waterloo.

While there, Beatrice suffered a fatal heart attack and passed away at age 50 on 8 May 1972. She was a remarkable pioneer, being the first female computer scientist in Canada. In 2014, she was posthumously awarded the Lifetime Achievement Award in Computer Science by the Canadian Association of Computer Science.

Irma Wyman

Born: 31 January 1928
Died: 17 November 2015 (aged 87)

Irma M. Wyman was born in Detroit, Michigan, the only child of a German family. Mother Marie and father Max worked in a bakery. She completed high school during the Second World War and, as there were few male students, it made it easier for her to enrol at university. In 1945, Irma was awarded a Regents Scholarship and was accepted into the College of Engineering at the University of Michigan, along with six other female students.

Unfortunately, her scholarship was not enough to cover her financial needs that included paying for books and accommodation. To supplement her income, during her studies Irma worked as a waitress and switchboard operator in her residence hall, later remarking that she was 'living as leanly as I could and working as much as I could, wherever I could'. She soon became aware of the discrimination against women when she did not gain equal access to resources and study partners in a field that was dominated by males. Despite a lack of support, her outstanding grades saw her qualify for membership in Tau Beta Pi, the engineering honour society. As women were not permitted to join, she was awarded with a 'Women's badge'. To make matters worse, one of her professors shared his view that women had no place in engineering and, that no matter what she did, she would fail his class. Naturally, she dropped his subject. But he wasn't alone in his thinking, as her mother received a letter from the dean of women, expressing extreme disapproval of Irma's choice of major.

In her third year of study, she worked on a missile guidance project at the Willow Run Research Center in Detroit. At the time, mechanical calculators were used to determine the trajectories, although that was about to change

253

with the emergence of computers, including the Mark II developed at Harvard University. Irma became attracted to the concept of computing:

> I became an enthusiastic pioneer in this new technology, and it led to my life's career... I grew up being told that I would never go to college, that I shouldn't get my hopes up, that there would be no possibility of me doing that. I felt that if I gave up, I would be rewarding all these people who said I couldn't do it, I shouldn't do it.

In 1949 she graduated as one of the first two women with a BSE EngMath from the University of Michigan's College of Engineering. The other, Mildred 'Dennie' F. Denecke, received a BSE Phys, and she and Irma became lifelong friends. Of the seven females that had started the degree, five either married and dropped out or changed their major.

After graduation, Irma couldn't find an employer who would hire a female engineer and so she continued working for the Willow Run Research Center. In the mid-1950s she joined a start-up company in Boston that was eventually acquired by Honeywell Information Systems based in Minneapolis, Minnesota. Initially based in Boston, this was to be her career profession and heralded the beginning of a long management role at Honeywell. Between 1953 and 1980 she became thoroughly familiar with every facet of the computer business, including design, manufacturing, maintenance, patents and sales. After she demonstrated the Datamatic 1000, a computer designed for commercial work with an ability to handle large tape files and tape sorts to US Treasury's Savings Bond division officials, they purchased one.

In 1980 Irma relocated to Honeywell's corporate headquarters in Minneapolis and was promoted in 1982 to the role of Chief Information Officer (CIO) and Vice-President, the first woman to hold that position. She retired in 1990 at age 62.

After retirement, Irma was ordained in 1990 as a Deacon in the Episcopal Church of Minnesota, and in 1998 was appointed as the first Archdeacon for the Diaconate in their history, serving in that position until 2008.

In 1996, she established the Irma M. Wyman Scholarship Fund at CEW+ (Center for the Education of Women) to support women in engineering, computer science and related fields at the University of Michigan. In 2001 she was awarded the Michigan Engineering Alumni Society Medal. In 2007 Irma relocated to Cornelia House at Episcopal Homes in St. Paul where she became an integral part of the community. In the same year she was awarded an Honorary Doctor of Engineering from the University of Michigan.

In a 2011 interview with CEW, she outlined her ambition to be a strong supporter of women in STEM fields, and her understanding of the difficulties and importance of being given a chance at success: 'Since my life had been transformed by a scholarship, I knew exactly what the impact of that was on a person. And being female, I wanted to assist other women who were perhaps getting into the same kinds of challenges that I was.'

After suffering a stroke, Irma passed away at age 87 on 17 November 2015 at United Hospital, St Paul, Minnesota.

Kateryna Yushchenko

Born: 8 December 1919
Died: 15 August 2001 (aged 81)

Kateryna L. Yushchenko was born in the former capital of the Cossacks in Chigirin, Soviet Union. Her father, Logvin Rvachev, was a teacher of history and geography. When Kateryna was aged 17, Logvin was arrested in 1937 as a Ukrainian nationalist, resulting in her being expelled from the first year of her course in the department of Physics and Mathematics at Kyiv University. The reason provided inferred that she was 'an enemy of the people'. Her parents were sentenced to ten years in prison, only overturned in 1954 with the death of Stalin and lack of evidence that they had committed any crime.

Although Kateryna was considered as the daughter of enemies of the people, she then applied to the University of Moscow and was accepted. However, she could not attend as they did not provide accommodation. As a result she relocated to Uzbekistan, where the local university was offering scholarships, room and board to anyone who wanted to study. And so, in the summer of 1938, she enrolled at the Uzbek State University in Samarkand, which during the war amalgamated with the Central Asia State University in Tashkent. She also found employment at a military plant that produced the scopes for tank guns. She graduated with a degree in mathematics in 1942.

At the conclusion of the war, Kateryna returned to Ukraine just in time for the opening of the Lviv Branch of the Institute of Mathematics of the Ukrainian Academy of Sciences. She was employed by Boris Vladimirovich Gnedenko in the Department of Probability Theory and in 1950 graduated with a PhD under the supervision of Boris Gnedenko and Viktor Glushkov, making her the first woman in the USSR to become a Doctor of Physical and Mathematical Sciences in programming. In the same year she was invited to join Gnedenko at the Kyiv Institute of Mathematics of the Ukrainian Academy of Sciences where he had been transferred.

In the following years, the Kyiv Institute was involved in the early construction of satellites that required complex calculations. To this end, they purchased a set of punch machines, installing them in the basement of the Ukrainian Academy of Sciences building. Kateryna was appointed as Director of this Computing Laboratory in Levedev where they built the first universally programmable electronic computer, MESM, in the Soviet Union and possibly in continental Europe.

In 1954 B.V. Gnedenko suggested that the Levedev Laboratory be transferred to the Institute of Mathematics. Kateryna became part of the group that operated the MESM, the computer comprising about 6000 vacuum tubes and having the ability to perform around 3000 operations per minute. It was 10 metres in length and 2 metres tall, occupying around 60 square metres.

As impressive as the MESM was for its time, it suffered from a low speed and insufficient memory, requiring the development of an internal 'high-level' programming language to interact better with humans. In the process, it became clear that the more complex tasks were difficult to solve just by writing simple machine programs. There was a problem in developing the high-level language: the absence of an appropriate translator for better human/computer communication. L.I. Kaluzhnin, a professor at Kyiv University, who taught the course on mathematical logic in the 1950–70s, made a significant advance in the understanding of this problem and formalised a scheme of interfacing with the program. Consequently, in 1955 Kateryna and V.S. Korolyuk created an 'Address language' which became the first fundamental achievement of the Scientific School of Theoretical Programming. The Address language was used extensively in the Soviet Union for more than two decades.

In 1961 Kateryna was the co-author (with B.V. Gnedenko and V.S. Korolyuk) of the first Soviet textbook on programming, *The Elements of Programming*. The book was published in 1961 and reprinted in 1964 when it was also translated and published in the GDR (German Democratic Republic), as well as in Hungary and in France in 1969. In 1976 Kateryna was elected as a Member of the USSR Academy of Sciences and member of The International Academy of Computer Science.

Kateryna received many honours for her achievements, including the Prize of the USSR Council of Ministers, the Prize of Academic Glushkov for her work in computing algebra, and the Order of Princess Olga, a Ukrainian civil decoration, featuring Olga of Kiev and bestowed to women for 'personal merits in state, production, scientific, educational, cultural, charity and other spheres of social activities, for upbringing children in families'.

To assist new computer programmers, Kateryna wrote an educational series of textbooks in the 1970s and was also a prolific researcher and author, serving as a mentor to 45 Doctors of Philosophy and 11 Doctors of Sciences. She held five Copyright Certificates, which developed eight State Standards of Ukraine. Her publications included over 200 manuscripts, including 23 monographs and training aids.

Kateryna passed away at age 81 on 15 August 2001.

Lixia Zhang

Born: 16 June 1951

Lixia Zhang was born in Shanxi in the People's Republic of China and was raised in the northern part of the country. When the Cultural Revolution closed high schools and colleges, she worked as a tractor driver on a farm, this being her first paid job. She later remarked: 'Luckily, my elders privately encouraged me to study and told me science moves humanity forward.' Taking their advice, she taught herself English and calculus, and in 1976 was awarded a Bachelor of Science degree from Heilongjiang University in Harbin, China. In 1978 she passed the nationwide graduate-school entrance exam with the highest scores and was selected to study in the USA. Life for her there had its challenges in the early times as her English was far from fluent and there were gaps in her knowledge.

Relocating, she enrolled at California State University, Los Angeles, graduating in 1981 with a master's degree in electrical engineering. She then attended Massachusetts Institute of Technology (MIT) where she completed her PhD in 1989 under the supervision of the eminent computer scientist David D. Clark who was also a pioneer of the Internet. Lixia described him as 'a magical teacher who guided and supported me for eight years. He taught me what the Internet is.'

During her studies, in 1986 she was the only woman and only student to attend the initial meeting of the Internet Engineering Task Force (IETF). Although her early work involved routing, her PhD dissertation considered quality of service. Following her doctorate, Lixia worked as a researcher at Xerox PARC (Palo Alto Research Center). Between 1994 and 1996 she was a member of the Internet Architecture Board and in 1994 won the Xerox Excellence in Science and Technology Award.

In 1999 Lixia devised the term 'middlebox', referring to any computer networking device that performs functions other than that of a regular internet protocol router. Her term is now widely used and includes firewalls and network address translators. She also designed a protocol for changing the settings in an experimental network setup, thereby forming the basis for the Resource Reservation Protocol (RRP). In September 1993, Lixia, along with co-authors Steve Deering, Deborah Estrin, Scott Shenker, and Daniel Zappala, published a ground-breaking article on the protocol, 'RSVP: A New Resource ReSerVation Protocol' in the journal *IEEE Network*, Vol. 7, Issue 5, pp.8-18. In 2002, it was selected as one of ten landmark articles, and it was reprinted with commentary in the 50th-anniversary issue of *IEEE Communications Magazine*.

Since 2006 Lixia has been a Fellow of the Association for Computing Machinery (ACM) and Institute of Electrical and Electronics Engineers (IEEE). She was again a member of the Internet Architecture Board between 2005 and 2009. In her final year she won the IEEE Internet Award and since 2010 has pioneered the design and development of a multi-campus research project Named Data Networking (NDN), a new internet protocol architecture funded by the National Science Foundation (NSF) in the USA.

In 2012, Lixia was appointed as the Jonathan B. Postel Professor of Computer Science at the University of California, Los Angeles. In 2014 she was featured in the Notable Women in Computing cards, her photo appearing on the four of diamonds.

She was selected in 2015 to be on the N2Women (Networking Networking Women) list of '10 Women You Should Know in Networking and Communications' and was acknowledged as one of the top 100 US computer scientists based on publication H-Index in 2018. Lixia won the ACM SIGCOMM (Association for Computing Machinery's Special Interest Group on Data Communications) Lifetime Achievement Award for 'pioneering work in Internet protocol development' in 2020.

Lixia lives with her husband, Jim Ma, in Sherman Oaks, California. They have two sons, Shawn, and Zane. She has a passion for reading especially the renowned Feynman Lectures on Physics series, remarking that they 'teach me not only physics, but how to look at problems and conduct research'. Her career goal is to help the growth of the Internet.

Bibliography

General

Alice, Margaret, *Hypatia's Heritage: A History of Women in Science from Antiquity to the Late Nineteenth Century* (USA: Beacon Press, 2001).

Biographies of Women Mathematicians <https://www.agnesscott.edu/lriddle/women/women.htm>. (An excellent website with links to many other resources.)

Contributions of 20th Century Women in Physics < http://cwp.library.ucla.edu/>. (Another website with excellent links.)

Croucher, John, *Women of Science: 100 Inspirational Lives* (Amberley, 2019).

Ignotofsky, Rachel, *Women in Science* (Berkeley: Ten Speed Press, 2016).

Jones, Claire G., Martin, Alison E., Wolf, Alexis, (eds.) *The Palgrave Handbook of Women and Science since 1660* (Palgrave McMillan, 2022).

Latta, Susan. M., *Bold Women of Medicine: 21 Stories of Astounding Discoveries, Daring Surgeries, and Healing Breakthroughs* (Chicago Review Press, 2017).

McGrayne, Sharon Bertsch, *Nobel Prize Women in Science: Their Lives, Struggles, and Momentous Discoveries* (USA: National Academies Press, 2001).

Ogilvie, Marylin Bailey, *Women in Science: Antiquity through the Nineteenth Century, A Biographical Dictionary with an Annotated Bibliography* (The MIT Press, 1990).

Rossiter, Margaret W., *Women Scientists in America: Before Affirmative Action, 1940-1972* (John Hopkins University Press, 1998).

Saini, Angela, *Inferior: How Science Got Women Wrong—and the New Research that's Rewriting the Story* (Beacon Press, 2017).

Swaby, Rachel, *Headstrong, 52 Women Who Changed Science and the World* (New York Broadway Books, 2015).

Wasserman, Elga R., *The Door in the Dream: Conversations with Eminent Women in Science* (Joseph Henry Press, 2000).

Yount, Lisa, *A to Z of Women in Science and Math* (Infobase, 1999)

Revolvy, <https://www.revolvy.com/>.

Sarah Allen

'Meet Sarah Allen, Presidential Innovation Fellow at The Smithsonian Institute' (Hackbright Academy, 14 November 2013) <https://blog.hackbrightacademy.com/blog/sarah-allen-2013-presidential-innovation-fellow-smithsonian/>.

'Sarah Allen Co-Creator of Adobe After Effects/Shockwave Flash Video' *Code Sync* <*https://codesync.global/speaker/sarah-allen/*>.

'Sarah Allen' *Linked in* <*https://www.linkedin.com/in/ultrasaurus*>.

Ruth Leach Amonette

'Biography for Ruth Amonette' *IBM* <*https://www.ibm.com/ibm/history/witexhibit/wit_hall_amonette.html*>.

Raftery, Tom, 'Can IBM continue to support blatant sexual discrimination?' Tom Raftery's – Things to Come <https://tomraftery.com/2012/04/>.

'Ruth Leach Amonette' *Monterey Herald* <*https://www.legacy.com/obituaries/montereyherald/obituary.aspx?n=ruth-leach-amonette&pid=2364302*>.

Kathleen 'Kay' McNulty Mauchly Antonelli

J J O'Connor and Robertson, E F (*Mac Tutor*, March 2021) <*Kathleen McNulty Antonelli (1921 - 2006) - Biography - MacTutor History of Mathematics (st-andrews.ac.uk)*>.

Harkin, Sofia, 'Kathleen McNulty Antonelli, a Pioneer of the Computer Revolution' (Lottie, 12 June 2017) <*https://www.lottie.com/blogs/strong-women/kathleen-antonelli-mcnulty*>.

'Kathleen 'Kay' McNulty Mauchly Antonelli' *Urban Funeral Home* < https://www.urbanfuneralhome.com/obituary/34700/Kathleen-Kay-Antonelli/>.

'Kay McNulty, ENIAC superhero' (*Code Like a Woman*, 22 August 2016) <*https://codelikeawoman.wordpress.com/2016/08/22/kay-mcnulty-eniac-superhero/.*>

Růžena Bajcsy

Abbate, Janet, 'Oral History Růžena Bajcsy 2002' (*IEEE History Center*, 9 July 2002) <*https://ethw.org/Oral-History:Ruzena_Bajcsy_(2002) *>.

'Ruzena Bajcsy' *Dplp* <https://dblp.org/pid/b/RuzenaBajcsy.html>.

'Professor Růžena Bajcsy' Memory of Nations <*https://www.memoryofnations.eu/en/bajcsy-ruzena-1933*>.

'Ruzena Bajcsy' Ncwit.org <*https://ncwit.org/profile/ruzena-bajcsy/*>.

Joan Ball

Hicks, Mar, 'Computer Love: Replicating Social Order Through Early Computer Dating Systems'. *Ada: A Journal of Gender, New Media, and Technology*, No. 10 (2016).
<*https://adanewmedia.org/2016/10/issue10-hicks/*>.
Hicks, Mar., 'The Mother of All Swipes' (*Logic Magazine*, 1 July 2017).
<*https://logicmag.io/sex/the-mother-of-all-swipes/*>.

Jean Bartik

Bartik, Jean Jennings, 'Pioneer Programmer: Jean Jennings Bartik and the Computer That Changed the World' (Truman State University Press, 2014).
'Jean Jennings Bartik' Computer History Museum <*https://computerhistory. org/profile/jean-jennings-bartik/*>.
'Jean Bartik, Biography' <*https://ethw.org/Jean_Bartik*>.
Juavinett, Ashley, '5 facts about Jean Bartik' (*Massive Science*, 7 October 2017).
<*https://next.massivesci.com/articles/jean-bartik-eniac-programmer/*>.
O'Connor, J J and Robertson, E F, (*Mac Tutor*, July 2012) 'Betty Jean Jennings Bartik'
<*https://mathshistory.st-andrews.ac.uk/Biographies/Bartik/*>.

Carol Bartz

Clancy, Heather. 'Icon: Carol Bartz, former CEO, Autodesk and Yahoo!' (*Smart Planet*, Issue 21, 1 July 2013)
Long, Robert M. 'Everything You Want to Know About the Life of Carol Bartz' (*Vizaca*, 23 February 2021) <*https://www.vizaca.com/life-of-carol-bartz/*>.
'Computer History Museum, Carol Bartz' <*https://computerhistory.org/profile/carol-bartz/*>.
Hasse, Javier, 'Former Yahoo CEO Carol Bartz Shares Advice for Cannabis Entrepreneurs: 'You Have To Have Some Cojones' (*Benzinga*, 18 July 2021). <*https://www.benzinga.com/markets/cannabis/20/07/16616614/former-yahoo-ceo-carol-bartz-shares-advice-for-cannabis-entrepreneurs-you-have-to-have-some-cojo*>.
'Wisconsin Women Making History' <https://womeninwisconsin.org/profile/carol-bartz/>.

Mavis Batey

Crypto Museum < *https://cryptomuseum.com/people/mavis_batey.htm*>.
Smith Michael, 'Mavis Batey obituary' (*The Guardian*, 21 November 2013) <*https://www.theguardian.com/world/2013/nov/20/mavis-batey*>.
'Cracking the codes of gardens: The life of Mavis Batey' <*https://london.ac.uk/news-and-opinion/leading-women/cracking-codes-gardens-life-mavis-batey*>.

'The Heroine Collective. Biography: Mavis Batey – Code-Breaker' *<http://www.theheroinecollective.com/mavis-batey/>*.

Gwen Bell

Bell, Gwen and Bell, Gordon, 'Guide to the Gwen Bell artifact and book collection' *<https://archive.computerhistory.org/resources/access/text/finding-aids/102733969-GBell/102733969-GBell.pdf>*.

Lee, J.A.N., 'Gwen Bell' (*IEEE Computer Society*, 1995). *<https://history.computer.org/pioneers/bell-g.html>*.

'Gwen Bell' (*Wikiwand*, 14 March 2021) *<https://www.wikiwand.com/en/Gwen_Bell>*.

Mary Blagg

Whitaker, Ewen A., *Mapping and Naming the Moon: A History of Lunar Cartography and Nomenclature* (United Kingdom: Cambridge University Press, 1999).

Bartels, Meghan, 'The Woman who Named the Moon and Clocked Variable Stars', *Astronomy*, (14 November 2016) *<http://www.astronomy.com/news/2016/11/mary-adela-blagg>*.

Christoforou, Peter, *English Astronomy Pioneer Mary Adela Blagg* (1858–1944), www.astronomytrek.com, (17 December 2016), *<https://www.astronomytrek.com/english-astronomy-pioneer-mary-adela-blagg-1858-1944>*.

Morgan, Barbara and Melrose, Massachusetts, 'Blagg, Mary Adela (1858–1944)', *Women in World History: A Biographical Encyclopedia*, (2002) *<https://www.encyclopedia.com/women/encyclopedias-almanacs-transcripts-and-maps/blagg-mary-adela-1858-1944>*.

Shears, Jeremy, 'Selenography and Variable Stars: Women & The RAS: Mary Blagg', Oxford Journals, Oxford University Press (1 October 2016) *<https://academic.oup.com/astrogeo/article/57/5/5.17/2738839>*.

Gertrude Blanch

Grier, David, 'Biographies of Women Mathematicians, Gertrude Blanch' (Agnes Scott College, 1 June 2019) *<https://www.agnesscott.edu/lriddle/women/blanch.htm>*.

Grier, David, Gertrude Blanch of the Mathematical Tables Project, *IEEE Annals of the History of Computing*, Volume 19, Issue 4, October 1997 pp 18–27.

Grier, David Alan, *When Computers Were Human* (Princeton, NJ: Princeton University Press, 2005).

O'Connor, J J and Robertson, E F, 'Getrude Blanch' (*Mac Tutor*, April 2009) *<https://mathshistory.st-andrews.ac.uk/Biographies/Blanch/>*.

Tropp, H, interview with Gertrude Blanch at the Aspen Hotel in Washington, D.C. on 16 May 1973 (Computer Oral History Collection, 1969-1973, 1977, Archives Center, National Museum of American History).

Sharla Boehm

Amberman, 'Finding Sharla Boehm' (*The Edtech Curmudgeon*, 12 May 2015) <*http://edtechcurmudgeon.blogspot.com/2015/05/finding-sharla-boehm.html*>.
'Sharla Boehm' < *https://en.wikipedia.org/wiki/Sharla_Boehm*>.

Kathleen Booth

'Kathleen Booth: British Computer Scientist', PeoplePill, <*https://peoplepill.com/people/kathleen-booth/*>.
'Kathleen Booth' *Centre for Computing History*, <*http://www.computinghistory.org.uk/det/32489/Kathleen-Booth/*>.
'Dr. Kathleen Booth (née Britten)' *IT History Society*, <*https://www.ithistory.org/honor-roll/dr-kathleen-booth-nee-britten*>.
Priddy, Jason, 'Kathleen Booth' (7 May 2019) <*https://medium.com/@BatmanPriddy/kathleen-booth-7bb303fb15be*>.

Anita Borg

Abbate, Janet, 'Oral-History: Anita Borg' (*ETHW*, 5 January 2001) <*https://ethw.org/Oral-History:Anita_Borg*>.
Anita Borg Institute for Women in Technology <*https://www.crunchbase.com/organization/anita-borg-institute-for-women-in-technology*>.
AnitaB.org, 'Our History' <*https://anitab.org/our-history/*>.
Mieszkowski, Katharine, 'Not just another nerdy white guy' (Salon, 10 September 2003) <*https://www.salon.com/2003/09/10/borg_memorial/*>.
Shade, Leslie Regan, 'Anita Borg American computer scientist' *Britannica* <*https://www.britannica.com/biography/Anita-Borg*>.

Ellen Broad

'Ellen Broad' <*http://ellenbroad.com/*>.
'Ellen Broad' Melbourne University Publishing <*https://www.mup.com.au/authors/ellen-broad*>.
'Ms Ellen Broad' (Australian National University, 10 August 2021) <https://cecs.anu.edu.au/people/ellen-broad>.

Joy Buolamwini

Farley, Amy, 'Meet the computer scientist and activist who got Big Tech to stand down' (*Forbes*, September 2020) <*https://www.fastcompany.com/90525023/most-creative-people-2020-joy-buolamwini*>.
'Joy Buolamwini' MIT Media Lab People <*https://www.media.mit.edu/people/joyab/overview/*>.
'Joy Buolamwini' *LinkedIn* <*https://www.linkedin.com/in/buolamwini*>.

'Joy Buolamwini: Founder, Algorithmic Justice League; Researcher, MIT Media Lab', Carnegie Corporation of New York <*https://www.carnegie.org/awards/honoree/joy-buolamwini/*>.

Alice Rowe Burks

'Alice R. Burks' (*Ann Arbor News*, 13 December 2013) <*https://obits.mlive.com/us/obituaries/annarbor/name/alice-burks-obituary?pid=187519874*>.
Lee, J.A.N., (*IEEE Computer Society*, 1995) <https://history.computer.org/pioneers/burks-ar.html>.
Stern, Nancy B., 'Oral history interview with Alice R. Burks and Arthur W. Burks' (Charles Babbage Institute, 20 June 1980)<*https://conservancy.umn.edu/handle/11299/107206*>.

Margaret Burnett

'Margaret M. Burnett' Oregon State University <*http://web.engr.oregonstate.edu/~burnett/*>.
Petersen, Chris, 'Margaret Burnett: Oral History Interview, Oregon State University ,(*Oral History Project*, 10 January 2017). <*https://scarc.library.oregonstate.edu/oh150/burnett/biography.html*>.

Karen Catlin

Amazon, Karen Catlin books <*https://www.amazon.com/Karen-Catlin/e/B01CAKHCD0%3Fref=dbs_a_mng_rwt_scns_share*>.
'Karin Catlin' (*Freejournal.org*, 2 June 2020) <*https://amp.ww.en.freejournal.org/53052530/1/karen-catlin.html*>.
'Karin Catlin', <*https://karencatlin.com/about/*>.
'An Interview With Karen Catlin' <*https://get.tech/blog/mystartintech-interview-with-karen-catlin/*>.
'Karen Catlin: Advocate for Women in Tech', SpeakerHub <*https://speakerhub.com/speaker/karen-catlin*>.

Beatrice Cave-Browne-Cave

Beatrice Mabel Cave-Browne-Cave, <*https://en.wikipedia.org/wiki/Beatrice_Mabel_Cave-Browne-Cave*>.
Bery, Mark, 'Mathematician Beatrice Cave-Brown-Cave' (*The Streatham Society*, 30 May 2021). <*https://www.streathamsociety.org.uk/blog/mathematician-beatrice-cave-brown-cave*>.
O'Connor, J J and Robertson, E F, (*Mac Tutor*, September 2021) <*https://mathshistory.st-andrews.ac.uk/Biographies/Cave-Browne-Cave_Beatrice/*>.

Edith Clarke

Brittain, James, *Scanning the Past: Edith Clarke and Power System Stability*, Proceedings of the IEEE, The Institute of Electrical and Electronics Engineers

Bibliography

Durbin, John, *In Memoriam: Edith Clarke*, Index of Memorial Resolutions and Biographical Sketches (Texas: University of Texas, 2012)

Layne, Margaret E., *Women in Engineering. Pioneers and Trailblazers* (Reston, Va.: ASCE Press, 2009)

Carey, Charles Jr., 'Edith Clarke', American National Biography Online, <*https://doi.org/10.1093/anb/9780198606697.article.1300295*>.

'Edith Clarke', *Revolvy*, <*https://www.revolvy.com/page/Edith-Clarke*>.

Riddle, Larry, 'Edith Clarke', Biographies of Women Mathematicians, Agnes Scott College, (26 February 2016) <*https://www.agnesscott.edu/lriddle/women/clarke.htm*>.

Mary A. Clem

'Mary Clem' Wikitia < *https://wikitia.com/wiki/Mary_Clem*>.

Iowa State University, *Plaza of Heroines* <*https://plaza.las.iastate.edu/directory/mary-a-clem/*>.

Tammi and Debbie, 'Mary Clem' <*https://brownanddunn.com/Women-In-Computer-History/mary-clem/*>.

Lynn Conway

Alicandri, James. *Forbes* <*https://www.forbes.com/sites/jeremyalicandri/2020/11/18/ibm-apologizes-for-firing-computer-pioneer/?sh=65b8cc7b67d5*>.

Krishna, Swapna, NOW <*https://now.northropgrumman.com/lynn-conway-computer-science-trailblazer-and-transgender-pioneer/*>.

'Lynn Conway' IEEE Computer Society <*https://www.computer.org/profiles/lynn-conway*>.

'Lynn Conway' IEEE Solid State Circuits <*http://ai.eecs.umich.edu/people/conway/conway.html*>.

Joëlle Coutaz

'Curriculum Vitae - Joëlle Coutaz' <*http://iihm.imag.fr/coutaz/coutazCV.pdf*>.

'Encounters with HCI Pioneers: a persona; photo journal' <*https://hcipioneers.wordpress.com/portfolio/coutaz-joelle/*>.

'Joëlle Coutaz's publications' Équipe Ingénierie de l'Interaction Humain-Machine <*http://iihm.imag.fr/en/publication/coutaz/*>.

Kate Crawford

Corbyn, Zoe. Interview with Kate Crawford (*Guardian*, 6 June 2021) <*https://www.theguardian.com/technology/2021/jun/06/microsofts-kate-crawford-ai-is-neither-artificial-nor-intelligent*>.

'Crawford, Kate'. *Atlas of AI* (Yale University Press, 2021).

Microsoft. Kate Crawford, Senior Principal Researcher <*https://www.microsoft.com/en-us/research/people/kate/*>.

Wood, Stephanie. AI's inherent risks. (*Sydney Morning Herald*, 20 August 2021) <*https://www.smh.com.au/national/a-lot-of-people-are-sleepwalking-into-it-the-expert-raising-concerns-over-ai-20210714-p589qh.html* >.

Klára Dán von Neumann

Ravilious, Kate, 'Weatherwatch: the unsung woman behind modern forecasting' (*The Guardian*, 13 March 2021) <*https://www.theguardian.com/news/2021/mar/13/weatherwatch-unsung-woman- behind-modern-forecasting-klara-dan-von-neumann*>.
'Klára Dan' Book of Days Tales <*https://www.bookofdaystales.com/klara-dan/*>.
'Witman, Sarah, 'Meet the Computer Scientist You Should Thank For Your Smartphone's Weather App' (*Smithsonian Magazine*, 16 June 2017). <*https://www.smithsonianmag.com/science-nature/meet-computer-scientist-you-should-thank-your-phone-weather-app-180963716/*

Eleanor Dodson

'Eleanor Dodson' *The Royal Society*. Biography <*https://royalsociety.org/people/eleanor-dodson-11342/*>.
Ferry, Georgina, 'Interview with Eleanor Dodson, computational methods developer of Protein Crystallography' (University of Oxford, 29 January 2020) <https://podcasts.ox.ac.uk/interview-eleanor-dodson-computational-methods-developer-protein-crystallography>.
'Professor Eleanor Dodson, FRS', University of York. <*https://www.york.ac.uk/chemistry/staff/academic/emeritus/edodson/*>.

Elizabeth Feinler

'Official Biography: Elizabeth Feinler' Internet Hall of Fame. <*https://www.internethalloffame.org/official-biography-elizabeth-feinler*>.
'Elizabeth Feinler and the History of the Internet' New York Historical Society. Women at the Center. 13 November 2020.
<*https://womenatthecenter.nyhistory.org/elizabeth-feinler-and-the-history-of-the- internet/*>.
Newnham, Danielle. 'Elizabeth Feinler and The History of the Internet'
<*https://daniellenewnham.medium.com/elizabeth-feinler-and-the-history-of-the- internet-83f4f7366787*>.

Christiane Floyd

Floyd, Christiane, Züllighoven, Heinz, Budde, Reinhard, Keil-Slawik, Reinhard. *Software Development and Reality Construction* (Springer, 1992).
'Christiane Floyd' ACM Digital Library <*https://dl.acm.org/profile/81100356037*>.
'Christiane Floyd' *dplp* <*https://dblp.org/pid/f/ChristianeFloyd.html*>.

Bibliography

'Pioneering Computer Scientist' Technische Universitat Berlin. <*https:// www.tu.berlin/en/about/themenportal-ueber-die-tu-berlin/2021/januar/ pioneering-computer-scientist/*>.

Sally Jean Floyd

Hafner, Katie, 'Sally Floyd, Who Helped Things Run Smoothly Online, Dies at 69' (*New York Times*, 4 September 2018). <*https://www.nytimes. com/2019/09/04/science/sally-floyd-dead.html*>.

Krishnan, Megha. (*The Daily Californian*, 10 September 2019) <*https:// www.dailycal.org/2019/09/10/she-was-filled-with-love-uc-berkeley- alumna-computer-scientist-sally-floyd-dies-at-69/*>.

'Sally Floyd' *ETHW* <https://ethw.org/Sally_Floyd>.

Alexandra 'Sandra' Illmer Forsythe

'Alexandra Illmer Forsythe' PeoplePill <*https://peoplepill.com/people/ alexandra-illmer-forsythe*>.

Margaret R. Fox

'Margaret R. Fox' IT History Society <*https://www.ithistory.org/honor-roll/ mrs-margaret-r-fox*>.

Ross, James. 'An Interview with Margaret Fox' 13 April 1983. <*https:// conservancy.umn.edu/bitstream/handle/11299/107292/oh049mf. pdf?sequence=1&isAllowed=y*>.

Timnit Gebru

Simonite, Tom. 'Wired' <*https://www.wired.com/story/google-timnit-gebru- ai-what-really-happened/*>.

'Timnit Gebru Biography' Fact Files. <*https://fact-files.com/timnit-gebru-wiki/*>.

'Timnit Gebru' Linked in. <*https://www.linkedin.com/in/timnit-gebru- 7b3b407*>.

Adele Goldberg

Abbate, Janet, 'Oral-History: Adele Goldberg' (*ETHW*, 3 July 2002) <*https:// ethw.org/Oral-History:Adele_Goldberg*>.

Morpling, 'Adele Goldberg: computer scientist' (*Computer Magazine*, 21 September 2018) <*https://computermagazineinfo.blogspot. com/2018/09/adele-goldberg-computer-scientist_43.html*>.

Adele Katz Goldstine

'Adele Goldstine, the Woman Who Wrote the Book' (*SWE Magazine*, 22 May 2019). <*https://alltogether.swe.org/2019/05/adele-goldstine-the- woman-who-wrote-the-book/*>.

'Adele Katz Goldstine' *ETHW* <*https://ethw.org/Adele_Katz_Goldstine*>.
Kathuria, Charvi, 'Tech Women: Meet Adele Goldstine, The Woman Behind ENIAC' (shethepeople, 14 December 2017) <*https://www.shethepeople. tv/news/tech-women-meet-adele-goldstein/*>.

Shafi Goldwasser

Rackoff, Charles, 'Shafi Goldwasser' M. Turing Award <*https://amturing. acm.org/award_winners/goldwasser_8627889.cfm*>.
'Shafi Goldwasser' Simons Institute, Berkeley. <*https://simons.berkeley.edu/ people/shafi-goldwasser*>.
'Shafi Goldwasser' MIT Computer Science & Artificial Intelligence Lab, 28 April 2020 <*https://www.csail.mit.edu/person/shafi-goldwasser*>.

Evelyn Boyd Granville

'Evelyn Granville: American mathematician' *Britannica.* <*https://www. britannica.com/biography/Evelyn-Granville*>.
Horowitz, AnneMarie 'Women Who Shoot for the Skies: Dr. Evelyn Boyd Granville' (Department of Energy, 16 July 2018*)* <*https://www.energy. gov/articles/five-fast-facts-about-evelyn-boyd-granville*>.
O'Connor, J J and Robertson, E F, *Mac Tutor*, 'Evelyn Boyd Granville' <*https://mathshistory.st-andrews.ac.uk/Biographies/Granville/*>.

Irene Greif

'Author: Irene Greif' Interaction Design Foundation <*https://www. interaction-design.org/literature/author/irene-greif*>.
'Biography: Irene Greif' Handwiki. <*https://handwiki.org/wiki/ Biography:Irene_Greif*>.
'Irene Greif'. IBM. <*https://www.ibm.com/ibm/history/witexhibit/wit_ fellows_greif.html*>.
'Irene Greif' American Academy of Arts and Sciences. <*https://www.amacad. org/person/irene-greif*>.
McCluskey, Eileen, 'Irene Greif '69, SM '72, PhD '75' (*MIT Technology Review*, 20 October 2008) <*https://www.technologyreview. com/2008/10/20/218022/irene-greif-69-sm-72-phd-75/*>.
Rosen, Rebecca J., The First Woman to Get a Ph.D. in Computer Science From MIT' *The Atlantic,* 6 March 2014) <*https://www.theatlantic.com/ technology/archive/2014/03/the-first-woman-to-get-a-phd-in-computer-science-from-mit/284127/*.

Margaret Elaine Heafield Hamilton

Corbyn, Zoë, 'They worried that the men might rebel. They didn't' (*The Guardian,* 14 July 2019) <*https://www.theguardian.com/technology/2019/ jul/13/margaret-hamilton-computer-scientist-interview-software-apollo-missions-1969-moon-landing-nasa-women*>.

George, Alice 'Margaret Hamilton Led the NASA Software Team that Landed Astronauts on the Moon' (*Smithsonian Magazine*, 14 March 2019) <*https://www.smithsonianmag.com/smithsonian-institution/margaret-hamilton-led-nasa-software-team-landed-astronauts-moon-180971575/*>.

Glorfeld, Jeff, 'Margaret Hamilton helped land the Eagle' (*Cosmos Magazine*, 9 August 2020). <*https://cosmosmagazine.com/technology/computing/margaret-hamilton-helped-land-the-eagle/*>.

Mary K. Hawes

'Proposing COBOL' National Museum of American History <*https://americanhistory.si.edu/cobol/proposing-cobol*>.

Grete Hermann

Herzenberg, Caroline, 'Grete Hermann: An early contributor to quantum theory' 19 December 2008. <*https://www.europeanwomeninmaths.org/wp-content/uploads/2016/02/gretehermann.pdf*>.

Herzenberg, Caroline, 'Grete Hermann: Mathematician, Physicist, Philosopher', American Physical Society 2008 April Meeting and HEDP/HEDLA Meeting, April 11-15, 2008,

Shipley, Patricia and Leal, Fernando. 'A Tribute to Grete Hermann' <*http://sfcp.org.uk/wp-content/uploads/2019/02/A_Tribute_to_Grete_Hermann.pdf*>.

Susan M. Hockey

Hockey, Susan, 'Is There a Computer in this Class?' September 1999. <*www.iath.virginia.edu/hcs/hockey.html*>

'Susan Hockey' European Association for Digital Humanities <*http://eadh-static.adho.org/people/susan-hockey.html*>.

'Susan Hockey' University of Oxford <*https://www.stx.ox.ac.uk/people/susan-hockey*>.

Dorothy Crowfoot Hodgkin

Byers, N., 'Hodgkin, Dorothy Crowfoot', Contributions of 20th Century Women to Physics <*http://cwp.library.ucla.edu/*>.

Dodson, Guy; Glusker, Jenny P.; Sayre, David (eds.), *Structural Studies on Molecules of Biological Interest: A Volume in Honour of Professor Dorothy Hodgkin* (Oxford: Clarendon Press, 1981).

Ferry, G., 'Hodgkin, Dorothy Mary Crowfoot', *Oxford Dictionary of National Biography online* (21 May 2009).

Glusker, J.P. and Adams, M.J., 'Dorothy Crowfoot Hodgkin' (1995) 48 (5), *Physics Today*, p. 80.

Hudson, Gill, 'Unfathering the Thinkable: Gender, Science and Pacificism in the 1930s', in Marina Benjamin (ed.) *Science and Sensibility: Gender* and *Scientific Enquiry, 1780–1945*, (Oxford: Basil Blackwell,1991), pp. 264–86.

Johnson, L.N. and Phillips, D., 'Professor Dorothy Hodgkin, OM, FRS' (1994) 1 (9), *Nature Structural Biology*, pp. 573–76

Opfell, Olga S., *Lady Laureate: Women Who Have Won the Nobel Prize* (Metuchen, NJ & London: Scarecrow Press, 1978), pp. 209–23.

Perutz, M., 'Professor Dorothy Hodgkin' (2009) 27 (4), *Quarterly Reviews of Biophysics*, pp. 333–37.

Frances Elizabeth 'Betty' Snyder Holberton

'Betty Holberton, ENIAC Programmer' Women in Computer Science. *<https://24094361.weebly.com/betty-holberton.html>*.

Kathuria, Charvi, 'Meet Betty Holberton, Pioneer in Computer Debugging' (Shethepeople, 9 December 2017). *<https://www.shethepeople.tv/news/betty-holberton-wait/>*.

Levy, Claudia, 'Betty Holberton Dies' (*The Washington Post*, 11 December 2001) *<https://www.washingtonpost.com/archive/local/2001/12/11/betty-holberton-dies/ad778f02-763a-4a68-b85f-68eacff97e0d/>*.

Erna Schneider Hoover

'Erna Hoover' - Biography, World of Computer Science, (2012) *<https://www.women.cs.cmu.edu/ada/Resources/Women>*.

'Erna Schneider Hoover - Computerized Telephone Switching System', Lemelson MIT, *<http://lemelson.mit.edu/resources/erna-schneider-hoover>*.

'Erna Schneider Hoover', Engineering and Technology Wiki *<https://ethw.org/Erna_Schneider_Hoover>*.

Nutt, Amy Ellis, 'Fame calls on 2 titans of telephony in NJ' (*The Star-Ledger*, 18 June 2008), *<https://www.nj.com/news/index.ssf/2008/06/fame_calls_on_2_titans_of_tele.html?>*.

'Queens of Tech', YouTube *<https://www.youtube.com/watch?v=mqIfLPqE3iU>*.

Grace Brewster Murray Hopper

Beyer, Kurt W., *Grace Hopper and the Invention of the Information Age* (1st ed.) (Cambridge, Massachusetts: MIT Press, 2009)

'Grace Hopper Biography. Mathematician, Military Leader, Computer Programmer', Biography, *<https://www.biography.com/people/grace-hopper-21406809>*

'Grace Hopper - United States Naval Officer and Mathematician', *Encyclopaedia Britannica*, *<https://www.britannica.com/biography/Grace-Hopper>*

Marx, Christy, *Grace Hopper: The First Woman to Program the First Computer in the United States*, Women Hall of Famers in Mathematics and Science (1st ed.) (New York City: Rosen Publishing Group, August 2003).

Norman, Rebecca, *Biographies of Women Mathematicians: Grace Murray Hopper* (Agnes Scott College, June 1997).

Williams, Kathleen Broome, *Grace Hopper: Admiral of the Cyber Sea* (1st ed.) (Annapolis, Maryland: Naval Institute Press, 15 November 2004).

Mary Jane Irwin

'Interview with Mary Jane Irwin' Computing Research Association. *<https://cra.org/cra-wp/interview-with-mary-jane-irwin/>*.

'Mary Jane Irwin' PeoplePill *<https://peoplepill.com/people/mary-jane-irwin>*.

McLellan, Paul, 'Mary Jane Irwin Receives the Kaufman Award' (*SemiConductor Engineering*, 10 October 2019). *<https://semiengineering.com/mary-jane-irwin-receives-the-kaufman-award/>*.

Mary Lou Jepsen

'Dr. Mary Lou Jepsen' *<https://www.maryloujepsen.com/>*.

'Mary Lou Jepsen' *Linked in*. *<https://www.linkedin.com/in/majepsen>*.

'Mary Lou Jepsen: optical scientist business executive' Prabook *<https://prabook.com/web/mary_lou.jepsen/263599>*.

Katherine Johnson

'Katherine Johnson (1918–2020)' (*Nature*, 2020, vol. 579, issue 7799, 341-341). *<https://www.nature.com/articles/d41586-020-00749-3>*.

'Katherine Johnson (1918-2020) Former NASA Research Mathematician' *NASA <https://solarsystem.nasa.gov/people/434/katherine-johnson-1918-2020/>*.

Shetterly, Margot Lee, 'Katherine Johnson Biography' (*NASA*, 25 February 2020) *<https://www.nasa.gov/content/katherine-johnson-biography>*.

Karen Spärck Jones

Bowls, Nellie, 'Overlooked No More: Karen Sparck Jones, who Established the Basis for Search Engines' (*New York Times*, 2 January 2019). *<https://www.nytimes.com/2019/01/02/obituaries/karen-sparck-jones-overlooked.html>*.

'Karen Spärck Jones' Computer Laboratory, University of Cambridge, March 2007. *<https://www.cl.cam.ac.uk/archive/ksj21/>*.

University of Cambridge. *<https://www.cl.cam.ac.uk/misc/obituaries/sparck-jones/>*.

Susan Kare

Hintz, Eric S., 'Susan Kare, Iconic Designer' (Lemelson Center, 4 May 2018). *<https://invention.si.edu/susan-kare-iconic-designer>*.

Lange, Alexandra, 'The Woman Who Gave the Macintosh a Smile'. (*New Yorker,* 19 April 2018) *<https://www.newyorker.com/culture/cultural-comment/the-woman-who-gave-the-macintosh-a-smile>.*
'Susan Kare' Famous Graphic Designers *<https://www. famousgraphicdesigners.org/susan-kare>.*

Mary Kenneth Keller

Ryan, Maeve. 'Sister Mary Kenneth Keller (PhD, 1965): The first PhD in computer science in the US', University of Wisconsin, Madison. Computer Sciences, School of Computer, Data & Information Sciences (18 March 2019). *<https://www.cs.wisc.edu/2019/03/18/2759/>.*
Sam, Abdullah, 'Mary Kenneth Keller' (Notes Read, 29 December 2020). *<https://notesread.com/mary-kenneth-keller/>.*
'Sister Mary Kenneth Keller' Center for Computer History. *<http://www. computinghistory.org.uk/det/47364/Sister-Mary-Kenneth-Keller/>.*

Maria Margaret Klawe

'Maria Klawe'. *<https://microsoft.fandom.com/wiki/Maria_Klawe>.*
'President Maria Klawe'. Harvey Mudd College. *<https://www.hmc.edu/ about-hmc/presidents-office/president-maria-klawe/>*

Sandra Kurtzig

'Kurtzig, Sandra, L.'. *Encylopedia.com. <https://www.encyclopedia.com/ education/economics-magazines/kurtzig-sandra-l>.*
'Oral History of Sandra Kurtzig'. Computer History Museum. (YouTube, 6 June 2018) *<https://www.youtube.com/watch?v=e5PDmiUfDp8>.*
Stromberg, Lisa. 'Sandra Kurtzig: The Original Silicon Valley 'Mompreneur" *The Huffington Post,* 8 July 2015) *<https://www.huffpost.com/entry/ sandra-kurtzig-the-origin_b_7749390>.*

Hedwig Eva Maria Kiesler ''Hedy Lamarr''

Barton, Ruth, *Hedy Lamarr: The Most Beautiful Woman in Film* (Lexington: University of Kentucky Press, 2010).
'Hedy Lamarr: Inventor of More than the 1st Theatrical-film Orgasm' (*Los Angeles Times,* 28 November 2010).
'Hollywood Star whose Invention Paved the Way for Wi-Fi' (*New Scientist,* 8 December 2011).
Lamarr, Hedy, *Ecstasy and Me: My Life as a Woman* (New York: Bartholomew House, 1966)
Rhodes, Richard, *Hedy's Folly: The Life and Breakthrough Inventions of Hedy Lamarr* (New York: Doubleday, 2012).
Shearer, Stephen Michael, *Beautiful: The Life of Hedy Lamarr* (New York: St. Martin's Press, 2010).
Young, Christopher, *The Films of Hedy Lamarr* (New York: Citadel Press, 1979)

Ailsa Land

'Ailsa H. Land' Informs. <*https://www.informs.org/Explore/History-of-O.R.-Excellence/Biographical-Profiles/Land-Ailsa-H*>.

Ferry, Georgina, 'Ailsa Land obituary'. (*The Guardian*, 14 June 2021). <*https://www.theguardian.com/science/2021/jun/14/ailsa-land-obituary*>.

'In memory Professor Ailsa Land (1927-2021)' The London School of Political Science and Political Science <*https://blogs.lse.ac.uk/condolences/*>.

Rosenhead, Jonathan and Végh, László. 'Remembering Aisla Land'. (*The Operational Research Society*, 15 June 2021). <*https://www.theorsociety.com/news/remembering-aisla-land-1927-2021/*>.

Henrietta Swan Leavitt

Haynes, Korey. 'Meet Henrietta Leavitt, the woman who gave us a universal ruler'. (*Astronomy*, 4 February 2019).
<*https://astronomy.com/news/2019/02/meet-henrietta-leavitt-the-woman-who-gave-us-a-universal-ruler*>.

'Henrietta Swan Leavitt American astronomer'. *Britannica*. <*https://www.britannica.com/biography/Henrietta-Swan-Leavitt*>.

'Henrietta Swan Leavitt - Biography, Facts and Pictures'. Famous Scientists. <*https://www.famousscientists.org/henrietta-swan-leavitt/*>.

O'Connor, J J and Robertson, E F, 'Henrietta Swan Leavitt' (Mac Tutor, August 2017).

Nicole Reine Lepaute

Boistel, G, 'Nicole-Reine Lepaute et l'Hortensia', *Les Cahiers Clairaut* 108 (2004), 13. <*https://cosmosmagazine.com/mathematics/the-comet-calculator-nicole-reine-lepaute/*>.

'Nicole-Reine Étable de la Brière Lepaute (1723–1788)' in *The Unforgotten Sisters*, Gabriella Bernardi, March 2016. <*https://www.researchgate.net/publication/315024924_Nicole-Reine_Etable_de_la_Briere_Lepaute_1723-1788*>.

Ogilvie, M and Harvey, J (eds.), Nicole-Reine Lepaute, *Biographical Dictionary of Women in Science* (Routledge, New York, 2000), 772-773. <*https://mathshistory.st-andrews.ac.uk/Biographies/Lepaute/*>.

Barbara Jane Huberman Liskov

'Barbara Liskov Wins Turing Award' (*MIT News*, 10 March 2009) <*https://news.mit.edu/2009/turing-liskov-0310*>.

Huberman (Liskov) and Barbara Jane, *A Program to Play Chess End Games* (PDF) (Stanford University Department of Computer Science, Technical Report CS 106, Stanford Artificial Intelligence Project Memo AI-65, 1968).

Liskov, B., 'Distributed programming in Argus' (1988) 31 (3), Communications of the ACM,. 31(3) (1988), 300–312.

'MIT's Magnificent Seven: Women Faculty Members Cited as Top Scientists (*MIT News Office*, 5 Nov 2002)

Oral-History: Barbara Liskov, Engineering and Technology Wiki, (12 September 2018) *<https://ethw.org/Oral-History:Barbara_Liskov_ (1991)>*.

Van Vleck, Tom, 'A.M. Turing Award Barbara Liskov' (2012), *<https:// amturing.acm.org/award_winners/liskov_1108679.cfm>*.

Joyce Currie Little

'Joyce Currie Little Interview: Overview' Computer Educators Oral History Project *<https://www.southwestern.edu/a/departments/mathcompsci/ OHProject/littleJC-overview.html>*.

'Joyce Little', Educause *<https://members.educause.edu/joyce-currie-little>*.

Little, Joyce and Granger, Mary 'Integrating CASE tools into the CS/CIS curriculum' (*ACM SIGCSE Bulletin*, Vol 41, No. 3, 1996). *<https:// towson.academia.edu/JoyceLittle>*.

(Augusta) Ada Lovelace (Byron)

'Ada Lovelace Symposium – Celebrating 200 Years of a Computer Visionary', Podcasts (UK: University of Oxford).

Baum, Joan, *The Calculating Passion of Ada Byron* (Archon, 1986).

Hooper, Rowan, 'Ada Lovelace: My Brain is More than Merely Mortal' (*New Scientist*, 15 October 2012) *<https://www.newscientist.com/article/ dn22385-ada-lovelace-my-brain-is-more-than-merely-mortal/>*.

Phillips, Ana Lena, 'Crowdsourcing Gender Equity: Ada Lovelace Day, and Its Companion Website, Aims to Raise the Profile of Women in Science and Technology' *American Scientist*, 99(6), (2011) 463.

Woolley, Benjamin, *The Bride of Science: Romance, Reason, and Byron's Daughter* (McGraw-Hill, 2002).

Marissa Mayer

Weinberger, Matt and Lesk, Paige 'The rise and fall of Marissa Mayer, the once-beloved CEO of Yahoo now pursuing her own venture' (*Insider*, 12 February 2020). *<https://www.businessinsider.com/yahoo-marissa-mayer-rise-and-fall-2017- 6?r=AU&IR=T>*.

'#35 Marissa Mayer' *Forbes* *<https://www.forbes.com/profile/marissa-mayer/?sh=15a3070a4c5e>*.

Doorey, Marie, 'Marissa Mayer, American software engineer and businesswoman'. *Britannica* *<https://www.britannica.com/biography/ Marissa-Mayer>*.

Marlyn Meltzer

Kathuria, Charvi. 'Tech Women: Meet Marlyn Wescoff Meltzer, ENIAC Programmer' (Shethepeople, 16 December 2017). *<https://www.shethepeople.tv/news/marlyn-wescoff-meltzer-eniac-programmer/>*.

'Marlyn Meltzer Biography' *ETHW. <https://ethw.org/Marlyn_Meltzer>*.

Sheppard, Alyson, 'Meet the 'Refrigerator Ladies' Who Programmed the ENIAC' *(MF, 13 October 2013). <https://www.mentalfloss.com/article/53160/meet-refrigerator-ladies-who-programmed-eniac>*.

Ann Katherine Mitchell

'Ann Mitchell (1922-2020) - Codebreaker, Social Reformer and Oxford Mathematician' University of Oxford, mathematical Institute *<https://www.maths.ox.ac.uk/node/36050>*.

'Ann Katherine Mitchell' PeoplePill *<https://peoplepill.com/people/ann-katharine-mitchell>*.

Maria Mitchell

Among the Stars: The Life of Maria Mitchell. Astronomer, Educator, Women's Rights Activist (Nantucket, MA: Mill Hill Press, 2007).

Bergland, Renée, *Maria Mitchell and the Sexing of Science* (Boston, MA: Beacon Press, 2008).

Gormley, Beatrice, *Maria Mitchell the Soul of an Astronomer* (William B. Eerdmans Publishing Co, Grand Rapids, MI, 1995).

Hoffleit, Dorrit, 'The Maria Mitchell Observatory - For Astronomical Research and Public Enlightenment' (pdf) *The Journal of the American Association of Variable Star Observer*, 30 (1), (2001) 62

McPherson, Stephanie Sammartino, 'Rooftop Astronomer: A Story About Maria Mitchell' (*Lerner Publishing Group*, 1 Aug 2011).

'Maria Mitchell's Gold Medal', Maria Mitchell Association, Nantucket's Science Center *<https://www.mariamitchell.org/about/awards/maria-mitchells-gold-medal>*.

Vera Molnár

Carlson, Wayne E.,' Computer Graphics and Computer Animation: A Retrospective Overview' *Pressbooks*, Chapter 9.2. *<https://ohiostate.pressbooks.pub/graphicshistory/chapter/9-2-vera-molnar/>*.

Chen, Min, 'The Artist Who Drew with Computers, Before Computers Were a Thing', 13 November 2017. *<https://www.surfacemag.com/articles/vera-molnar-in-thinking-machines-at-moma/>*.

'Vera Molnar', *MoMA <https://www.moma.org/artists/37083>*.

'Vera Molnár' *<http://www.veramolnar.com/>*.

Sudha Murthy

Mudde, Raggi. 'Sudha Murthy- An Iconic Women, Philanthropist, and Author' 1 December 2016. <*https://www.karnataka.com/personalities/sudha-murty/*>.

'Sudha Murthy' Team Leverage Edu. <*https://leverageedu.com/blog/sudha-murthy/*>.

'Sudha Murthy' Starsunfolded. < *https://starsunfolded.com/sudha-murthy/*>

Susan Hubbell Nycum

Parker, Donn B. and Susan H. Nycum. 'Computer Crime' 4 May 2018 <*http://130.18.86.27/faculty/warkentin/SecurityPapers/Robert/Others/ParkerNycum1984_CACM27_4_ComputerCrime.pdf*>.

'Susan H. Nycum'. Silicon Valley Arbitration & Mediation Center. <*https://svamc.org/member/susannycum/*>.

'Susan H. Nycum' *League of Coders.* <*http://wit.library.cornell.edu/show.html?id=68*>.

Yost, Jeffery. 'An Interview with Susan H. Nycum'. 5 June 2013. <*https://conservancy.umn.edu/bitstream/handle/11299/162871/oh432shn.pdf?sequence=1&isAllowed=y*>.

Ellen Lauri Ochoa

'NASA Astronaut Dr. Ellen Ochoa'. *Johnson Space Center.* <*https://www.nasa.gov/centers/johnson/about/people/orgs/bios/ochoa.html*>.

'Biography of Ellen Ochoa'. Scholastic. <*https://www.scholastic.com/teachers/articles/teaching-content/biography-ellen-ochoa/*>.

'Ellen Ochoa' NASA Biography. <*https://www.nasa.gov/centers/johnson/pdf/716572main_Ellen_Ochoa_Biography.pdf*>.

Cathy Helen O'Neil

O'Neil, Cathy. 'Weapons of Math Destruction' (Penguin, 2017). <*https://www.penguin.com.au/books/weapons-of-math-destruction-9780141985411*>.

TED Talk. 'The era of blind faith in algorithms must end'. TED Talk, April 2017. <*https://www.ted.com/talks/cathy_o_neil_the_era_of_blind_faith_in_big_data_must_end*>

Christine Paulin-Mohring

'Biography: Christine Paulin-Mohring' *HandWiki.* <*https://handwiki.org/wiki/Biography:Christine_Paulin-Mohring*>.

'Christine Paulin-Mohring' *MathSciNet.* <*https://www.mathgenealogy.org/id.php?id=128359*>.

'Christine Paulin-Mohring', Short Biography. *<https://www.lri.fr/~paulin/bio.html>*.
'Women Who Code. 9 programming languages and the women who created them'. *ARN.* *<https://www.arnnet.com.au/slideshow/574529/pictures-9-programming-languages-women-who-created-them/>*.

Radia Perlman

'Rita Perlman'. Internet Hall of Fame. *<https://internethalloffame.org/inductees/radia-perlman>*.
Rosen, Rebecca J., 'Radia Perlman: 'Don't Call Me the Mother of the Internet." *The Atlantic.* *<https://www.theatlantic.com/technology/archive/2014/03/radia-perlman-dont-call-me-the-mother-of-the-internet/284146/>*.
'Who is: Radia Perlman – The Mother of Internet' (*Recab*, 4 March 2014). *<https://recab.com/who-is-radia-perman-the-mother-of-internet/>*.

Rózsa Péter

Albers, Donald J.; Alexanderson, Gerald L.; Reid, Constance, eds., *Rózsa Péter 1905–1977, More Mathematical People* (Harcourt Brace Jovanovich, 1990).
Andrásfai, Béla, 'Rózsa (Rosa) Péter' (1986) 30 (2–3), *Periodica Polytechnica Electrical Engineering*, 30(2-3) (1986), 139–145.
Morris, Edie and Harkleroad, Leon, 'Rózsa Péter: Recursive Function Theory's Founding Mother' (1990) 12 (1), *The Mathematical Intelligencer*, 12(1) (1990), 59–64.
'Rózsa Péter: Founder of Recursive Function Theory', *Women in Science: A Selection of 16 Contributors* (San Diego Supercomputer Center, 1997)
Tamássy, István, 'Interview with Róza Péter' (1994) 4 (3), *Modern Logic*, 277–280.

Maria Petrou

Kittler, Josef, 'Maria Petrou, IAPR Fellow'. IAPR. *<https://iapr.org/members/newsletter/Newsletter13-01/index_files/Page652.htm>*.
Vitner, Richard. 'Maria Petrou obituary' (*The Guardian*, 4 December 2012). *<https://www.theguardian.com/technology/2012/dec/04/maria-petrou>*.
Vinter, Richard, 'Tribute: Maria Petrou' (Imperial College London, 12 November 2012). *<https://www.imperial.ac.uk/news/116147/tribute-maria-petrou/>*.

Rosalind Wright Picard

Jewell, Wendy. 'Rosalind Picard' *My Hero* *<https://myhero.com/Rosalind_Picard_2014>*.

MIT Faculty Personnel Record. (9 November 2021). *<https://web.media. mit.edu/~picard/CV-Picard.pdf>*.

Ramsay, Peter, 'MIT Professor Rosalind Picard: Atheist to Faith in Christ' (19 June 2020) *<https://heaven4sure.com/2020/06/19/rosalind-picard-mit-atheist-christ/>*.

Johanna Camilla ('Hansi') Piesch

'Johanna (Hansi) Piesch'. Yumpu *<https://www.yumpu.com/en/document/read/46998739/johanna-hansi-piesch>*.

'Johanna Piesch' *<https://de.zxc.wiki/wiki/Johanna_Piesch>*.

'Johanna Piesch: Austrian librarian, physicist, mathematician and informatics pioneer'. PeoplePill. *<https://peoplepill.com/people/johanna-piesch/>*.

Lee, J A N, 'Johanna (Hansi) Piesch' IEEE Computer Society *<https://history.computer.org/pioneers/piesch.html>*.

Hu Qiheng

'Hu Qiheng', China Internet Museum. *<http://en.internet.cn/character/person/hqh.html>*.

'Hu Qiheng', Freedomology. *<https://www.freedomology.org/hu-qiheng/>*.

'Qiheng Hu' (Internet Hall of Fame, 2013) *<https://www.internethalloffame.org/inductees/qiheng-hu>*.

Virginia Marie ('Ginni') Rometty

'Virginia M. (Ginni) Rometty' IBM *<https://www.ibm.com/about/ginni/>*.

'Ginni Rometty: CEO, IBM' *Forbes*. *<https://www.forbes.com/profile/ginni-rometty/?sh=3442d86346ea>*.

Lev-Ram, Michal 'IBM's Ginni Rometty: The way we hire must change—and we must do it now' (*Fortune*, 19 June 2020) *<https://fortune.com/2020/06/19/ibms-ginni-rometty-the-way-we-hire-must-change-and-we-must-do-it-now/>*.

'Virginia M. Rometty' (Horatio Alger Association, 2016) *<https://horatioalger.org/members/member-detail/virginia-m-rometty>*.

Jean E. Sammet

Fisher, Lawrence M., 'Jean E. Sammet 1928-2017' (Communications of the ACM, July 2017, Vol. 60 No. 7, p. 22) *<https://cacm.acm.org/magazines/2017/7/218860-jean-e-sammet-1928-2017/fulltext>*.

Lee, J.A.N. 'Jean E. Sammet' IEEE Computer Society. *<https://history.computer.org/pioneers/sammet.html>*.

Sammet, Jean E., 'The Early History of Cobol' in Wexelblat, Richard L., ed., *History of Programming Languages*, Academic Press, New York, 1981.

Sammet, Jean E., 'The Beginning and Development of FORMAC', *ACM SIGPIAN Notices* Vol. 28, No. 3, 1993, pp. 209-230.

Bibliography

Lucy Sanders

Gershon, Eric, 'Inquiry – Lucy Sanders' (*Coloradan Alumni Magazine*, 1 June 2017) <*https://www.colorado.edu/coloradan/2017/06/01/inquiry-lucy-sanders*>.

'Lucy Sanders' *NCWIT.org* <*https://ncwit.org/profile/lucy-sanders/*>.

'Lucy Sanders (MCompSci'79)' Computer Science, College Of Engineering And Applied Science, University of Colorado <*https://www.colorado.edu/cs/2020/02/13/lucy-sanders-mcompsci79*>.

Moore, Paula 'For Lucy Sanders, computing and giving back are family traditions' (*Denver Business Journal*, 11 November 2016). <*https://www.bizjournals.com/denver/news/2016/11/11/for-lucy-sanders-computing-and-giving-back-are.html*>.

Patricia Selinger

'Patricia Selinger' IBM <*https://www.ibm.com/ibm/history/witexhibit/wit_fellows_selinger.html*>.

'Dr. Patricia G. Selinger' *IT History Society* <*https://www.ithistory.org/honor-roll/dr-patricia-g-selinger*>.

Hamilton, James, 'Interview Database dialogue with Pat Selinger' (ACM Digital Library, Communications of the ACM, Volume 51, Issue 1, 2December 2008 pp 32–35) <*https://dl.acm.org/doi/10.1145/1409360.1409373*>.

Priti Shankar

'Margarida Priti Shankar' Geni <*https://www.geni.com/people/Margarida-Priti-Shankar/6000000002851257546*>.

Professor Priti Shankar. *Yumpu.* <*https://www.yumpu.com/en/document/read/11615083/professor-priti-shankar*>.

Singh, Surjit, 'A Tribute to Prof Priti Shankar' (Guftagu @ Amolak. in, 27 October 2011) <*https://amolak.in/web/a-tribute-to-prof-priti-shankar/*>.

Stephanie 'Steve' Shirley

Cameron, Lauri, 'How a Woman Named 'Steve' Became One of Britain's Most Celebrated IT Pioneers, Entrepreneurs, and Philanthropists', IEEE Computer Society <*https://www.computer.org/publications/tech-news/research/dame-stephanie-steve-shirley-computer-pioneer*>.

'Dame Stephanie' <*https://www.steveshirley.com/*>.

'Dame Stephanie Shirley Entrepreneur and philanthropist'. TED speaker. <*https://www.ted.com/speakers/dame_stephanie_steve_shirley*>.

'Oral-History:Dame Stephanie (Steve) Shirley' *ETHW* <*https://ethw.org/Oral-History:Dame_Stephanie_(Steve)_Shirley*>.

Megan Smith

Megan Smith Director's Office. *MIT Media Lab People.* <*https://www.media.mit.edu/people/msmith/overview/*>.
Megan J Smith. Linked in. <*https://www.linkedin.com/in/msmith21*>.
Megan Smith (Google[x]) at Startup Grind. (YouTube, 13 February 2014). <*https://www.youtube.com/watch?v=SYid0vRYV0k*>.

Cynthia Jane Solomon

'Cynthia Solomon' The Tinkering Studio. <*https://www.exploratorium.edu/tinkering/tinkerers/cynthia-solomon*>.
'Cynthia Solomon: computer Scientist' PeoplePill <*https://peoplepill.com/people/cynthia-solomon*>.
'Cynthia J Solomon' Nuwber <*https://nuwber.com/person/563a7892a219445d52be3c8c*>.

Frances Spence

Kathuria, Charvi 'Tech Women: Meet ENIAC Programmer Frances V Spence' (shethepeople, 21 December 2017).
<*https://www.shethepeople.tv/news/tech-women-meet-eniac-programmer-frances-v-spence/*>.
'Mrs. Frances Spence (née Bilas)' *IT History Society* <*https://www.ithistory.org/honor-roll/mrs-frances-spence-ne-bilas*>.

Janese Swanson

'Janese Swanson High-Tech Girls Toys' *Lemelson-MIT* <*https://lemelson.mit.edu/resources/janese-swanson*>.
Billiam, 'Girl Tech Toys Were So Cool & So Connected' (YouTube, 15 April 2021) <*https://www.youtube.com/watch?v=qtR1Ijyv7yE*>.
'Janese Swanson: Inventing a Better Way'. Esme <*https://esme.com/single-moms/solo-mom-in-the-spotlight/janese-swanson-inventing-a-better-way*>.

Janet Taylor

Alger, K. R., 'Mrs Janet Taylor – Authoress and Instructress in Navigation and Nautical Astronomy' (1804-1870)' (1982) 6, Fawcett Library Papers, LLRS Publications.
Croucher, John and Croucher, Rosalind F., *Mistress of Science* (Stroud: Amberley Pub., 2016).
Croucher, John and Rosalind, 'Mrs Janet Taylor and the 'Black Art' of Compass Adjusting in Mid-19th Century England' (2018) *International Journal of Maritime History*, 30 (2), 234–251.

Croucher, John and Croucher, Rosalind F., 'Mrs Janet Taylor and the Civil List Pension' (2013) 21 (2), *Women's History Review*, 253–280.

Croucher, John and Croucher, Rosalind F., 'Mrs Janet Taylor's 'Mariner's Calculator': Assessment and Reassessment', *British Journal for the History of Science*, 44(4) (2011) 493–507.

Croucher, John, 'An Exceptional Woman of Science', *Bulletin of the Scientific Instrument Society* 84 (2005), 22–27

Ruth Teitelbaum

Haigh, Thomas; Mark, Peter; Rope, Crispin, *Eniac in Action: Making and Remaking the Modern Computer* (Cambridge, MA: MIT Press, 2016), 26.

Martin, Gay, *Recent Advances and Issues in Computers* (Phoenix, Arizona: The Oryx Press, 2000), 106-107.

'Ruth Teitelbaum', Engineering and Technology History Wiki, (25 February 2016), <*https://ethw.org/Ruth_Teitelbaum*>.

'Ruth Teitelbaum', *Revolvy*, <*https://www.revolvy.com/page/Ruth-Teitelbaum*>.

Janie Tsao

Athulya, 'Live Together, Work Together : The Husband-Wife Duo Behind Success of Linksys' (Your Tech Story, 17 October 2019) <*https://www.yourtechstory.com/2019/10/17/live-together-work-together-husband-wife-duo-behind-success-linksys/*>.

'Janie Tsao: Co-founder, Vice President of Worldwide Sales, Marketing and Business Development'. Linksys. <*https://newsroom.cisco.com/dlls/2004/bio_linksys_janie_tsao.pdf*>.

Dana Lynn Ulery

'Dr. Dana L. Ulery' IT History Society <*https://www.ithistory.org/honor-roll/dr-dana-l-ulery*>.

'Dana Lynn Ulery: computer scientist management consultant'. Prabook <*https://prabook.com/web/dana_lynn.ulery/235360*>.

Irina Nikivincze, 'Dana Ulery: Pioneer of Statistical Computing and Architect of Large' (IEEE Annals of the History of Computing Complex Systems, Apr.-June 2017, pp. 91-95, vol. 39) <*https://www.computer.org/csdl/magazine/an/2017/02/man2017020091/13rRUB7a191*>.

Ulery, Dana L., *BuyIt Software Development Plan: A C-BASS Component* (PN, 1999).

Manuela Maria Veloso

Chklovski, Tara 'An Interview with Manuela Veloso: AI and Autonomous Agents' Technovation. < *https://www.technovation.org/blogs/an-interview-with-manuela-veloso-ai-and-autonomous-agents/*>.

Veloso, Manuela M., Home Page, Carnegie Mellon University. *<http://www. cs.cmu.edu/~mmv/>.*

Reese, Hope 'Leading the Robot Invasion of the Old Boys' Club' (The Cut, 13 December 2021). *<https://www.thecut.com/2021/12/trailblazers-manuela-veloso-artificial-intelligence.html>.*

Mary Allen Wilkes

Damer Bruce 'DigiBarn TV: Mary Allen Wilkes programming the LINC computer in the mid-1960s' (YouTube, 26 April 2011) *<https://www. youtube.com/watch?v=Cmv6p8hN0xQ>.*

Johanns, Kate 'Pioneers in Tech: Mary Allen Wilkes, first to WFH with a computer' (Smarter MSP, 14 May 2021*) <https://smartermsp.com/ pioneers-in-tech-mary-allen-wilkes-first-to-wfh-with-a-computer/>.*

'Mary Allen Wilkes: American Computer Scientist' PeoplePill *<https:// peoplepill.com/people/mary-allen-wilkes>.*

'Mary Allen Wilkes: Biography' ETHW *<https://ethw.org/Mary_Allen_ Wilkes>.*

Sophie Wilson

'Dr. Sophie Wilson Broadcom, Cambridge' University of York. *<https:// www.cs.york.ac.uk/equality-and-diversity/heroes-of-computer-science/ drsophiewilson/>.*

'Sophie Wilson' Celebsagewiki *<https://www.celebsagewiki.com/sophie-wilson>.*

'Sophie Wilson: Biography' The Royal Society *<https://royalsociety.org/ people/sophie wilson-12544/>.*

'Sophie Wilsom' Centre for Computing History *<http://www. computinghistory.org.uk/det/6615/Sophie-Wilson/>.*

Anna Winlock

Byrd, Mary, E. 'Anna Winlock' SAO/NASA Astrophysics Data System (ADS) p. 254. *<http://adsabs.harvard.edu/full/1904PA.....12..254B>.*

Geiling, Natasha 'The Women Who Mapped the Universe and Still Couldn't Get Any Respect' (*Smithsonian Magazine*, 18 September 2013). *<https:// www.smithsonianmag.com/history/the-women-who-mapped-the-universe-and-still-couldnt-get-any-respect-9287444/>.*

'Winlock, Anna (1857–1904)' *Encyclopaedia.com <https://www. encyclopedia.com/women/encyclopedias-almanacs-transcripts-and-maps/ winlock-anna-1857-1904>.*

Beatrice Worsley

'Beatrice Worsley' Centre for Computing History *<http://www. computinghistory.org.uk/det/45797/Beatrice-Worsley/>.*

Campbell, Scott M., 'Beatrice Helen Worsley: Canada's Female Computer Pioneer', IEEE Annals of the History of Computing (October–December 2003), pp. 51–62.

'Meet Beatrice Worsley, Our First Female Computer Scientist' (Herevolution, 11 May 2015) <*https://www.hervolution.org/stemspark-meet-beatrice-worsley-our-first-female-computer-scientist/*>.

Raymond, Katrine 'Beatrice Worsley' (The Canadian Encyclopedia, 25 October 2017) <*https://www.thecanadianencyclopedia.ca/en/article/beatrice-worsley*>.

Irma Wyman

'Irma M. Wyman' Center for The Education Of Women +, University of Michigan <*http://www.cew.umich.edu/news-story/irma-m-wyman/*>.

'The Venerable Dr. Irma M. Wyman', *StarTribune* <*https://www.startribune.com/obituaries/detail/110908/*>.

Bjorhus, Jennifer 'Obituary: Irma Wyman was Honeywell's first female CIO, Episcopal deacon' (*StarTribune*, 24 November 2015) <*https://www.startribune.com/irma-wyman-honeywell-s-first-female-cio-episcopal-deacon/353286831/*>.

'Irma M. Wyman Bequest Creates STEM Legacy at CEW+' Leaders & Best Impact, University of Michigan <*https://leadersandbestimpact.umich.edu/story/ripple-effect/*>.

Katerina Yushchenko

'Kateryna L. Yushchenko' History of Computing in Ukraine <*http://en.uacomputing.com/persons/yushenko/*>.

Videla, Alvaro, 'Kateryna L. Yushchenko – Inventor of Pointers' (Pioneers of the Computing Age, 8 December 2018). <*https://medium.com/a-computer-of-ones-own/kateryna-l-yushchenko-inventor-of-pointers-6f2796fa1798*>.

Briman, Shimon, 'How a Jewish woman and a Ukrainian woman launched the computer age' Ukrainian Jewish Encounter <*https://ukrainianjewishencounter.org/en/how-a-jewish-woman-and-a-ukrainian-woman-launched-the-computer-age/*>.

Lixia Zhang

'Lixia Zhang' PeoplePill <*https://peoplepill.com/people/lixia-zhang*>.

'Lixia Zhang' IETF Datatracker <*https://datatracker.ietf.org/person/Lixia%20Zhang*>.

'Lixia Zhang' UCLA Computer Science Department <*http://web.cs.ucla.edu/~lixia/bio.html*>.

Photographic Credits

Sarah Allen: Date: 2012, Author: Brian Ireley, Source: The Smithsonian Institution

Ruth Leach Amonette: Date: 1944, Author: n/a, Source: Bryant Digital Commons

Kathleen McNulty Antonelli: Kay McNulty in her high school graduation portrait, Date: 1938. Source: High School Graduation Photo

Ruzena Bajczy: in her office at the University of California, Berkeley, Date: 2013, Franc Salina

Jean Bartik: Betty Jennings Bartik operating the ENIAC's main control panel while the machine was still located at the Moore School. Date: *c.*1944, U.S. Army Photo from the archives of the ARL Technical Library.

Carol Bartz: at her first Yahoo! employee all hands meeting, in Sunnyvale, California, Date: 2009 Yahoo! Blog from Sunnyvale, California, USA Source: Yahoo!

Mavis Batey: Courtesy of the Batey family via Bletchley Park Trust

Gwen Bell: Gwen Bell with plaque at the Computer History Museum's 35th anniversary. Date: 2014, CHM with permission of Gordon Bell

Mary Adela Blagg: in her youth, Date: before 1898. Photographer unknown, *https://www.atlasobscura.com/articles/how-do-moon-craters-get-names*

Gertrude Blanch: Portrait of the American mathematician Gertrude Blanch, Date: c 1938, Author: Momoman 7, Source: Own Work

Sharla Boehm: Date: 1957, Author: Tenley Boehm Bourke, Source: The uploader on Wikimedia Commons received this from the author/ copyright holder

Kathleen Booth: Date: n/a probably 1978, Source & Author: Lakehead University Archives, Lakehead University Photograph Collection. The University photographs Ceremonies folder UG6 H I 1 to 16.

Anita Borg: Date: n/a, Author: n/a, Source: AnitaB.org

Ellen Broad: Date: 2017, Author: Amanda Thorson, Source: Amanda Thorson Photography.

Joy Buolamwini: at Wikimania in Cape Town, South Africa, Date: 2018, Author: Niccolo Coranti, Source: own work

Alice Burks: Date: 2001, Author: Robert KS, Source: English Wikipedia editor Robert KS,

Margaret Myers Burnett: at the ACM CHI Conference, Date: 2017, Author: NCWIT, Source: Margaret Burnett

Karen Catlin: Date: 2021, Source & Author: Karen Catlin

Beatrice Cave-Brown-Cave: at Girton College Date: 1919, Author: College staff picture of 1919, Source: https://issuu.com/girtoncollege/docs/girton_college_the_year_2014-15/13

Edith Clarke: Date n/a, Author: n/a, Source: Photo courtesy of the Society of Women Engineers Archives, Walter P. Reuther Library, Wayne State University

Lynn Conway: Date: 2006, Author: Charles Rogers, Source: http://ai.eecs.umich.edu/people/conway/LynnPhotos/Lynn2006.jpg,

Kate Crawford: Date: 2009, Author: andresmh, Source: Flickr: Kate Crawford

Klára Dán von Neumann: Date: n/a, Author: n/a, Source: Los Alamos National Laboratory

Eleanor Dodson: at the time of her admission as Fellow of the Royal Society, Date: 2003, Author: n/a, Source: Eleanor Dodson via Tony Wilkinson

Elizabeth 'Jake' Feinler , Date: 2011, Source & Author: Elizabeth Feinler

Christiane Floyd: speaking at a conference at the HTW Berlin, Date: 2015, Author: WiseWoman, Source: Own work

Sally Floyd: Date: 2008, Author: Carole Leita, Source: ICSI

Sandra Forsythe: Date: n/a, Author: n/a, Source: Stanford University

Margaret R. Fox: Date: 1983, Source; National Institute of Standards and Technology, U.S. Department of Commerce, Author: National Institute of Standards and Technology, U.S. Department of Commerce

Timnit Gebru: Scientist Timnit Gebru, Date: 2018, Author: TechCrunch, Source: https://www.flickr.com/photos/52522100@N07/30671211838

Adele Goldberg: Adele Goldberg speaking at PyCon, Date: 2007, Author: Terry Hancock, Source: http://www.freesoftwaremagazine.com/articles/thrills_chills_and_pictures_from_pycon_200

Shafrira Goldwasser: Date: n/a, Source & Author: Weizmann Institute of Science

Evelyn Boyd Granville: Date: 1945, Author: n/a, Source: Smith College Special Collections, Student publications and student publications records – Yearbooks 1945

Irene Greif: at an informal family event, Date: 2015, Author: Igreif11, Source: Own work

Margaret Hamilton: Date: 1995, Author: Daphne Weld Nichols, Source: Photograph of Margaret Hamilton taken by photographer Daphne Weld Nichols

Mary K. Hawes: COBOL: Initial Specifications for a Common Business Oriented Language. Source: Government Printing Office/Wikicommons

Grete Hermann: Date: c 1935, Author: n/a, Source: Archiv der Sozialen Demokratie der Friedrich-Ebert-Stiftung, 6/FOTA189903

Susan Hockey: Date: n/a, Author: n/a, Source: Library of Congress

Dorothy Crowfoot Hodgkin: Date: 2010, Author: University of Bristol, Source: https://www.flickr.com/photos/bristoluniversity/45949493842/

Betty Holberton: then Betty Snyder, programming the ENIAC in building 328 at the Ballistic Research Laboratory, Date:1947 to 1955, Author: n/a, Source: US Army Photo

Erma Schneider Hoover: Date: n/a, Author: n/a, Source: Reused with permission of Nokia Corporation and AT & T Archives

Grace M. Hopper: Date: 1984, Author: James S. Davis, Source US Navy

Mary Jane Irwin: Date: c 2006, Author: Chuck Fong, Studio 2 Photography, Source: Mary Jane Irwin

Mary Lou Jepsen: Dr Mary Lou Jepsen. Co-founder, One Laptop Per Child, Date: 2014, Author: Kenneth C. Zirkel, Source: Own Work

Katherine Johnson. Also Katherine Coleman Goble Johnson, Date: 1983, Author: NASA, Source: https://crgis.ndc.nasa.gov/historic/File:1983-L-04373.jpg

Karen Sparck Jones: photographed in front of the University of Cambridge Computer Library, Date: 2002, Author: en:user: Markus Kuhn Source: http://en.wikipedia.org/wiki/Image:Karen_Sp%C3%A4rck_Jones.jpg

Susan Kare: at the 2019 National Design Awards at Cooper Hewitt, Date: 2019, Author: Cooper Hewitt, Source: https://www.youtube.com/watch?v=0ok6bxLPOTk&t=57s

Mary Kenneth Keller: upon the occasion of the award of PhD, University of Wisconsin, Madison, WI, Date: 1965, Source: & Author The Clarke University Archives

Hedwig Eva Maria Kiesler 'Hedy Lamarr': publicity photo for film *The Heavenly Body*, Date: 1944, Author: n/a, Source: eBay

Maria Klawe: Date: 2015, Author: Craig Stanfill Source: President Maria Klawe at Graduation,

Sandra Kurtzig: Date: 2014, Author: tiernantech, Source https://www.flickr.com/photos/8786051@N03/15405815705/

Ailsa Land: Date: 2010, Author: LSE Library Source: https://www.flickr.com/photos/lselibrary/4437665957/

Henrietta Swan Leavitt: Date: n/a, assumed middle age, Author: n/a, Source: Cepheid Variable Stars (weber.edu)

Nicole-Reine Lepaute: Date: n/a, Author: n/a, Source: http://www-history.mcs.st-and.ac.uk/PictDisplay/Lepaute.html

Barbara Jane Huberman Liskov: Date: n/a, Author: Jason Dorfman, Source: Barbara Liskov

Joyce Currie Little: Date: n/a, Author: n/a, Source: https://iscap-edsig.org/edsig/fellows/littlej.php

Ada Byron Lovelace: Augusta Ada King Countess of Lovelace, daguerreotype portrait, Date: 1843, Author: Antoine Claudet, Source: https://blogs.bodleian.ox.ac.uk/adalovelace/2015/10/14/only-known-

Megan Smith: Date: 2014, Author: Chuck Kennedy, White House photographer, Source: https://www.whitehouse.gov/sites/default/files/microsites/ostp/megan_smith_portrait.jpg,

Cynthia Solomon: Date: 2017, Author: Cynthia Solomon, Source: Cynthia Solomon's personal files

Frances Spence: then Frances Bilas, operating the ENIAC's main control panel while the machine was still located at the Moore School, Date: c 1944, Source & Author: U.S. Army Photo from the archives of the ARLTechnical Library

Janese Swanson: Date: c 2020, Author: Bill Wyland Galleries, Source: Dr Janese Swanson

'Janet' Jane Ann Ionn Taylor: Date: n/a, Source: Courtesy of John and Rosalind Croucher, Sydney, Australia.

Ruth Lichterman Teitelbaum: crouching, wiring the right side of the ENIAC with a new program, Date; probably 1944, Source & Author: U.S. Army Photo from the archives of the ARL Technical Library

Janie Tsao: Date: n/a, Source: Mashbac

Dana L. Ulery: Date: 2008, Source: Own Work, Author: Dlu776

Manuela Veloso: speaking at the Turing centennial conference at Manchester, Date: 2012, Author: David.Monniaux, Source: Own work

Mary Allen Wilkes: Date: 2015, Author: n/a, Source: Mary Allen Wilkes' personal archives

Sophie Wilson: Date: 2013, Author: Chris Monk, Source: https://www.flickr.com/photos/101251639@N02/9669448671

Beatrice Worsley: 'Trixie' Worsley, Date: 1958, Author: Canada Pictures Ltd, Source: the University of Toronto Archives from the J.N. Patterson Hume Fond, B2007-0007/001P(03).

Irma Wyman: Date: c 1998?, Author: n/a, Source: Irma Wyman

Katerina Yushchenko: Date: 2012, Author: Writing_About_Charity_wikicontest_2012_-_30.JPG: Amakuha; derivative work: Makakaaa, Source: Writing About Charity wikicontest 2012 - 30.JPG

Lixia Zhang: Date: n/a, Source & Author: Lixia Zhang